Computer-assisted Text Analysis

New Technologies for Social Research

New technologies are transforming how social scientists in a wide range of fields do research. The series, New Technologies for Social Research, aims to provide detailed, accessible and up-to-date treatments of such technologies, and to assess in a critical way their methodological implications.

Recent volumes include:

Computer Analysis and Qualitative Research
Nigel G. Fielding and Raymond M. Lee

Computer Modelling of Social Processes
edited by Wim B.G. Liebrand, Andrzej Nowak and Rainer Hegselmann

Neural Networks
An Introductory Guide for Social Scientists
G. David Garson

Computer-assisted Text Analysis
Roel Popping

Computer-assisted Text Analysis

Roel Popping

SAGE Publications
London • Thousand Oaks • New Delhi

SAGE Publications Ltd
6 Bonhill Street
London EC2A 4PU

SAGE Publications Inc
2455 Teller Road
Thousand Oaks, California 91320

SAGE Publications India Pvt Ltd
32, M-Block Market
Greater Kailash - I
New Delhi 110 048

British Library cataloguing in Publication data

A catalogue record for this book is available from the British Library

ISBN 0 7619 5378 7
ISBN 0 7619 5379 5 (pbk)

Library of Congress catalog card number available

Typeset by A.Barát
Printed by The Cromwell Press Ltd, Trowbridge, Wiltshire

37. Om het bestaande te begrijpen, d.i. te vergelijken en te ordenen maken wij er van een beeld.

(In order to understand what is existing, i.e., to compare and to order, we build an image of it.)

38. Onze voorstelling van het bestaande is niet het bestaande zelf, maar een beeld er van.

(Our notion of the existing is not the existing itself, but an image of it.)

39. Het woord-symbool is de zinnelijke representatie van de voorstelling van het bestaande.

(The word-symbol is the sensual representation of the performance of the existing.)

Frederik van Eeden (1975 [1893]) *Rede-kundige grondslag van verstand-houding.* (Logical foundation of understanding.) Utrecht: Het Spectrum.

Contents

Preface

This book contains an introduction into recent developments in the field of analysis of textual data with emphasis on constructing a data matrix that is appropriate for statistical analysis. The book is especially intended for investigators from the social sciences. When computer supported text analysis was introduced, some major differences compared to the conventional way of analysis were stressed. In the first years of the computer supported analysis the texts segments were not only available on paper, but also in electronic form. The assigning of the text segments then was mainly based on finding matches between words or phrases in texts and words or phrases in so-called dictionaries. This task was no longer performed by human coders, who needed an intensive training.

In the meantime however, more types of computer assisted text analysis became available. In many situations the investigator again or still, starts with texts on paper, and the assigning is again performed by coders. These coders assign the words or phrases as intended by the sender of the message. The word or phrase counts are not only the main point of interest, relations between concepts are receiving more and more attention. The availability of several research strategies makes it much easier to find a method that matches the research question at hand. In case one is interested in concept occurrences, one might use thematic text analysis. This is the kind of analysis that is still applied most today. The newer types of analysis are denoted as semantic text analysis, network analysis of evaluative texts, the analysis of cognitive maps. The semantic analysis applies in case text is used as a source of information about relational characteristics. In case the research question requires that text blocks are depicted as sets of interrelated concepts, the network analysis can be used. The focus is on the types of substantive inferences afforded by these approaches.

General topics concerning text analysis that must be mentioned for completeness, but that have been discussed in previous publications before and have not changed, are only shortly discussed.

The name of the author of a text refers to the person who composed that text, and who is responsible for all the errors and omissions that might be found. In general this author is not the person who wrote everything by him- or herself alone. With respect to the present book, many people have in some way contributed to the text. They did so by offering ideas, discussing topics, commenting on parts that were written. It is impossible to mention everybody by name. Wim Liebrand contributed the idea for the example about fairness and injuries in sports. Ivan Gadourek commented on the first chapters, he put me back to reality where I wanted to escape. Carl Roberts commented on many chapters, this has been appreciated very much. The figures are drawn by Chris Beukema.

A considerable part of the text was written in hours that were actually reserved for the family. Marika, Attila és Gergő nevében köszönjük a türelmét, thank you for your patience. My mother showed much interest in this book. Sadly, she could not witness its appearance. The dedication is all that I can now offer.

1

Text analysis: What and why?

Text analysis encompasses a class of techniques for the social scientific study of communication. From one point of view text analysis, or content analysis, can be contrasted with observation.[1] Central to it is not the material, the visible, the audible, but the invisible: the world of meanings, values, norms as these are made accessible by symbolic behaviour (language, literature, plastic art, music). The 'content' in content analysis is the material's meaning, i.e., the social significance behind the visible or audible symbols in papers, books, film, recordings, pictures, paintings, or behind human activities in radio- and television broadcasts or in films. The focus is especially on the content of the message, by preference in mass communication where the message is addressed to many other people.

Originally text analysis was used primarily to draw conclusions regarding the source of the message. Sources were often a collectivity, such as an organization, or a government. (See for example George [1959b].) However, communication is more broadly understood as involving message, channel, audience, as well as source. In fact, these four aspects of communication represent the most common contextual variables used in analyses of texts and transcripts (Roberts, 1997b).[2]

Beyond examining symbolic content within various contexts, text analysis is used in bringing structure to an enormous amount of rather unstructured information. This allows the investigator to make explicit various aspects that might not be noticed by a lay observer. In this way a better understanding can be gained in certain aspects of societal processes.

But the meaning of text analysis remains illusive. One might ask whether sensory perception can have the invisible and immaterial as its object. The analysis of content does not focus on behaviour, but on recording and comparing artifacts of attributes produced by human behaviour, both individually, and interactively. Its fundamental characteristic is that it is concerned with the communicative act *post hoc*.

Background

The first well-documented case of a quantitative analysis of printed material probably occurred in Sweden in the 18th century, an analysis in which religious symbols in songs were counted (Krippendorff, 1980: 113). Analysis of newspaper content started at the beginning of the 20th century, and has been depicted as developing in five 'methodological' stages (Van Cuilenburg, 1991: 72):

I.	Frequency-analysis, until the 1950s;
II.	Valence-analysis, in the middle of the '50s;
III.	Intensity analysis, in the '50s and '60s;
IV.	'Contingency analysis', starting from 1960;
V.	Computer analysis, starting from the end of the sixties.

Up to the fifties text analysis was used to describe texts in a simple way. Investigators restrict themselves to questions like 'how frequently does a specific word or theme appear in a text?' and 'how many articles deal with this specific topic (criminality, environmental problems)?' A flourishing-period in this frequency analysis stage was around World War II, as Allied governments sponsored considerable research into the content of Nazi propaganda. These analyses were not only useful for the war effort, but formed the basis of much scholarly research in the early 1950s.

Soon thereafter investigators began valence analysis in which they asked questions about whether words are positively or negatively valued (e.g., 'friend' versus 'enemy'), and whether *pro* or *contra* themes receive attention. Pro and contra were soon differentiated to the extent that themes and words were discussed in texts in a positive or negative way. In this way attempts were made to reveal the 'evaluative load' of texts.

Text analysis came to its third stage, that of intensity analysis, when themes and words were assigned weights (generally in the range 0–1) to indicate the relative strength of evaluations and assertions. For example, 'Will be' involves an assertion of higher intensity than does 'Might be', leading one to assign respective weights of 2/3 and 1/3 to instances of these phrases. This leaves 'room' for a verbal expression having a higher value (namely 'Are') with a weight of 1.

Text analysis remained a descriptive research method until about 1960. Investigators addressed almost exclusively questions about how often (frequency) and in which way (pro or contra, intensity) a specific theme appears in a text. Statistical research techniques available at the time, especially association and correlation analysis, allowed research questions regarding occurrences of specific themes in texts. This involves investigating the associations (or 'contingency') between textual characteristics. Reasoning in such contingency analyses was depicted as simply noting that 'the connection between the specific characteristics A and B in the text denotes this specific fact X.'

In the late 1960s, investigators started using the computer. Numerous analyses of textual data were performed by a group of researchers at Harvard University. These text analyses were almost exclusively performed using The General Inquirer, a mainframe computer program for classifying and counting words/phrases within discrete 'meaning categories.'[3] During the late 1960s and 1970s these word-count text analysis methods were often misused, as frequencies of words/phrases-taken-out-of-context were tabulated, collapsed into meaning categories, correlated, and (at times dubiously) interpreted.[4] In the wake of such misuses there was a decline of confidence in the promise of text analysis research, which consequently came to appear with decreasing frequency in mainstream social science journals.

Today a great deal of research is only possible with the computer. Text or content analysis without the computer implies an enormous amount of work. De Sola Pool (1980: 245) once remarked: 'I stopped doing content analysis before Phil Stone had developed the General Inquirer, because it was too hard. The amount of work involved for the product was enormous.' In contrast in 1979 investigators at the Free University in Amsterdam hired 50 coders, who *within a month* were able to code over 400,000 different data items from 5400 newspaper articles with the use of a computer program (Van Cuilenburg, 1991: 73). Investigators using the General Inquirer have been able to accomplish similar feats. Tasks that were in the past performed using pencil and paper have been taken over by the computer. Data are coded and stored with software assistance. Once all data have been coded, they are immediately available for statistical analysis. Numerous texts that have long been available as data files on a computer system, can now quickly be entered into programs for text analysis.[5]

Schrott and Lanoue (1994) investigated several developments in the field of text analysis in the period 1970–1993. They did so based on a text analysis of 3005 abstracts of research papers in social sciences. An enormous expansion of the number of research papers was found in the period from 1977 until 1986 in which text analysis was used in the pursuit of applied research. After that time, the number decreased slowly. Especially in communication research the use of text analysis has increased over time, but in political science the reverse is found. In the 1990s there is a dramatic increase in the use of the method in sociology. The authors also investigated whether social scientists relied exclusively on text analysis in their research, or whether they employed other methods besides text analysis. They found a growing trend toward mixed approaches among many researchers. Far more descriptive text analyses have been performed compared to theory-driven ones. In a descriptive analysis words or themes are counted that are of relevance according to the investigator, these words and themes become clear during the coding process. A theory-driven analysis starts from a dictionary (in which words and phrases are linked to themes) that was developed in advance and is based on some theory. In communication sciences a substantial increase of both types is found. In sociology however, a slight preference for descriptive text analysis prevails.

New developments, in which the computer is used, have increased rapidly. Now there are apparently successful efforts to generate automatic summaries of texts (Brandow, Mitze and Rau, 1995; McKeown and Radev, 1995). This is a first step in the direction of completely automated data collection. Brandow et al. have developed an Automated News Extraction System (ANES) that automatically summarises news stories. The system identifies the most relevant sentences in a news story by statistical analysis of so-called 'signature words'. Two hundred and fifty documents were examined by using the system. The resulting extracts were read and judged independently by at least one analyst with the corresponding full-text document serving as the basis for judging the acceptability of the extract content. In 74% of all cases it was concluded that ANES produced acceptable extracts. Although these developments may someday find application in text analysis methodologies, they are still under construction and are not themselves methods of analysis.

Contrasts

Writings on text analysis can be viewed as a dialogue in which several rather general but contrasting pairs of terms return again and again. Among the most important of these contrasts are those between deduction and induction, quantitative and qualitative, manifest and latent, intension and extension, denotation and connotation, description and interpretation. These contrasts will be discussed in this section. Their impact on text analysis will become clear in later chapters.

Deduction and induction. Empirical research projects often have a deductive character. Here conclusions are reached by reasoning from general to particular. This implies that a general theory with respect to some topic is formulated and hypotheses are derived. It is then tested whether these hypotheses can be confirmed for a sample drawn from some well-defined population. Confirmation is based on the strength of one's statistical inference. As a result the investigator may conclude with a known probability of being in error that the hypotheses (and, by extension the theory) hold in the population from which the sample was drawn. This method of knowledge acquisition is often called the hypothetico-deductive research strategy.

The contrasting strategy is used when the investigation has an inductive character. Here the investigator follows a method of reasoning which results in general laws inferred from particular facts or instances. The investigator builds a theory that accounts for patterns that occur within a restricted research domain. The research then proceeds to investigate whether this theory still holds in another (comparable) domain, or whether it is to be modified to account for patterns in both domains. Theory development precedes as new domains are explored for new anti-theoretical patterns.

In most research projects one of these two approaches is followed. Sometimes both are used, for example, when an inductive pilot study is followed by a deductive main investigation.

Quantitative and qualitative. The distinction between qualitative and quantitative refers to the methods applied by social scientists. Quantitative methods are those that follow deductive reasoning, that use inferential statistics, and that are confirmatory. Qualitative methods on the other hand are inductive, non-statistical, and exploratory. The qualitative approach is very important when the investigator wants to describe a specific situation, change, or development in a case study, or to perform a pilot study in which hypotheses and theories are formulated. Moreover qualitative and quantitative approaches can be used very well together in one project. On the one hand, qualitative analysis may be used to improve ideas concerning the raising of the research problem, the definition of concepts and categories, the determination of the appropriate tools for analysis. A quantitative study may then be used in which these analytic tools are applied to the research problem. On the other hand, qualitative research can be used to bring to life concrete illustrations of both typical and anomalous cases glossed over in a quantitative text analysis.[6]

Manifest and latent. The manifest meaning of a word refers to the surface meaning of that word. Investigating manifest content involves the analysis of what is undeniably present. This content refers to any meaning that is universally attached to a word or an expression, independent of the intentions of the source of the message or the expectations it aroused in the receiver of the message.

An investigator might also be interested in the latent character of a message: in the deeper layers of content's meanings, in what is written between the lines, in what George (1959b: 27) called the 'behavioural and situational' contexts of content. Here behavioural context refers to the goal the source pursues. Situational context encompasses information on who the source is, for whom the message is meant, under which circumstances the message is sent, and so on. Take for example the sentence 'He looked blue from cold.' The manifest content of the word 'blue' denotes a colour, while the latent content refers to the fact that the person is extremely cold. This latent content is inferred as the word is mentioned within a situational context related to temperature and the known physiological consequences thereof. Graber (1989: 144) formulates the issue as follows: 'Senders and receivers routinely interpret messages in ways that go beyond the manifest content. They extract additional information such as the intentions and mood of the source, the power relationships between source and receiver expressed through the language format, and the likely consequences of the message.' Such inferences give insight into the qualities of the communication's source, yet they also reveal that the messages investigated are approached in the context of a conceptual system that serves as an ordering principle for the observations.

Intension and extension. Words have a specific intension and extension. The intension of a word is the set of essential properties which determines correct and incorrect usages of the word in conjunction with other words (Lyons, 1977: 159). A word's extension is the class of empirical things to which it is correctly applied (Lyons, 1977: 158). Lyons presents the sentence 'Anything that is canine is a dog' as an intensional definition of the class of dogs. Poodles and sheep-dogs possess this quality, and are therefore part of the extension of the word 'dog'. This example illustrates the hierarchical relation between intension and extension: one can not determine the extension of a word when its intension is not known. One might run into problems when words are used that have several intensions. 'Democracy' is a form of government, but it also stands for 'freedom of expression', depending on how it is used. Moreover, there are words, like 'belief' and 'love', whose extension is hard to identify.

Denotation and connotation. The denotation of a word posits a fixed relation between the word and the object it refers to: 'By the denotation of a lexeme ... will be meant the relationship that holds between that lexeme and persons, things, places, properties, processes and activities external to the language system' (Lyons, 1977: 207). It refers to the standard or conceptual meaning of a word. In contrast, words and sentences are more than mere names for objects. Particularly in social scientific research they must also be explained in the context in which they appear. This contextually determined meaning (or evaluative load) is the text's connotation: the meaning suggested in addition to the text's denotative meaning. In most such research both the interpretation of the word and of the context are considered.

Connotation, however, might also include a secondary denotation. Apart from the fixed interpretation words can also have a variable interpretation, that might even hold for a small group of people in a specific setting. For most people 'pot' is something to keep flowers in, but for some groups it refers to a drug.

A fixed interpretation of words is an interpretation that holds for all members in a language community, while a variable interpretation only holds for a part of that community. This variable interpretation is especially met in evaluations. For example, the denotation of 'South African' is clear, but its connotation is not. For older people it might refer to racial separation, while for younger people it might indicate cooperation between races. The evaluative interpretation of words, however, can also be identical for all members of a language community. A word like 'friend' always has a positive interpretation; a word like 'enemy' always a negative one.

Based on distinctions between fixed and variable interpretation of words, and between referential and evaluative functions of words, four elements in the interpretation of words can be distinguished. In Table 1.1 the fixed interpretations of words fall in cells a and c of the table, whereas variable interpretations fall in cells b and d. Denotations are referential and fixed. The table's other cells depict the three types of connotation that words can have.

Description and interpretation. A description is 'a picture in words'. It is a factual representation of what is shown. In analyses of texts, it implies that the investigator exclusively addresses questions about how often and in which way a specific word appears in a text. As soon as one begins explaining what the

Table 1.1 *Four elements of interpretation of words*

function	interpretation	
	for all	for some
referential	a denotation	b secondary denotation
evaluative	c fixed evaluation	d variable evaluation

Source: Van Cuilenburg & Noomen, 1984: 101

word means or why it is used in some way, one is involved in interpretation. Interpretation is always of a message 'as intended by' someone (the source) and with respect to someone (the receiver). The researcher's ability to empathetically understand texts' sources and audiences becomes especially important when the latent content of a text is investigated.

A definition

Despite some differences in the nature of their subject matter, more recent texts on content or text analysis are consistent in their portrayal of this type of analysis as involving the quantification of qualitative data for the purpose of affording statistical inferences. In this book I further restrict my discussions to the analysis to texts, and will therefore use the term text analysis. Text analysis is a research technique for making replicable and valid inferences from text to their context.

A much broader definition was presented by Shapiro and Markoff (1997: 14). They define content analysis as 'any systematic reduction of a flow of text (or other symbols) to a standard set of statistically manipulable symbols representing the presence, the intensity, or the frequency of some characteristics relevant to social science.' This definition follows after a detailed discussion on issues that have been raised in definitions of text analysis. These issues they discuss are mentioned, followed by the position I take.

The symbolic objects that are studied. In this book text is studied. Text should be interpreted in a broad way. It is for example text from an article, lecture, broadcast on radio or television, new media like the internet, and so on. Lindkvist (1981: 26 ff) distinguishes between three definitions of 'text':

1. every *semiotic* structure of meaning (... Such a concept includes not only language but music, architecture, picture, event, and social actions);
2. every *linguistic* means of expression (thus music, for example, is excluded for the text concept);
3. *written* language (which would exclude, for example, audiovisual language [e.g., transcripts of broadcastings – rp]).

This book uses the second definition above.

The intellectual products. The emphasis is on statistical inference. This allows the investigator to follow a hypothetico-deductive research strategy.

The quantitative versus qualitative issue. Markoff and Shapiro discussed the distinction based on level of measurement (see footnote 5). With respect to this distinction both quantitative and qualitative analysis are allowed.

Manifest or latent content. Both forms of content are allowed.

The object of investigation. In most situations the source of the text is investigated, but this should not exclude the text itself, neither the audience or the receivers of the text.

The terms that serve to remind us of the identification of text analysis as a scientific pursuit. Here the analysis should be systematic and should use methods that are replicable and valid.

Some specific definitions follow. In his book on content analysis Krippendorff (1980: 21) uses almost the same definition as above. He has replaced 'text' by 'data', however. Therefore his newer definition is broader. In an earlier definition Krippendorff (1978: 70) used the term 'text', but restricted the object to the source. In their definition Stone et al. (1966: 5) refer to 'characteristics in text', they also exclude other symbolic material. The definition used in this book is different from the one by Berelson, who considered content analysis 'a research technique for the objective, systematic and quantitative description of the manifest content of communication' (Berelson, 1971: 18). The word 'manifest' has disappeared, therefore investigating the latent meaning and considering the connotation of the text is no longer excluded. This allows interpretation.[7] The word 'quantitative' has also disappeared from the definition. Both quantitative and qualitative data, based on level of measurement are allowed. Replicability, as used by Krippendorff, implies the requirement to be 'objective' and 'systematic'. Objectivity implies that every stage in the research process is based on explicitly formulated rules and procedures. In other words, the content of the text must be accentuated, and the investigator's values and beliefs must not bias the result of the analysis. Being systematic implies inclusion and exclusion of categories according to consistently applied rules.

Exclusions

Text as referring to the semiotic structure of meaning (other than what can be found in actual text) is not considered in the book. Illustrations of some studies in which this definition is followed, include Simonton's (1994) investigation of melodic structures. He used the computer to calculate the two-note transition probabilities for the first five-note pairs of over 15,000 themes by almost 500 classical composers. This measure of melodic originality was validated against conventional musical wisdom: melodic originality was higher in first-movement themes in comparison to themes in later movements; it was higher in composers' later works in comparison to their earlier works; and it was high in the early Baroque, late Romantic, and early Modern periods, but relatively low throughout the Classical period.

Also dealing with melodic style is a study by Whissell (1996), who developed a computer program to assist with emotional stylometric analysis. She reports on an analysis of Beatles lyrics, an analysis that confirms popular and critical belief that the lyrics of John Lennon are less pleasant and sadder than the lyrics of Paul McCartney.

The coding scheme proposed by Bales (1950) for scoring behaviour during interactions has been widely applied. A coding system for paintings produced by psychiatric patients is proposed by Hacking et al. (1996). In their system, each painting is overlaid with a grid. For each of 20 squares in the grid, coders assign values for: presence of various colours; brightness of colours; line thickness; percentage of space covered; and emotional tone. Patients' use of yellow, orange, and line thickness distinguishes among diagnostic categories.

Another excluded form of text analysis is one in which the computer has no specific role other than in the analysis of spacial measures. In such research investigators look at where texts of interest appear in a journal (which page, which column), how much space they occupy, the size of the heading, information about authors, and so on. Here the content of the text itself is not the important issue, but its outline. For example Gutteling et al. (1991) compared four Dutch newspapers on the coverage of environmental risks during 1977–1984. They report facts like the finding that one paper contained 3 times more articles on environmental risk and devoted about 5 times more lines than another paper. Articles in two national and in two local newspapers, published in the period 1977–1984 were surveyed. The investigators examined the number of articles on environmental risks, the amount of lines of text, the coverage of incidents, and the coverage of risks.

Another comparable but much older study is the one by McQuail (1977) who investigated factors affecting the maintenance of the independence, diversity and editorial standards of newspapers and periodicals in Great Britain. For several newspapers McQuail lists over time the number of pages as the percentage of space used for editorial issues and for advertisements. The editorial issues such as news and features are split in sub-issues. As an example, Table 1.2 informs about the way the amount of total print in *The Times* was used in 1947 and 1975.

Finally, Cronin, Davenport and Martinson (1997) counted the genders of article's authors and of persons cited in the articles, or whose contributions to the articles were acknowledged.

Table 1.2   *Total print into categories of editorial space and advertisements in The Times in 1947 and 1975*

	1947	1975
Editorial space	60%	65%
News	41%	39%
Home news	21%	18%
Other news	20%	21%
Features	7%	16%
Other	12%	10%
Advertisements	40%	35%

Based on McQuail (1977: 16–17)

Logistical issues

In his contribution to the Festschrift for Lasswell, Janowitz (1969: 157) mentions three sets of barriers, listed in ascending order of importance, to the development of text analysis as a quantitative technique: (a) organizational and administrative, (b) substantive, and (c) methodological and theoretical. Janowitz states that organizational and administrative components are threshold factors not satisfactorily solved (in 1969), so there is no acceptable format for the generation and retrieval of essential text analysis data. Janowitz is very brief here. When discussing this issue, I will also refer to general organizational and administrative components that are directly related to the computer assisted text analysis. With respect to substantive barriers it is necessary that data be gathered covering a long historical period for a particular source or a particular medium. Janowitz asserts that 'quantitative studies ... have a value which is directly proportional to the time span covered' (Janowitz, 1969: 158). The longer the time span, the better the investigator can demonstrate transformations in, for example, human values. Data sets covering such a long period are hardly available. I agree on this point. Most text analysis studies I am aware of cover a period of less than five years, many cover even a few weeks. Lindenberg's (1976) study on depersonalization is a notable exception, as it is an investigation in which a data set covering a long period is used. Lindenberg used the sample years 1852 through 1969 in a text analysis of *The New York Times* to locate changes in frequency of occurrence of different kinds of actors and recipients of action (targets). He was able to show over time a supra-individualization of actors and an abstraction and anonymization of targets. Actors become independent from targets, and vice versa. This could only be shown in a study covering such a long period in time. Other studies that cover long periods are performed by Danielson and Lasorsa (1997) and much earlier by Sorokin (1937). This latter study was re-analysed by Klingemann, Mohler and Weber

(1982). The studies will be discussed in this text. These substantive barriers are related to the design of the study, not to the (text analysis) method used. Therefore no computer program can be used to level this barrier.

Furthermore, Janowitz argues that while many technical questions have been attacked, e.g., reliability, methodological questions are still hardly explored. Besides this, there is a gap between 'theory' and 'empirical data'. Janowitz has illustrated this point by presenting some examples. Important elements here are the fusion of text analysis with other methodologies, and the way in which an investigator looks at the data, e.g., the manifest or latent content is considered. I hope to show that progress is being made with respect to some methodological questions and that the gap between theory and empirical data is becoming smaller. Progress has been possible due to new developments that rely heavily on the computer.

Incorporating latent meaning and connotation into analyses has consequences, especially for the validity of results. Van Cuilenburg and Noomen (1984) point to the relation between text analysis and theory. Text analysis is more manifest and less latent when fewer assumptions, hypotheses, and theoretical constructions are placed between the rerendering of the text in specific terms (the coding) and the final conclusions regarding the text. They indicate here that text analysis is not theory-neutral. Where latent intention is coded, theoretical relevance is high, but reliability is low. Conversely, when manifest content is coded, reliability is high, but theoretical relevance might be lower (Galtung, 1971: 70).

Quantitative text analysis is especially suited for a hypothetico-deductive research strategy. Several kinds of hypotheses are important in this type of text analysis (see also Krippendorff (1980: 50 ff). The first concerns the (frequency of) occurrence of specific concepts in text someone wants to make inferences about. This type can be used to distinguish between different groups (males versus females, newspaper X versus newspaper Y) or between time periods. In the second type of hypothesis the connections between different concepts that occur in blocks of text are regarded. Especially here, many changes have occurred over the last years in the way text analysis is performed. Investigators doing contingency analysis considered the co-occurrence of concepts in a text block. Today the relation between two concepts is made explicit in the coding process. The third type of hypothesis concerns relations between the results of content inferences and the results of other studies whether for the purposes of validation in the spirit of multiple operationalism or to establish connections between textual and non-textual matter.

Steps in a quantitative text analysis

Below is a list of steps that are required in performing a quantitative analysis.[8]

1.   Consider the research problem thoroughly.

2.   Develop testable hypotheses, and decide how you want to operation-
      alize the set of concepts that will be used. A qualitative pilot study
      can be part of this process. The operationalization starts as you note
      phrases that recur.
3.   Evaluate the relevance of the representative sample of texts you have
      obtained for the research project. Define the recording units.
4.   Define both concepts as well as a set of coding rules that indicate
      when texts should be classified according to each concept. Try to
      synthesize conceptual categories and coding rules; ask yourself what
      is the rationale for coding the data in this way.
5.   Collect and do the initial coding of the data. In many situations
      coders are indispensable, therefore the investigator must take care to
      ensure that coding rules are applied in a consistent way. To realize
      this, coders must be trained. The investigator must guarantee that
      inter- and intra coder agreement is high. It is also useful to evaluate
      the coding scheme using a sample of texts. When necessary, coding
      rules may be revised.
6.   Complete coding the data.
7.   Perform statistical analyses on the encoded data.
8.   Interpret the results of the analyses: What do they mean? What are
      their implications?
9.   Write a report on the results.
10.   Consider whether the research objectives have been met.

The breath of potential text analysis applications can be seen on this partial
list compiled by Berelson (1971: 27 ff):

Characteristics of content-substance[9]
*   To describe trends in communication content;
*   To trace the development of scholarship;
*   To show international differences in communication content;
*   To compare media or 'levels' of communication;
*   To audit communication content against objectives;
*   To construct and apply communication standards;
*   To aid in technical research operations;
Characteristics of content-form
*   To expose propaganda techniques;
*   To measure the 'readability' of communication materials;
*   To discover stylistic features;
Producers of content
*   To identify the intentions and other characteristics of the communicators;
*   To determine the psychological state of persons or groups;
*   To detect the existence of propaganda;
*   To secure political and military intelligence;
Audience of content
*   To reflect attitudes, interests, and values of population groups;

Effects of content
- To reveal the focus of attention;
- To describe attitudinal and behavioural responses to communications.

In this chapter the rise of text analysis until the beginning of the computer era has been briefly described and defined. In text analysis research a specific terminology is used. This terminology will be further expanded in the next chapter. In the computer era three quantitative approaches to text analysis can be distinguished, namely the thematic, semantic, and network approaches. These approaches are introduced in the third chapter. The fourth, fifth and sixth chapters are devoted to the elaboration of one of these respective approaches. The approaches involve own questions with respect to reliability and validity, this is the topic of Chapter 7. The relation between text analysis and related kinds of analysis follows in the next two chapters. The first of these is on the relation to qualitative analysis, the second one on the relation to linguistics and information retrieval. Chapter 10 contains conclusions. The book ends with an overview of available computer programs for text analysis.

Notes

1. Until a strict definition is given the terms text analysis and content analysis will be used interchangeably.
2. Expanding on Lasswell's (1948) delineation of communication research Holsti (1969: 24) argued that communication is composed of six basic elements: a *source* or sender, an *encoding* process which results in a *message*, a *channel* of transmission, a *detector* or recipient of the message, and a *decoding process*. Although text analysis is performed on the message, the results may be used for inferences about all the other elements of the communication process.
3. The General Inquirer was soon followed by other text analysis programs, all of which operated more or less in the same way. Klein (1996) discusses the development in these early software packages in more detail.
   In Europe these are packages like COCOA (COunt and COncordance on Atlas), EVA (Electronic Verbal Analysis), COFTA (COmpiler For Text Analysis), LDVLIB (Linguistische Daten Verarbeitung [linguistic data processing] LIBrary). Differences among these packages are mainly technical, and are not reviewed here. They all generate more or less the same output, and run on mainframe computers. More recent packages of this genre, namely Textpack and Intext, will be described in Chapter 4. Also see Burton (1981a, 1981b, 1981c, 1982) for historical placement of people and events in the US relevant for the computer production of concordances and indexes.
4. Kelly and Stone (1975) attempted to solve this problem with the development of software for disambiguating the various meanings words can take.
5. See the first chapter of Krippendorff (1981) and the second chapter of Stone et al. (1966) for more details on historical developments in, and applications of text analysis. Readers familiar with the German language might also read the first chapter in Lisch and Kriz (1978). Stone (1997: 40 ff) presents an overview of computer assisted text analysis since the early 1960s.

6. Quantitative and qualitative analyses are also distinguished in another way, based on the level of measurement. From this point of view variables having scale points on at least an ordinal level of measurement allow quantitative analyses. In this situation the investigator might compute correlations (rank or product-moment) between different variables. In the situation of qualitative research the variables have nominal categories, or binary categories (occurs or does not occur).

The single occurrence or non-occurrence of a word can even be the main topic in an investigation. This holds if one is for example investigating when and where a specific kind of propaganda starts. Here the singularity argument is important. Topics that hardly occur, or that are 'strikingly missing', can reverse the scale for the meaning of the text that is investigated.

Within content analysis George (1959b) has introduced the terms 'frequency content analysis' for the quantitative approach, and 'non-frequency content analysis' for the qualitative approach. Relations between such qualitative variables can be analysed by using log-linear or logit models. This type of research is especially suited for a hypothetico-deductive research strategy. Both methods, quantitative and qualitative, yield data matrices from which probabilistic inferences can be drawn.

7. Galtung remarks that even in case a manifest analysis is performed, it is not precluded that the experienced coder adds to the code his own interpretation of what is communicated (Galtung, 1979: 69).

8. More or less similar lists have been presented by Weber (1990: 21 ff), and by Bierschenk and Bierschenk (1976: 11).

9. Not listed here is the application of text analysis methods to open-ended survey questions. Greater validity can be attained in the encoding of such data as symptomatic, rather than more subjective criteria are applied on this interpretation.

2

Further conceptual foundations

In performing a text analysis several techniques are used that need to be explained. Here the main notions are discussed. Text analysis as well as some fundamental contrasts have already been defined in the previous chapter. Still requiring definitions are units, concept categories, and (ways of) coding.

Units

In a text analysis study texts are broken down into units. A unit is a single group of words regarded as complete in itself. Units that constitute the basis for analysis are called units of analysis. The unit of analysis is that which one wants to characterize. The actual choice of the unit is primarily determined by the theoretical and practical purposes of the investigation. Often the main heading (including sub-heading) on the first page of a newspaper is taken as unit of analysis. One's theoretical argument is then generally that this heading contains all information that was considered by the newpaper's editors to have been most important during that day. Of course, a practical argument for the choice is that the heading is short and easy to identify.

Three additional kinds of units are: sampling units, recording units, and context units. Krippendorff (1980: 57 ff) describes sampling units as 'those parts of the observed reality or of the stream of source language expressions that are regarded independent of each other.' These units, that are also known as text blocks, have physically identifiable boundaries. They are the parts of a text population that are assigned unique numbers and are sampled with known probability.

Recording units, also called coding units or text units, are 'the specific segment of content that is characterized by placing it in a given category' (Holsti, 1969: 116). In encoding, text coders record whether or not text segments have one or more attributes. Such text segments are recording units that, for example, might be indicative of aggressive tendencies, economic subject matter, etc. Weber (1990: 21–23) notes that such attributes could be noted in various types of the recording unit, such as the word, word sense, sentence, theme, paragraph, or whole text. To this list Weber might have added the grammatical clause, i.e. a part of a sentence with its own inflected verb and associated subject and object.[1] Recording units can be repeated measures within a sampling unit.[2]

Context units indicate the body of text to be considered in characterizing a recording unit. In manual text analysis the context unit is usually not made explicit. Here, contextual information is sought when deemed intuitively necessary. For example: 'since we are in a work context, we will examine the meaning of job satisfaction and not religious satisfaction' (McTavish and Pirro, 1990: 248). In computer assisted analysis the context is generally read as adjacency, i.e., it is determined by a prespecified number of words preceding and following the word being encoded. In this way context can be defined in many ways (Klein, 1996: 73–74):

- The context consists of the text line in which the word that is considered is found;
- The context goes up to the next punctuation mark in the text. Punctuation marks are comma's, colons, semicolons, dots, question or exclamation marks;
- The context is the complete sentence;
- The word that is considered is centred on a line as defined in an editor program;
- A certain number of words before and after the word that is investigated is shown;
- As previously, but extended with some further criteria:
  - When a punctuation mark is found in the range of words following the word that is investigated the context ends;
  - The context ends after the line;
  - The context ends when a mark for the end of the sentence is found.

When a computer program is used, the program's limitations usually dictate the context that will be used.

Units from different levels of analysis may be included in each other. More than one unit of analysis can be employed in one study. This is illustrated by taking the example of books. The first unit of analysis is that of the book itself, the second one is the level of the chapters in the book, the third level is that of the paragraphs. In case this is the lowest level, the paragraph, is the recording unit. Often the investigator will continue until the level of the sentence. In such a case the paragraph might be the sampling unit. Within this sampling unit several recording units, the sentences, may be found. The chapter might also be used as context unit for the paragraph.

Next is the unit of enumeration, the unit in terms of which texts' attributes are quantified (Cartwright, 1953: 440). The unit of enumeration and the recording unit are identical when the investigator's data are counts of recording units within certain concepts. When seeing the number 5 in one's data matrix, the question 'Five what?' is asking for one's enumeration unit (e.g., 5 words –

here identically one's recording unit – indicative of some conceptual category like aggression). Cartwright (1953: 441) gives an example where the two units are not identical: 'One might characterize an entire editorial on foreign aid as predominantly favourable or unfavourable and then, for purposes of quantification, count the number of column inches of the editorial. In this case a column inch would be the unit of enumeration, whereas the editorial as a whole would be the recording unit' (Cartwright, 1953: 441). In this case 5 would not be 5 editorials (or even 5 words) favourable to foreign aid, but 5 column inches of such text.

The units must in practice be delineated and identified. There are several ways to do this (Krippendorff, 1980: 61–62). Among these are the *physical units* that are physically delineated (for example, an issue of a newspaper, or a letter), and the *syntactical units* that are 'natural' to the grammar of a communications medium. Examples are words, or news items in a broadcast. *Referential units* are defined by particular objects, events, persons etc. to which an expression refers. So, prime minister Thatcher may be referred to by 'Margaret Thatcher', 'the Iron Lady', 'the leader of the Conservative party', or if the context is unambiguous by 'she'. Each expression denotes the same person though in different ways. It is unimportant whether the reference is made directly or indirectly in one word or in a phrase.

Referential units imply that a data language is used that merely recognizes objects and their attributes. Due to the complexity of natural language objects and attributes are sometimes hard to identify. For this reason complex sentences might be split into sentences that possess a certain structure. These are *propositional units*. Say we have the sentence 'The aggressive thief threatens the police officer.' This is now read as two nuclear sentences: 'The thief / is / aggressive.' and 'The thief / threatens / the police officer.' These units are used when the semantic and the network approach to text analysis are applied.

Previously I quoted Holsti as saying that recording units are placed in categories. When recording units and categories have been established, coding can start. I now turn to a discussion of concept categories.

Concept categories and dictionary formulation

Every time one performs a content analysis of texts, words and phrases must be aggregated into categories that correspond to theoretical concepts of interest to the researcher's theory. These concept categories are very basic in text analysis.

A concept is a unit of thinking in relation to a referent (Schmidt, 1995: 4). Often it is restricted to one word that names to a specific 'something,' that condenses relevant information. For example Carley defines it as 'a single idea, or ideational kernel, regardless [of whether] it is represented by a single word or a phrase' (Carley, 1986: 146; 1993: 81). Very often a concept refers to more than one thing, e.g., a chair is something one sits on, but it can also refer to one's position (e.g., a committee leader or a professor). The concept is a unit of meaning. It is used as the basic unit for the meaning content, what is meant, of a piece of text. The concept in its proper meaning is assigned to a concept category. The term 'theme' is generally used for broader classes of concepts. Weber (1984: 140) proposed to reserve the term 'category' for groups of concepts which have similar meanings and/or connotations, and the term 'theme' for clusters of concepts with different meanings or connotations, but that taken together refer to some theme or issue.

Four issues related to the concept deserve attention. Syntactic relations among concepts may be of interest. Second, one's research problem should (in part) drive the development of concept categories. Third, rules for assigning text-characteristics to these categories must be developed. This implies the need for dictionaries. Finally, the texts themselves may (via a more inductive reasoning process) drive dictionary development. Let us consider the issues in more detail.

Concept categories are operationalized by words and phrases. Single words are useful when the investigator wants to contrast the results in a specific text with general usage, or usage in another text. Phrases merely reflect the fact that meanings often require more than one word to be located in texts. Concept categories can be ordered as genus and species. The extent to which the species are fine-grained depends on one's research problem.

An investigator may also be interested in the syntactic relations among concepts. This relation is, for example, found when the co-occurrence of noun-concepts and verb-concepts which indicate a type of action are investigated. If one wants to investigate whether workers strike more or threaten to strike more than clerks, one might compare on the one hand the co-occurrence of the noun 'worker' and the verb 'strike', and on the other hand the co-occurrence of the noun 'clerk' and again the verb 'strike'. It is even possible to have this restricted to concepts alone, now the issue is how the concept is valenced. An example of a negative valence is the word 'loafer' to indicate a striker.

The research problem drives the development of the concept categories. Here is decided how fine-grained the categories have to be.

The words and phrases that are used to operationalize concepts are called search entries. These are the entries that are looked for in a text. A dictionary consists of concept categories and the corresponding search entries. It is a concrete representation of the investigator's theory as is related to verbal data. The construction of dictionaries is considered in more detail in Chapter 4.

The concepts that are used in an investigation should be derived (deductive-ly) from theory,[3] but frequently they are also based on occurrence in the empirical condition that is investigated (inductively). Only occasionally are authors explicit about the way they build their concepts. Banks (1976: 386) explains how in his research he came to a set of categories. He describes it as a stepwise process, starting with tentative categories. The categories were revised several times. This was not only because of the theoretical relevance of the categories, but also because of requirements set for the categories (especial-ly, that they be exclusive and exhaustive). Key issues here are fixed versus interactively constructed dictionaries. Also at issue is whether dictionary entries are grounded in theory or in the texts themselves. If they are fully grounded in the theory, and therefore derived from that theory, they can be formulated in advance. In such cases mainly the manifest meaning of concepts is coded. In case the dictionary is also inductively based on texts, it will be more likely to capture the latent meaning in text as well.

For a long time it was assumed that dictionaries have to be grounded in theory. This was the philosophy behind the development of the Lasswell Value Dictionary and the Harvard IV Psychosocial Dictionary, for example (Weber, 1990). These are both general dictionaries, as they are not developed for one specific investigation. Today dictionaries are also based on concepts found in the data.

Coding

Coding is 'the process whereby raw data are systematically transformed and aggregated into units which permit precise description of relevant content characteristics' (Holsti, 1969: 94). That is, it is the processes in which recording units are identified and linked to the conceptual categories. The rules by which this is accomplished serve as the operational bond between the investigator's data and his theory and hypotheses. If coding is performed by humans, it is necessary that the coder is able to accurately identify the recording units (e.g., clauses). The coder also has to apply the concept categories correctly.

A main problem in the coding phase of an investigation is related to the ambiguity of texts. Simply put, many words have more than one meaning (i.e., they are homomorphic or ambiguous). For example, Weber (1990: 44) reports four different senses of the word *state*:

- state (noun; body politic or area of government);
- situation (e.g., state of science);
- to state (verb; to declare);
- 'united states' (idiom; handled by the second sense of United).

Text analysis software that automatically distinguishes among these usages requires sophisticated disambiguation capability (Kelly and Stone, 1975).

When coding is performed by human coders, these persons make several decisions based on coding instructions provided by the investigator. Unfortunately, these instructions are usually not reported, leaving details of the coding process closed to public scrunity. Such details are inevitably instructive when reported, however. Hak and Bernts (1996) analysed transcripts of discussions between coders and showed how these often led to coding decisions that are not fully justified by formal coding instructions. They argue that coders often base their coding decisions on criteria that emerge during the training and in discussion with other coders. These criteria typically go beyond the formal, written coding instructions. Therefore, they believe, high levels of inter-rater reliability may often represent little more than a training artifact. Coding instructions must form the basis of all coding decisions. If coding decisions are problematic, better coding instructions are called for. Instructions will differ depending on the instrumental or representational approach and on the nature of ambiguity in texts.

Instrumental versus representational approach

At issue in the instrumental versus representational distinction is 'whether' one chooses to apply one's own theory or one's sources' theories to the texts under analysis. This distinction was originally made by Osgood and has recently been refined by Shapiro (1997). In the instrumental view texts are interpreted according to the researcher's theory. The approach ignores the meanings that the texts' authors may have intended. When the representational perspective is applied, texts are used as a means to understand the author's meaning.[4]

The instrumental approach can be illustrated with the work of Gottschalk and his colleagues (Gottschalk et al., 1975; Gottschalk, 1997). This work involves assigning psychological scores based on the results of a text analysis of their speech. These scores are calculated based on word usages indicating distinctive characteristics, according to the theoretical perspective of the investigators. More generally, when an instrumental perspective is applied, texts are interpreted according to the researcher's theory. In terms of Osgood: 'As a matter of fact, we may define a method of text analysis as allowing for "instrumental" analysis as if it taps message evidence that is beyond voluntary control of the source and hence yields valid inferences despite the strategies of the source' (Osgood, 1959: 75). Thus, the instrumental approach to text analysis tends to use texts to identify individual and societal characteristics about which society members may be unaware.

The representational approach can be illustrated using Carley's (1986, 1988) study of dormitory residents. Based on interviews with students she extracted topics salient in their speech. She recorded which topics the students related to other topics. In this way she was able to construct a cognitive map in line with what the student said. Using a representational approach the researcher focuses less on specific wording than on the context within which the texts originated. When a text is analysed representationally, *the researcher attempts to map the meaning intended by its source.* This mapping cannot be accomplished unless the coder understands the social context within which the text originated.

Today many investigators still follow the instrumental view as shown by Shapiro. If the researcher using an instrumental approach knows his or her theory well enough, he or she ought to be able to fully automate it. This would give rise to a 'fixed dictionary' of conceptual categories with a one-to-one correspondence with words and phrases in texts. Researchers using the representational approach must develop *ad hoc* dictionaries that contain concepts that reflect the perspectives of the texts' authors. Coders must use sympathetic 'understanding' (or 'Verstehen') to encode the texts according to the meanings their sources intended. At issue is no longer 'how' to encode text (instrumental approach), but 'whether' one chooses to apply one's own theory or one's sources' theories to the texts under analysis.

Ambiguity

Ambiguity refers to the situation in which an expression can have more than one meaning. 'Spring' denotes a place where water flows, but also a season of the year. From Schrodt et al. (1994) we learn that the words 'accuse' and 'deny' lack ambiguity, but that 'force' and 'attack' are very problematic. This is because the latter terms can be used both as nouns and as verbs. Ambiguity complicates the encoding process in any analysis of texts.[5] More specifically, methodological problems due to idiosyncratic, illocutionary, and relevance ambiguity will inevitably arise as one obtains quantitative representations of texts.[6]

Rigorous statistical analyses of data encoded from texts require that raters, once trained, should encode the same texts identically. When computers were first enlisted in the encoding process, it was soon discovered not only that they afforded perfect inter-rater (actually, inter-computer) agreement, but that they did so at a cost to the quality of the encoded data. In short, computers are dumb. Upon encountering a sentence such as, 'You'll eat your words!', they obediently classify the word, 'eat,' as an occurrence of the concept, 'consume,' instead of as 'regret' (as in the sentence, 'You'll regret your words.'). Until the coder (or computer) has been trained to recognize such idiomatic uses of words, ambiguity will remain in the process of classifying these words under one or another concept.

Problems of idiomatic ambiguity date back to debates on whether social scientists should quantify the manifest or latent content of qualitative data. Later on the debates evolved into a truce between practitioners of the already discussed instrumental versus representational approaches to text analysis (Shapiro, 1997). Because the instrumental approach to text analysis requires only the single theoretical perspective of the analyst, words and phrases can be automatically classified as concept occurrences according to a theory-based dictionary that the analyst has developed for just such classification (Stone et al., 1966; McTavish and Pirro, 1990). To reduce the likelihood of misclassification, software routines have been developed to disambiguate idioms before dictionary classifications are made (Kelly and Stone, 1975). This should lessen criticism of the instrumental approach. Idiomatic ambiguity is far less problematic when the representational view is applied, i.e., when the coder does the final classifying.

In some text analyses the investigator encodes not only concepts, but also grammatical relations among sentence components. After removing idiomatic ambiguities from texts, most linguistic interrelations among words, phrases, and clauses can be unambiguously identified according to the grammar of the language in which the texts were written. Yet, even if one grants that surface grammar can be unambiguously represented, illocutionary ambiguity will arise for researchers who take a representational approach to text analysis. This is because such researchers must accommodate linguistic ambiguities that arise between the words under analysis and the intentions of the persons who uttered them – ambiguities that are grounded in the very structure of language itself and that can only be clarified in the light of the context in which they are expressed. Examples of this kind of ambiguity are: *'Stop!'*, which may refer to 'what I am doing' or to 'how I am doing it', and *'John bought that camera.'*, as indicative of 'an awful purchase' or just of 'a purchase'. See Roberts (1997c) for a more rigorous treatment of such illocutionary ambiguities in language.

In Chapter 6 on semantic text analysis it is explained how texts can be encoded into networks. In addition to performing idiomatic and illocutionary disambiguation, the investigator may also apply what might be called a 'network grammar' to texts. For example, if a network were to be constructed entirely of identity relations (i.e., if a network grammar of identity relations were to be applied to a text), the researcher would need to develop 'relevance rules' for deciding which statements in the texts indicate identity relations among concepts (e.g., 'the government's fiscal policy is the reduction of spending'), and which do not (possibly, 'the government's fiscal policy has resulted in the reduction of spending'). Only statements (i.e., concept-relations) relevant to the grammar of the network under construction are then encoded according to this grammar. As with idiomatic and illocutionary ambiguity, relevance ambiguity must also be exhaustively addressed in the coding instructions developed by researchers.

Conclusion

Most topics that are important for performing a text analysis have now been mentioned. Taken together these topics constitute much of the conceptual framework within which an investigator can organize a text analysis study (Krippendorff, 1980: 25 ff). The framework consists of:

- The data as communicated to the analyst;
- The context of the data;
- How the analyst's knowledge partitions the reality;
- The target of the text analysis;
- Inference as the basic intellectual task;
- Validity as ultimate criteria of success.

This last validity issue has yet to be discussed, of course. A general discussion follows in Chapter 7. When it is crucial for a specific development in computer assisted text analysis, a discussion of validity is incorporated in the treatment of that development. For now, let us turn to an overview of recent developments for the content analysis of texts.

Notes

1. A sentence might consist of several clauses. Instead of sentence the more general term 'discourse' is also used. A discourse is a collection of statements in a text in which relations are made between subject and object. A sentence having only one clause is called a nuclear sentence.

   Inflected verbs can be recognized as any words that change form when the person and/or tense of the clause is changed. An example: The word, 'go', in 'I go.', and the word, 'goes', in 'He goes.', are inflected verbs because they change form when the subject changes from first to third person.

2. When such nesting occurs, dependencies among recording units within the same sampling unit are preserved. In a newspaper editorial several interrelated topics may be discussed, for example. Although each topic is identified individually, the statistical analysis must be performed on the level of the sampling unit, here the editorial.

3. The research line is indicated by Berelson (1971: 164–65) in a very clear way: 'The hypotheses derive from the nature of the problem and in a sense help to refine it. The general categories for analysis are contained in the hypotheses and they in turn are translated into concrete, specific indicators for purposes of actual analysis. The actual results are then generalized and applied to the level of the categories and thus constitute a test of the hypotheses under investigation.'

4. The contrast between instrumental and representational was first introduced at the Allerton House Conference in 1955, where the terms were related to communication. This contrast differs from the distinction that is made in the text, where the terms indicate a view on coding.

   In the view as introduced at the Allerton Conference, instrumental refers to 'that which is manipulated' (De Sola Pool, 1959b: 207), where Shapiro emphasizes the representation of texts according to the researcher's theory. The representational perspective on communication referred then to 'any content feature which ... indexes ... something about the source' (De Sola Pool, 1959b: 207). The message directly represents the sender's ideas and intentions. In the view of Shapiro the central issue is the representation of the text as intended by the sender.

5. Schrodt et al. (1994) pay particular attention to the disambiguation of very short common words. The word 'by' has 28 additional meanings, the word 'in' has 31, and for the word 'to' 25 meanings were found.

6. These three types of ambiguity are discussed in detail in Roberts and Popping (1996). See also later chapters.

3

Recent approaches to quantitative text analysis

It was around 1980 that a variety of new approaches to text analysis appeared. These approaches were made possible thanks to the advent of micro computers and computer packages, both of which have since become increasingly powerful and convenient. In particular, packages for software development have changed from being number oriented to text (string) oriented.

The main approach until that time had been the thematic approach. In this approach texts are quantified as 'counts' of words and phrases that were classified according to a set of general themes. Within the thematic approach it has become easier now to investigate the latent content of a message. The recent quantitative text analysis methods involve not only the identification of alternative themes, but also the encoding of relations among themes in texts. These relational methods for encoding texts are strikingly similar. In each case, a Subject–Verb–Object (or S–V–O) syntax is applied during the encoding process, or even a Subject–Valence–Verb–Object (S–V–V–O) syntax in which the valence can reflect negation, evaluation, intensity, etc. Unlike thematic text analysis, such 'clause-based text analysis' affords inferences about how texts' sources use words in their speech or writings. The new text analysis methods differ primarily according to the research purposes to which each's relationally encoded texts can be applied.

The new approaches can for the greater part be classified in two main groups. The first one is of semantic text analysis methodologies. In these methodologies variables indicate interrelations that themes may have in texts. The second approach of network text analyses methodologies affords variables that characterize entire networks of semantically linked themes.

The three approaches (thematic, semantic, and network) are introduced briefly in this chapter. In the next three chapters each is discussed respectively in greater detail.[1]

Thematic text analysis

Thematic text analysis (sometimes referred to as traditional text analysis) is the term for any text analysis in which variables indicate the occurrence (or frequency of occurrence) of particular concepts. Practitioners of thematic text analysis usually reserve the term 'theme' for broader classes of concepts. The theme can be considered as subject and as attribute (Stone, 1997: 36). In case it is a subject the analysis is concentrated on a specific referent (e.g., the president, the US, British foreign policy, communism). Themes as attributes are indicated by their measures of quantification. Stone remarks '"Theme" continues to be used in a loose, general way for analysing patterns in text' (1997: 37). Thematic text analysis allows the investigator to determine what, and how frequently, concepts occur in texts. The method is particularly useful when the investigator is interested in the prominence of various concepts in texts, possibly reflecting broad cultural shifts.

The information in concepts

The data matrix in a thematic text analysis has one row for each randomly sampled block of text, and one column for each theme that may occur in these text blocks. Say the following sentence comprises a text block:

'I always play fair.'

If an investigator is interested in the concept, SELF-REFERENCE, this sentence contains one occurrence of the concept, namely the word 'I'. However, investigators will most likely have numerous concepts they are interested in, and a dictionary containing lists of corresponding words and phrases that reflect each.

Cells in a thematic data matrix reflect the number of occurrences of a particular concept within a specific block of text. An example of a data matrix that results is presented in Table 3.1.

ID-numbers correspond to text-blocks. If Concept 1 were SELF-REFERENCE and the first text block were the sentence 'I always play fair,' the '1' in the associated cell would indicate a single occurrence of SELF-REFERENCE in this text-block. Once concept occurrences have been encoded, the frequency and their co-occurrences can be investigated.

If the instrumental approach is followed, the dictionaries are available before the actual coding process starts. As these dictionaries contain all concepts and their corresponding search entries, the coding process is easy to automate. The representational approach however, does not imply on beforehand a predetermined relation between concepts and search entries. These relations depend on the context in which a search entry is used. Therefore this approach is hard to automate. This approach also allows not only to detect new search entries for

Table 3.1 *A data matrix for a thematic text analysis*

ID-number	Concept 1	Concept 2	Concept 3
1	1	0	0
2	0	0	1
3	1	2	1
4	0	3	2
5	0	0	0
.	.	.	.
.	.	.	.
.	.	.	.

concepts in the texts, but also new concepts might be derived from information in the texts.

Methods

In thematic text analysis one can report occurrences and co-occurrences of concepts. Occurrences indicate the prominence of themes. When compared across contexts they can afford inferences about, for example, culture's changing themes, ideas, issues, and dilemmas (Namenwirth and Weber, 1987) or differences between media in representation news content about the same issue (Klein, 1996). Looking at co-occurrences means looking at associations among themes. This analysis is known as contingency analysis. In this type of analysis the goal is to calculate associations among occurrence measures, and to infer what the resulting pattern of association means. Problems occur if these inferences are about how concepts are related. Assume the following text block is investigated: 'The man likes detective stories, but his wife prefers love themes.' The concepts MAN (represented by 'the man') and LOVE THEME (represented by 'love themes') co-occur in this block, but no relation between the two is specified. For such inferences relations should have been encoded *a priori*, not via *ad hoc post hoc* looks at the texts.

Semantic approach to text analysis

In the thematic approach concepts are counted, in the semantic approach relations among concepts are also encoded. These relations are found in clauses. The advantage of this approach over the traditional thematic one is that it 'preserves the complex relations between parts of text and thus preserves much of the narrative flavour of the original text. ... The relational properties of data collected using a semantic grammar make it possible to analyse words and their interrelations statistically' (Franzosi, 1989: 137).

The move from a thematic to a semantic text analysis expands the types of questions that a researcher can answer. Referring to propaganda techniques in making this point, Roberts (1989: 169) notes that in a thematic analysis a possible research question would be: 'What themes are mentioned in propaganda that are not mentioned in other communications?' Using the semantic approach the question can be extended to: 'What syntactic strategies are used by political leaders when their policies fail (or succeed)?' Unlike the former question, the latter asks about concrete relations among concepts used within different social contexts.

The information in clauses

Semantically encoding data requires that one fit concepts that occur in a clause into a semantic grammar. The concept of clause is the usual one here, namely a sentence or part-of-a-sentence that (explicitly or implicitly) contains an inflected verb, an optional subject and/or object, plus all modifiers related to this verb, subject, and object. Take the sentence: 'The lower the prices, the more the customers.' This sentence is comprised of two clauses, because it implicitly contains two inflected instances of the verb to be ('the lower the prices are, the more the customers will be there'). Thus one determines the number of clauses in a text by counting its implicitly and explicitly inflected verbs. A semantic grammar is a template into which codes for concepts are fit. For example, let us consider a four-position semantic grammar for encoding opinion statements appearing in newspaper editorials. The grammar specifies the following four syntactic components:

- *Agency*   the initiator of an activity;
- *Position*   the position regarding the agency's activity;
- *Action*   the activity under consideration;
- *Object*   the target of this activity.

Applying this template to the sentence 'People don't listen to each other enough,' would require assigning the concepts '*people*' to the component agency, '*ought to*' to the position component, '*listen*' to the action component, and '*people*' to the object component. Other examples are *Unemployed people* (agency) *cannot* (position) *improve* (action) *their standard of living* (object), and *gasoline taxes* (object) *must not* (position) *be raised* (action). (Note that in this last sentence no agency is encoded, because no manifest raiser of taxes was mentioned.)

This semantic grammar has the Subject–Modal–auxiliary–verb–Verb–Object (or S–M–V–O) form used in linguistic content analysis (Roberts, 1989, 1997c). The work of Markoff et al. (1974) on *cahiers de doléances* of 1789 applies a

V–O form of semantic grammar, whereas Franzosi applies a S–V–O (or what he refers to as a Subject–Action–Object) form to narratives on Italian labour disputes. In most of these cases valence information (regarding negation, evaluation, etc.) is subsumed under the verb component. For this reason one sometimes refers to a semantic grammar as having a Subject–Verb–Valence–Object (S–V–V–O) form. By taking texts relational characteristics into account, semantic text analysis improves upon thematic text analysis methods and overcomes many of its problems. Based on a thematic text analysis, co-occurrence of subject and object can be identified, in the semantic text analysis the relation is specified and might be investigated.

Table 3.2 *A data matrix for a semantic text analysis*

ID-number	Agent	Position	Action	Object
1	12	07	34	12
2	08	03	22	88
3	14	03	34	70
4	10	01	35	70
5	16	11	29	52
.	.	.	.	.
.	.	.	.	.
.	.	.	.	.

Table 3.2 illustrates the type of data matrix produced when texts are semantically encoded. Note that numbers in the cells of this matrix correspond to specific concepts. For example, 'People don't listen to each other enough' could be encoded under the first ID using 12 as the code for 'person,' 7 for 'ought,' and 34 for 'listen.'

Methods

Semantically encoded data can be used to make inferences about the conditions under which texts' authors take specific positions on others' intentions. For example, when a government's totalitarian leadership initiates a public relations campaign to 'democratize' its image in the US press, such data could be used to test whether a significant increase had occurred from before to after the campaign in the odds that US news stories describe the regime (subject) attempting (position) to heed (action) its citizens (object).

Investigators have used the semantic approach for a wide variety of purposes. For example, Gottschalk (1997) uses the approach in generating scores on various scales indicating psychological traits like anxiety or hostility. Roberts (1989, 1997a) has developed a generic semantic grammar to facilitate coders' disambiguation of illocutionary ambiguities in natural language. Bierschenk (1991) applies a semantic grammar to create a topological representation of the mentality a text presents, a topology generated using cluster analysis. Other investigators collect data (concepts and their relations) in a more direct way.

Network approach to text analysis

A third type of variable is afforded within network text analyses, or map analysis. Network text analysis originated with the observation that after one has encoded semantic links among concepts, one can proceed to construct networks of semantically linked concepts. When concepts are depicted as networks, one is afforded more information than the frequency at which specific concepts are linked in each block of text; one is also able to characterize concepts and/or linkages according to their position within the network. For example, let us imagine that we construct a network of concepts in which all linkages indicate causal relations. Assigning the names concept A and concept B to any pair of concepts in the network, one could develop a measure of 'the causal-salience of concept A on concept B' as the proportion of 'all sequences of causal linkages with concept A as the cause' in which concept B is the effect. Note how such a measure draws on more than isolated semantically-linked concepts in blocks of text. It incorporates information on all concepts and links within network representations of text-blocks. Thus a data matrix might be generated from a network that contained variables that measured the causal-salience of each pair of its concepts.[2]

Figure 3.1 contains an example of a network.[3] Let us assume that all lines in the network represent causal relations. Concept A has both a direct and an indirect (via B) influence on concept C, concept A has a direct influence on concept B, and concept B has a direct influence on concept C. There are four lines of influence. If these all get the same weight, the influence of concept A on concept C is 0.5 (due to the direct and the indirect lines), and the influences of concept A on B and of concept B on C are each weighted 0.25, because there is only one line between each of these pairs of concepts.

The data matrix in Table 3.3 is one that might have been generated based on a sample of networks all of which contained these three concepts. The causal salience measures in the first row of the matrix correspond to the network depicted in Figure 3.1. The numbers in the other rows denote causal salience measures for other networks in the sample.

The information in networks

A link between concepts might indicate an unspecified association between two concepts, but links can also denote specific relations between concepts. (Carley, 1993: 94 ff) lists four formal properties that links may have: meaning (the

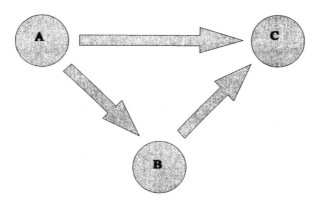

Figure 3.1 *A network of causal relations among concepts*

Table 3.3 *A data matrix for a network text analysis*

ID-number	A on B	A on C	B on C	B on A	C on A	C on B
1	.25	.50	.25	.00	.00	.00
2	.25	.00	.50	.00	.25	.00
3	.00	.00	.25	.25	.50	.00
4	.00	.00	.00	.50	.25	.25
5	.00	.25	.00	.50	.00	.25
.	.	.	.	.	.	.
.	.	.	.	.	.	.
.	.	.	.	.	.	.

content, such as 'is friends with'), directionality (one- or two-way), strength (to be defined as: intensity, certainty, frequency, and so on), and sign (positive, negative). By using scores on these properties the information in networks can be represented.

When the concepts have been identified and the properties that can exist between concepts have been defined, coding can start. Clauses are coded using these concepts and relations. The resulting network serves as the representation of the model. The data found for the network can be analysed statistically. For all pairs of concepts the scores on the four properties can be stored in a data matrix like the one in Table 3.3.

Methods

At this moment two network methods are available that allow statistical inferences, namely cognitive mapping and network evaluation approaches. These methods start from different positions.

Cognitive mapping involves extracting linguistic relations from texts or transcripts and then representing the 'mental models' or 'cognitive maps' that individual sources had in their memory at the time the relations were expressed. The idea of mental models has had extensive treatment in the social sciences (cf. Goffman, 1963; Blumer, 1969; Minsky, 1975; Johnson-Laird, 1983; Gentner and Stevens, 1983; etc.). The following are three key theoretical assumptions drawn from this literature into cognitive mapping methodology:

- Mental models are internal (i.e., subjective) representations;
- Linguistic expressions reveal mental models;
- Mental models can be represented as networks of concepts.

Within a cognitive map, the meaning of a concept is the aggregate set of relations it has to all other concepts that make up a conceptual network. Mental models are dynamic structures that are constructed and expanded as individuals make inferences and gather information. They contain both specific information about particular items, and general (or social) knowledge. A transcript of an individual's speech is a reflection of the individual's mental model at a particular point in time. Accordingly, such texts may be thought of as a sampling of information from the individual's memory.

The map comparison method (Carley, 1986) affords not only graphic descriptions of individuals' mental models, but also comparisons among models maintained by various social groups. Texts are parsed into clauses and words and phrases are assigned to meaning concepts. The investigator begins by identifying concepts and the types of relationships that can exist between pairs of these concepts. Then texts are encoded using these concepts and relationships. The resultant coded data can then be displayed graphically as mental models or compared across groups of individuals.

Encoded data can be compared as unions or intersections of S–V–V–O statements among groups of individuals. The union of all statements consists of all statements that occur in the networks, even if it is only once in one network. The intersection of statements consists of the statements that occur in all the networks. If a statement is missing in only one network, the statement is not in the intersection. The union of statements uttered by members of a group comprise the group's total knowledge on a particular topic. When statements intersect among the mental models of all members in a group, they comprise the knowledge on which group members hold a consensus. For example, among residents of an M.I.T. dormitory, Carley (1986: 166–9) found the concept of 'ideal dormitory supervisor' universally associated with concepts such as 'genuine,' 'honest,' and 'not artificial' for one group of residents (the 'heads'),

but with concepts such as 'analytic,' 'mature,' and 'gets high grades' for another
(the 'gnerds'). This type of text analysis is particularly useful for drawing
inferences about group consensus (when the frequency of maps containing the
same proposition approaches the number of group members) and group
dissension (when this frequency approaches zero).

The network evaluation approach was first elaborated by Van Cuilenburg et
al. (1986). The method has its roots in evaluative assertion analysis (Osgood et
al., 1956). Osgood et al. start from the position that every language has three
kinds of words:

- 'common meaning terms'
  These are words that have a common evaluative among 'reasonably
  sophisticated users of the language.' For example, the common meaning
  of words such as 'peace' is always positive; whereas that of words like
  'enemy' is always negative in connotation.
- 'attitude objects'
  These are with no fixed evaluative meaning. For example, a word like
  'car' is likely to be evaluated differently by different people.
- 'verbal connectors'
  These are words that indicate the association ('it is...') or dissociation ('it
  is not...') of attitude objects with common meaning terms or with other
  attitude objects.

By investigating how attitude objects are associated or dissociated, one can
investigate how these attitude objects are valued in a text. For this it is
necessary to parse texts into nuclear sentences, in which the three above-men-
tioned word-types can be found. After that, nuclear sentences can be recombined
in a way that reveals structure in the text. Osgood et al. (1956) referred to two
forms of nuclear sentences:

Attitude Object / Verbal Connector / Common Meaning Term

and

Attitude Object$_1$ / Verbal Connector / Attitude Object$_2$.

Let us again use the sentence: 'The aggressive thief threatens the police officer.'
In the previous chapter we have seen that this is read as two nuclear sentences:
'The thief / is / aggressive.' and 'The thief / threatens / the police officer.' The
first sentence contains a common meaning term (aggressive), the second one
does not.

The network evaluation approach has especially been used to investigate how
newspapers report on issues in which governments are involved. Van Cuilenburg, et al. (1986) report about the conflict as represented in the media between
the USA. and Iran at the time Khomeiny had taken over power from the Shah.

They found that the media were positive about the performance of the USA (the US-president said correctly) and negative about both Khomeiny (terroristic revolution; religious fanaticism) and the Shah (dictatorial power).

Other distinctions

Carley (1994) makes a distinction among conceptual, procedural, relational, and emotional analysis. The conceptual analysis is identical to what I have called the thematic analysis. Relational analysis includes both the semantic and the network approaches as already defined. I consider the emotional analysis as a special kind of relational analysis, namely one in which the relation between concepts expresses some emotion (John loves Mary).

Procedural analysis is different. It focuses on the process of identifying procedures and actions that are present in a text. It therefore provides information about the structure of a given task and the repertoire of actions that an individual can draw upon when engaging in a task. Carley distinguishes two distinct procedural approaches: decision based and plot based.

In decision based procedural analysis the investigator tries to capture the explicit and implicit policy that is followed in performing a task. This kind of analysis is also known as protocol analysis (Ericsson and Simon, 1994).[4] The plot based procedural analysis focuses on the story or plot in articles or books. For example, ethnographic analyses are part of this group of analyses (Griffin, 1993; Heise, 1991). These analyses are not quantitative analyses any more, but a kind of qualitative text analysis technique.

Many other distinctions hold for which similar remarks can be made. These analyses focus on description and interpretation. The methods applied in these analyses are generally referred to as methods for qualitative research. In Chapter 8 attention is called for this type of research.

Example data

Each of the next chapters will take up one of the three approaches in detail. In each a single data set will be analysed (then reanalysed) using a computer program suited to the approach at hand. The entire data set is analysed according to the thematic and semantic approach, and parts of it are used in analyses using the network approach. In this way benefits and limitations of the approach should become clear. It is not my purpose to discuss or even compare the computer programs used in the analyses. Software descriptions are given in the appendix.

The data set consists of 40 text blocks that were spoken by sportsmen about injuries and fair play in sports. The data to be analysed together are sometimes indicated as the corpus. The data were collected for this example. The theoretical notion is based on Liebrand et al. (1986), who tested the hypothesis that people always perceive themselves as acting more fairly than other people doing sports. Simply put, people think, 'I am fair and they are unfair.' The main concepts of interest are self reference, other reference, fair, unfair, seriousness of incident, injury, and aggression. Although more are possible, these few concepts will suffice in illustrating the three approaches to text analysis. The data are as follows:

1. He made a sliding, and as he started too late, he hit me against the ankle. I had an enormous pain.
2. By accident I smashed the ball into the audience. Fortunately nobody was hurt.
3. One should not listen to the audience, too often their advice is to do someone harm, or they already do it themselves by hissing.
4. Playing cards is not dangerous, nobody can hit you with them like with a ball.
5. The players of the other team were unfair, they caused a crash.
6. I always play fair.
7. The only problem is that you never know what your opponent does.
8. I'm always very cautious. I would feel very bad in case I would kick someone into hospital.
9. You should never lose your mind.
10. I always have to remember it is just a game, therefore I have to keep it fair.
11. They were very brutal.
12. He hit me in an awful way, I became dizzy, and had to consult a physician. This is no boxing any more.
13. He hooked Johnny in such a way that he fell, and broke his leg.
14. When you are running there quite alone, you sometimes feel very lonesome.
15. You train every day, there is no time left for other activities.
16. They tried to make us afraid by yelling very hard.
17. He fell, and said that I had hurt him and he had a lot of pain. I'm convinced he is lying.
18. I played far too long, therefore a muscle in my knee got sprained.
19. When I went down skiing I fell and broke my leg.
20. It was wet, therefore I fell and broke my arm. I should have been more cautious.
21. He is an awful person, in the boxing match last week he beat his opponent on the head so that he got brain damage.
22. I like a rough play, but it should be fair. If so, nobody gets injured.
23. Rugby players learn how to fall, so they hardly have problems.
24. He yelled: knock him down.
25. During the training the gymnastics player fell out of the rings.
26. At the end of a football match I always have so many blue spots on my legs.
27. The opponents are always intimidating us. They really try to make us afraid of them.
28. I always train alone, so you miss talking to other people.

29.   I like swimming, it is very good for your condition.
30.   At the end of a match I am always out of breath. It gives you a good feeling.
31.   The boy could not stand that he was losing, so he started playing in a way that was not fair.
32.   I don't understand why people like wrestling, those people almost kill each other.
33.   She was losing the match, therefore she became very angry and started yelling at the referee.
34.   He pushed his shoulder against the other cyclist, so this person fell badly and had a concussion of the brain.
35.   Normally speaking, she is very friendly, but in the field she always is a fury.
36.   If I can prevent a goal made by the others by tackling someone, I won't do it. Sorry.
37.   It is part of the game to be fair.
38.   In a hurdle-race you have to stay in the middle of your track, if you do so you can't hurt anybody, and nobody can hurt you.
39.   After a quarter of an hour I got a ball in my stomach, which causes an enormous pain.
40.   It was wet, therefore I slipped on the course, and broke my arm.

Notes

1. In the first chapter it was mentioned that communication consists of six basic elements. With respect to one of these, the message, different parts are distinguished: intent, content, relation/sign, grammatical form. These parts will get attention in the following three chapters as the various approaches are discussed.
2. Other types of variables that network text analysts have added to their data matrices include measures of themes' 'conductivity' – the number of linkages that the theme provides between other pairs of themes, and indicators of theme linkages that are logically implied, but not explicitly stated in each block of text.
3. In fact Figure 3.1 contains only one type of network, although it is the most frequently occurring one. A full overview is shown in Figure 3.2 below.

   The network in Figure 3.2 contains several levels. In general the analyses are on the level of points p and r. These refer to concepts as used by the researcher. These concepts, however, refer often to complete networks on another (more detailed) level that is not used in the analyses. For example, point p might refer to the concept 'labour market'. This market consists of parts that also constitute a network, but that are not used, like employees looking for a new job, and employers looking for new workers. Part A in Figure 3.2 might represent this network. In the same way the network in part X is represented by point r.

   Note: The network from Figure 3.1 is identical to part A in Figure 3.2, only the graphical representation is rotated.
4. A specific way of coding which comes close to decision analysis is applied by Gallhofer et al. (1986). They tried to derive a decision-makers' decision tree on the basis of his argumentation.

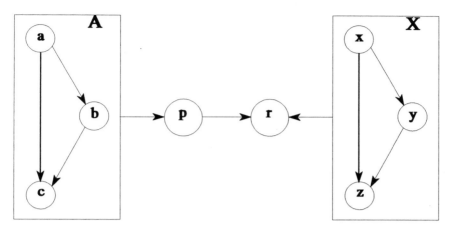

Figure 3.2 *Types of networks*

4

Thematic text analysis

In many studies, research hypotheses are tested by investigating the (frequency of) occurrences of certain themes in text blocks. The basic assumption is that there is a relation between the occurrence of themes and the interest in these themes by the producer of the text. Often a comparison between specific groups is made, even in a specific time period. In his introductory texts on computer-aided text analysis Weber (1984, 1990) uses an example in which occurrences of 'wealth' in the Democratic and Republican platforms are compared for the period 1844–1980. In a figure he shows for each party the percentage of various categories of words in each party's platforms over time. With respect to economic matters (WEALTH-TOTAL) he showed that before 1896 the parties varied diametrically in their concern (as indicated by the absence of similar patterns in percentage of words used to indicate these economic matters), and that after 1896 the parties show similar levels of concern. Since 1952 there was a tendency to move opposite again.

Commercial television stations get most of their money from advertising. Many advertisement blocks are centred around the news programs. For these stations it is important that many people look at the news. A distinctive style might attract more people. Klein (1996) investigated differences in news presentation between commercial television stations and the public ones in Germany on three subsequent days in 1986. He investigated the news brought by two public and two commercial stations during the main presentations. These start between 6:30 p.m. and 8:00 p.m. The data consisted of the transcripts of the messages. Messages were identified according to sender, day, and sequence number in the news. In total, 252 messages were analysed. The author applied 16 concepts to these messages. Coding according to the instrumental approach was performed by using the program Intext. Differences among the four TV-stations were first indicated by comparing the mean frequency of occurrence of each concept. After that statistical technique of correspondence analysis was applied. The 16 concepts and the four TV-stations together were represented in a three dimensional space. Messages on the public stations were more likely to be political news and involving conflict than were messages on the commercial ones. Messages on the commercial stations were more likely to be sensation, remarkable events, sex and love affairs than were messages on the other stations. One station even takes an extreme position, as it gives far more attention to these themes than any of the other stations. One public station emphasized most of all factors like actuality (relevant news that just occurred) and scientific argumentation, the other one especially the consequences of what had happened.

Differences between men's and women's speech on prime-time television were investigated by Sly (1991). Her data consisted of 50 transcribed conversations from one-minute segments randomly selected from prime-time viewing hours during 1990 across the three main US television networks: ABC, CBS, and NBC. Prime-time viewing hours are defined as extending from 7 p.m. to 10 p.m. on Monday through Saturday and from 6 p.m. to 10 p.m. on Sunday. Segments were only included in the sample if they contained some conversation and were at least partially non-commercial. A representational approach was used to identify significant differences between what men spoke of and what women spoke of on prime-time television. For each concept she could compare the difference between the mean frequency of occurrence in the male and female groups by applying a t-test for the difference between two independent means. She found among other things that many more of the transcripts contained male-only speech than female-only speech. When this fact is taken into account, by adjusting for female-only and male-only minutes, there are no notable differences between themes in male and female speech. However, a co-occurrence analysis suggested that female speech is more structured than male speech both before, and to a lesser degree after, the absence of female or male speakers is taken into account. Sly's findings further suggested that speech on prime-time television is structured differently according to gender.

Other illustrative applications of thematic text analysis, in which the computer is not necessarily used, can be found in Smith (1992). The text analyses in this book are primarily applied to the measurement of motivation and personality. Part II of Stone et al. (1966) contains many text analysis studies from the beginning of the computer era, of which make use of the General Inquirer.

This chapter begins with presenting the instrumental approach in the thematic text analysis. First, an explanation is given of how a thematic text analysis is organized, and then a discussion follows regarding specific directions that have developed since the 1960s. The representational approach is dealt with in the second part of the chapter.

The instrumental approach

Benefits of computer-assisted over hand-coded text analysis have frequently been formulated in a way that is suited for the instrumental view (Weber, 1984: 17; Heinrich, 1996: 327). The rules for coding text are made explicit and the computer provides perfect coder reliability in the application of these rules. The computer acts as a clerk who does not have to be familiar with the topic under investigation. With respect to the first program for computer-assisted text analysis, The General Inquirer, this was stated as follows: 'It is useful to liken the Inquirer to an energetic, compulsive, but stupid clerk who has been trained in text analysis mechanics. This clerk has no ideas of his own but waits for the specification of concepts and scoring procedures supplied by the investigator. Once these instructions are received and not found to be self-contradictory, the clerk is able to apply them systematically to endless amounts of data' (Stone et al., 1966: 68).

Wood (1980: 275, modifying the view presented by Holsti) argued that such analysis is appropriate when: (1) explicit and unambiguous coding instructions can be formulated, although they may not have to be available *a priori*, (2) the unit of analysis is the word or the delineated word phrase and inferences are to be based on frequency of occurrence, (3) the analysis includes a large number of content concepts, and (4) there is no reason to suspect beforehand that more than one coding operation will be necessary, or that one data set will be used for a series of investigations.

When the analysis starts many decisions have already been made. Variables have been constructed based on operationalizations of notions from the theory. Coding instructions have been formulated. Units of analysis and enumerations have been decided upon.

Investigators often want to know which words appear in the texts and with what frequency. Many investigators focus their activities on the most frequently occurring words. Table 4.1 contains the words from our example data set that appear at least twice.[1] Note that personal pronouns and articles arise most in the texts.

Three aspects of such a frequency list that deserve attention are mentioned by Weber (1984: 129). I will add two other aspects:

1. *Omitting words*. The computer program that generated the list might have been instructed to omit words like 'a' and 'the', forms of the verb 'to be' as 'is' or 'was'. These are words that are usually substantively uninteresting. Several programs use a list of words that should be excluded from the analysis. These words are called stop-words, go-words or trivial-words.[2] Personal pronouns are generally also part of such a list, but because they are important in the example, they are not excluded here. In Table 4.1 stop-words are listed in italics. If they were not to have been entered into the list, the size of this list would indeed have been considerably reduced.

2. *Word-endings*. Computer programs often do not identify word-endings, leaving them to list words as they are. Weber reports that 'Republican' and 'Republicans' appear as separate entries. Such fine breakdowns must be kept in mind when using the word lists. Table 4.1 contains the words 'started', 'losing', and 'boxing', which are verb forms. If these words are relevant with respect to the research question, and a program is used

Table 4.1   *Ordered word frequency list from the example data set generated by using Intext (only words appearing twice or more are included)*

49 .	4 like	2 One
33 ,	4 hurt	2 *no*
26 I	4 *do*	2 *never*
24 *the*	4 *can*	2 *more*
19 *a*	4 broke	2 me
16 He	3 way	2 make
13 *is*	3 us	2 made
12 you	3 *too*	2 m
11 *to*	3 *This*	2 losing
11 *of*	3 t	2 leg
11 *and*	3 started	2 *into*
10 it	3 Playing	2 him
10 *in*	3 people	2 good
8 *very*	3 pain	2 game
8 *so*	3 *on*	2 *for*
8 *always*	3 *If*	2 feel
6 they	3 hit	2 enormous
6 *that*	3 his	2 end
6 my	3 got	2 down
6 *have*	3 ball	2 cautious
6 fell	3 *At*	2 *but*
5 *was*	2 yelling	2 brain
5 *therefore*	2 *would*	2 boxing
5 other	2 *with*	2 became
5 *had*	2 *When*	2 *be*
5 fair	2 wet	2 awful
5 *By*	2 *were*	2 audience
5 *an*	2 train	2 arm
5 '	2 *there*	2 *are*
4 your	2 them	2 *am*
4 *should*	2 someone	2 alone
4 She	2 players	2 *against*
4 *not*	2 person	2 afraid
4 nobody	2 *out*	
4 match	2 opponent	

Note: Intext presents the words in alphabetical order, and not in order of frequency of occurrence

can identify word-endings, this problem can be solved for these words.

3.   *Low- and high-frequency words.* There are many more low-frequency than high-frequency words. In general one will be interested in words that occur with high frequency. These might operate as indicators for specific concepts. Depending on the goal of the investigation, words that hardly occur may also be interesting. The moment a word is first

mentioned might delineate a substantive change in discourse – a finding common in propaganda analyses.

4. *Breaking down words.* Words may be broken down in unusual ways. In Table 4.1 the word 't' is found three times. Once the word 'don' is found. Let it be clear the original word was 'don't'. The other single 't''s are part of the words 'can't' and 'won't'. The single 'm' that is found twice comes from 'I'm'. The single apostrophe is considered as a separation mark in Intext. These words should have been added to the list of trivial words. This was not done here to show that one should be cautious with respect to specific marks used in words.[3]

5. *Broader group.* Words might be part of a broader group that is more interesting. For example a text might contain names of boys and girls. What is interesting is not 'Joe', 'Andy' or 'Doris', but 'boy' or 'girl'. This can be handled in the dictionary, or in a more direct way by replacing the names in the original text either manually or using a program such as MECA's Translate.

Word lists such as that in Table 4.1 can be useful in drawing preliminary conclusions. Often the inventory is useful in developing the list of concepts and related search entries to be used in a final investigation. Search entries then become actual words or phrases to be identified in the texts.

Key word in context lists

In many situations it is not enough to see just the words that appear in the texts. To interpret them accurately, the context in which they appear must also be clear. Only in context can one judge whether words that occur are used in a consistent way. In case a word is used in a way inconsistent with other usages of the word the context is likely to give information about the content category that corresponds to a specific meaning of the word. The context in which each occurrence of a word to look for appears is shown in the so-called key word in context, or KWIC, lists provided by computer programs. Wood (1984: 291) lists some other features of KWIC lists. They provide an identification field for locating the texts within which key words appear. Moreover, they can serve as an inclusion or exclusion list during the coding process. Table 4.2 contains an example of a KWIC list, sometimes called a concordance (Weber, 1984: 130) for the word 'I.' Each occurrence of the word 'I' is presented between the words that precede and follow it. Some KWIC software allows multiple-word search entries, not on just single words, to be centred in these lists. In the instrumental approach KWIC lists can be used to set up search entries during dictionary development.[4] They are routinely used by investigators to verify *post hoc* whether their interpretations are valid.

Table 4.2 *Key word in context list of the search entry ' I ' generated with Intext*

```
1  late , he hit me against the ankle . ·  I  ·had an enormous pain . *tarted too
1  . Fortunately nobody was* By accident·  I  ·smashed the ball into the audience
1                                      *·  I  ·am always playing fair . *
1  feel very bad in case I would kick s*·  I  ·' m always very cautious . I would
1  kick s* I ' m always very cautious . ·  I  ·would feel very bad in case I would
1  tious . I would feel very bad in case·  I  ·would kick someone into hospital .
1  a game , therefore I have to keep it*·  I  ·always have to remember it is just
1  emember it is just a game , therefore·  I  ·have to keep it fair . * have to re
1  physici* He hit me in an awful way , ·  I  ·became dizzy , and had to consult a
1  in . I ' m c* He fell , and said that·  I  ·had hurt him and he had a lot of pa
1  d hurt him and he had a lot of pain . ·  I  ·' m convinced he is lying . * I had
1  muscle in my knee got sprained . *  *·  I  ·played far too long , therefore a
1  my leg . *                 * When·  I  ·went down skiing I fell and broke
1                 * When I went down skiing·  I  ·fell and broke my leg . *
1  ve been more * It was wet , therefore·  I  ·fell and broke my arm . I should ha
1  , therefore I fell and broke my arm . ·  I  ·should have been more cautious . *,
1  e fair . If so , nobody gets injured*·  I  ·like a rough play , but it should b
1  y leg* At the end of a football match·  I  ·always have so many blue spots on m
1  alking to other people . *          *·  I  ·always train alone , so you miss t
1  r your condition . *                *·  I  ·like swimming , it is very good fo
1  you a good fee* At the end of a match·  I  ·am always out of breath . It gives
1  wrestling , those people almost kill*·  I  ·don ' t understand why people like
1  rs by tackling some one , I won '* If·  I  ·can prevent a goal made by the othe
1  by the others by tackling some one , ·  I  ·won ' t do it . Sorry . *goal made
1  uses an e* After a quarter of an hour·  I  ·got a ball in my stomach , which ca
1  my arm . *      * It was wet , therefore·  I  ·slipped on the course , and broke
```

Note: The word that is investigated is placed in the middle of the line between dots. Intext generates a KWIC-list for all the words in the dictionary at once. The number preceding each line refers to the corresponding concept, here the SELF-REFERENCE

Dictionaries

The design of a dictionary, composed of concepts and corresponding search entries, involves the differentiation and specification of theoretical ideas. A dictionary is a concrete representation of the investigator's theory as it is related to verbal data.[5] Here it does not matter whether one uses one or several concepts. Theoretical hypotheses must be expressed as discrete concepts that will be at the heart of the text analysis (Wood, 1980: 281). Finding these concepts in a way that they fit perfectly to the theory is a time consuming process. Therefore generally several versions of one dictionary are available.

General dictionaries have advantages listed by Weber (1984: 132):

1. They are a standardized classification instrument;
2. They minimize the time needed for dictionary construction, validation, and revision;
3. They provide flexibility regarding the concepts employed.

In the past some general dictionaries have been constructed from specific theoretical points of view. They thus contain concepts as intended by their creator's theories. Well known examples of such dictionaries are the Lasswell Value Dictionary (LVD) and the Harvard IV Psychosocial Dictionary (Weber,

1990). The LVD was especially used from the mid 1960s through the late 1980s, the other dictionary from the early 1960s through the early 1980s. Stone et al. (1966) have described earlier dictionaries. The first editions of the Harvard Psychosocial Dictionary were in part based on Parsonian and Freudian concepts, while the Lasswell Value Dictionary is based on Lasswell and Kaplan's (1950) conceptual scheme for political analysis. It was constructed primarily for the analysis of political documents such as newspaper editorials and party platforms.[6]

Unfortunately, little research has been done to comparatively evaluate the validity of these dictionaries (Weber, 1990). On the other hand these general dictionaries provide the investigator with concepts into which most words of most texts can be classified. Their use thus saves time in dictionary construction, and affords some degree of comparison across research projects.

Investigators often have no use for such standardized concepts. Anticipating problems at the advent of computerized text analysis methodologies De Sola Pool (1959b: 213) wondered 'how ready we are to establish standard measures ... in content analysis. Such a measure is convenient when many researchers are working on the same variable, and when someone succeeds in working out good concepts for that variable. It is doubtful that either of those criteria can be met in most areas of content analysis'. Holsti (1969: 102) also listed arguments for not using such standard concepts, among them the desire for originality among investigators who are not willing to adopt categories developed by others, and an insufficient consensus on theory, such that concepts are often developed to fit the data at hand.

Another problem is that the dictionaries may be too general, covering a broader area than is needed for most investigations. They also do not seem to be time and place bound. Especially search entries might receive another connotation over time, and in one culture a search entry might have another meaning than in another culture. Therefore an investigator has to wonder whether a dictionary developed for the research he or she is going to perform might be preferred. This dictionary can be far more specific than a general one.

Concept categories

The concept category is defined in Chapter 2 as existing of words and phrases that are aggregated and that represent a theoretical concept relevant for the investigator's theory. Several concept categories together that refer to different aspects of a broad topic constitute a dictionary.

Wood (1980: 276) distinguishes *a priori* and *a posteriori* coding schemes. The *a priori* coding scheme implies that the concepts and entries are available before coding starts. The scheme to be used should be justified theoretically, and therefore the investigator's concepts should be used. This is the position taken by Holsti (1969) when he states that 'explicit and unambiguous coding instructions could be formulated.' In fact, it is the position taken by all who developed dictionaries in the instrumental text analysis tradition.

Most concepts and their search entries are not developed at one moment. In part they will be based on a preliminary analysis of the texts to be coded, on a sample of these texts, or, on a sample of similar texts. Once the investigator is satisfied with the concepts and search entries the definitive coding of the texts starts. Note that in this procedure concepts and search entries are available before the coding starts. Many text analysis programs perform the analysis at once using information available in specific files (a file containing concepts, a file containing search entries, a file containing trivial words, etc.). If a new search entry is added, the complete analysis must be repeated.

Investigators are always interested in at least one hypothesis. Therefore they can construct a set of concepts based on this hypothesis. Klein, who was mentioned at the beginning of this chapter, investigated hypotheses about the presentation of news. He developed 16 concepts that were relevant to measure relevant characteristics in the news presentation (e.g., consequences of events, conflict, romantics, age, science). The dictionary that is specifically developed to measure such characteristics usually has high validity and reliability (Weber, 1984: 132).

Concepts can be relatively narrow and be captured in only few search entries. An example of such a concept is SELF-REFERENCE. This concept only contains first person pronouns. A concept like EMOTION is very broad, it contains search entries like love, hate, envy, and so on.

Sometimes concepts are hierarchically related within a dictionary. The higher level refers to a theme, and the lower levels refer to specific concepts of the theme. For example the higher level might be 'unfair behaviour', and the lower levels refer to ways in which this is demonstrated: 'verbal intimidation', 'bodily harm', and so on.[7] Moreover, hierarchical concepts can be approached by allowing concepts to have two parts, for example one would get 'unfair:verbal' and 'unfair:physical'. Once entered into a data base or spreadsheet program, these concepts can easily be split in separate variables.

Constructing a dictionary

The construction of a dictionary involves two stages. In the first stage the investigator decides what concepts will be used. This depends on the theoretical frame of reference under consideration. Concepts were discussed above. If one is going to create a dictionary with numerous concepts, two things need specific attention. The investigator must make sure that the concepts are well-defined and span the meaning space of the texts, and that words are assigned to concepts with high validity.

In the second stage search entries are specified that belong to each of the concepts. In this second stage two sub-questions must be answered (Stone et al., 1966: 152):

- How can one obtain a list of possible search entries for the concept?
- How is one to decide which entries to select for the concept?

Finding the search entries is an empirical problem. In part the aspirant entries are easy to imagine based on examples at hand. They are also found when the total list of words in the texts is investigated. Here the investigator concentrates on very frequently occurring words or on specific words. The investigator will not recognize all relevant words at once, but might only be aware of them after the program has already run using the search entries defined up to that moment. The reverse situation is also possible, irrelevant words are not recognized immediately. In several cases a search entry will have to be modified or even deleted. Modification often consists of changing a search entry: the root of a noun, the stem of a verb, or just a combination of words (in a fixed order). The KWIC method can be used in finding search entries.

In the selection of the entries several problems in the use of dictionaries become evident. Words with an identical stem but different endings can have an identical meaning. In some situations the investigator is not concerned with the words themselves, but with combinations of different words, that is with concepts. Later in this chapter solutions for these problems of different endings and word phrases are discussed.

We have implicitly begun to answer the second of Stone et al.'s questions. Search entries should be assigned to concepts with high validity. Here one easily runs into problems, however. Words are used in specific linguistic and subcultural contexts. If the dictionary were developed for a specific project, the validity would probably be high as the specific words' and phrases' meaning are considered. But, if a general dictionary is used, this dictionary might not cover the meaning of words and phrases that holds for that specific language or culture. This is not a problem from an instrumental perspective, however.

Search entries. Let us assume that the set(s) of concepts to be used have been determined. Now one or more search entries have to be defined for each concept. A search entry consists of a word or a phrase that is indicative of the concept. In Table 4.3 are presented two concepts, SELF-REFERENCE and OTHER-REFERENCE, together with the corresponding search entries. These concepts and their search entries constitute a dictionary. The concepts will be labelled using the tags SELF and OTHER.[8] Text analysis dictionaries consist of concept names, the definitions or rules for assigning search entries to concepts, and the actual assignment of specific entries.

Coding is as follows:

Self-ref.

1.　He made a sliding, and as he started too late, he hit **me** against
　　the ankle. **I** had an enormous pain.　　　　　　　　　　2

Table 4.3 *Search entries for the concepts* SELF-REFERENCE *(01) and* OTHER-REFERENCE *(02)*

01	" I "	01	" our "	02	" his "
01	" me "	01	" our's "	02	" her "
01	" mine "	01	" ourselves "	02	" they "
01	" my "	01	" us "	02	" their "
01	" myself "	02	" he "	02	" opponent "
01	" we "	02	" she "	02	" this boy "

27.   The opponents are always intimidating **us**. They really try to make **us** afraid of them.   2

Other-ref.

1.   **He** made a sliding, and as **he** started too late, **he** hit me against the ankle. I had an enormous pain.   3

27.   The opponents are always intimidating us. **They** really try to make us afraid of them.   1

Note, in Table 4.3 the word 'opponent' is entered as a search entry for the OTHER-REFERENCE. In text block 27 'opponents' is not coded as OTHER-REFERENCE because the word is different from the word in the dictionary. Later in this chapter types of search entries will be introduced. Investigators have to address certain problems that arise in the creation of any concept or set of concepts. These problems stem from the ambiguity of both the concept definitions and of the search entries that are to be assigned to concepts.

The search entries that are used for the concept SELF-REFERENCE include words that are hardly used, like 'ourselves.' Depending on the task one can even prefer to split the reference in entries referring to the plural form ('selves') and to the single form ('self'). The plural form might refer to 'member identification with a group', a theoretical construct (Stone et al., 1966: 138). The list of entries for OTHER-REFERENCE contains pronouns, but also concrete persons (Johnny, opponent) or groups of persons (opponents, which clearly should have been in the list). These concrete ones can only be derived from the data. The way in which the entries have to be organized in a file depends on the computer program that is used.

Disambiguation. A concept might be indicated by different search entries, but the reverse is also possible. A search entry might refer to different concepts.[9] In this situation search entries can be disambiguated by adding some characteristics. For example, spring#1 denotes the season, and spring#2 refers to a source of water. The entry 'fan' is even more complicated. It may refer to a ventilator, to a follower, but also to something that is evaluated in a positive way. So, here three characteristics are needed.

In this latter example a new element is introduced. A judgment is given that is not found directly in the text itself. Fan is associated with a positive connotation. According to the Stanford Political Dictionary (Stone et al., 1966: 189) the word 'pure' has a positive affective connotation, and the word 'scandal' has a negative affective connotation. Such connotations are not found in the text itself, they are defined by the investigator. It is also conceivable that one search entry has several different connotations. For many people the word 'pot' as something to keep flowers in is considered in a positive way. But when it refers to a drug the connotation is evaluated in a negative way. Again this evaluation generally is not found directly in the text.

Information from the context is necessary to judge which meaning is intended. Methods are available in some computer programs to help identify which meaning is the correct one. Decisions are made based on the presence or absence of certain (combinations of) words around the word under investigation. This process is known as *disambiguation*.[10]

Idiomatic ambiguity is very hard to automate. I repeat that in a sentence such as, 'You'll eat your words!', the word, 'eat,' in most situations will be coded as an occurrence of the theme, 'consume,' instead of as 'regret'. Until the computer has been trained to recognize such idiomatic uses of words, ambiguity will remain in the process of classifying these words.

Suffix removal. Before it was noted with regard to search entries that the stem of a word might have different endings. This problem is solved by suffix removal, that is, by removing parts of words in texts so that only the stem remains. The problem might also be solved by using more complex search entries, such that other parts of words than only the end may vary. For example, 'car' and 'motorcar' might be identical entries. Both methods are only applied if the word as found in the text does not appear in the dictionary.

Two notes of warning are called for here: Suffix removal works fine for the English language. However, if text in another language is analysed it may not be useful. Grammatical forms in Slavonic languages, for example, are so complex to render suffix removal almost useless. Furthermore the investigator must be aware that due to suffix removal words might be included that are certainly not wanted. Using 'car' and 'motorcar' as identical entries, implies that also 'Madagascar' is identical. Here is a problem of validity. This is also discussed in the next section.

An alternative for the suffix removal might be to transform all inflected forms of words in the text into uninflected forms, pronouns will be converted to proper nouns, etc. Such is possible if lists exist that contain all possible transformations. When this alternative is followed details of the text will be lost.[11]

Complex search entries. Suffix removal is but a specific illustration of the more general topic of search entries. Words can have not only different endings, but also different beginnings. To allow for this, 'wild-card'-like search entries have been introduced, i.e., search entries that are not completely specified. The unspecified part is generally indicated by an asterix (*) or a question mark (?). Such wild-cards preclude the need to enter all search entries containing a particular sub-string. Instead, a general one, covering the others can be used. Table 4.4 shows how this works in Intext (Klein, 1992: 484).

Table 4.4 *Types of search entries*

type of search entry		search entry	found string(s)
1.	single word	'_attractive_'	attractive
2.	parts of single words		
2.1	in prefix position	'_attractive'	attractive, attractively
2.2	in suffix position	'attractive_'	attractive, unattractive
2.3	in infix position	'attractive'	attractive, unattractively
3.	word sequence	'_attractive person_'	attractive person
4.	word root chains	'<attractive person>'	unattractive person
5.	using wild-cards (?*)	'attra?tive'	attractive, attraktive
6.	case insensitive	U'attractiv'	Attraktivität, attractive

Note, the underscore '_' should be read as a space in the search entry

Source: Adapted from Klein (1992: 484)

The type mentioned under 2.1 in Table 4.4 (i.e., part of single words in prefix position), is in many programs denoted as word root. The word 'opponents' from the sample data set could thus be found using the search entry, '_opponent', where the underscore indicates a preceding space. Klein also refers to combined lists of search entries and specific expressions. Case folding implies that no difference is made between upper and lower case letters. The advantages of using the above search entries he mentions are:

1. The number of search entries is reduced;
2. The concept system can be read more easily;
3. There is no need to specify each grammatical form of a word;
4. The coding is faster;[12]
5. The concept system can be better maintained.

Klein is also aware of some disadvantages:

1. Case folding (i.e., insensitively) may lead to unwanted multiple coding;
2. Double or multiple search entries are difficult to find.

These disadvantages indicate that ambiguity might be introduced. When search entries are parts of single words, specific words may be coded that should not be. In any case, when wild-card search entries are used, the investigator must be aware of unintended effects this might have.

A more complex type of search entry is the word root chain. Here word roots have to appear in a specific order and within a specific distance. There are three options: (1) Word roots occur in words that immediately follow each other. (2) Word roots follow each other within a text unit, but not necessarily immediately. (3) Word roots occur within the text unit, and their order does not matter. An example of the first type is 'terrible politic*', indicating 'terrible politics', 'terrible politicians', and so on. With respect to the second type the maximum allowed distance between the roots has to be entered. The type would cover phrases like 'terrible young politicians'. The third type would also cover the phrase 'politicians are terrible'.

For example, the search entry, '_our', will cover the words 'our', 'ours', 'ourself', and 'ourselves'. Here the type of search entry is in prefix position. The entry '_my' will cover 'my' and 'myself'. But it also covers words like 'mystery' and 'myth', which are absolutely not self-references. In such cases search entries should not be used in this way.

In conclusion, complex search entries seem to have advantages as they allow to keep the dictionary simple. On the other hand, ambiguity is introduced in many ways. Not only because of the multiple coding problems that Klein refers to, but also because many search entries might be included without the investigator being aware of it. Examples of these unintended search entries are the already mentioned ones 'Madagascar,' 'mystery,' and 'myth.'

Negations. Another problem in many texts is that they contain negations, e.g., 'not going' instead of 'staying'. Often this problem is solved in a very *ad hoc* way. Words up to a specific distance from the word under investigation are selected. If in this list of selected words an even number of negations is found, the negations are ignored. In cases where an odd number of negations is found, a single negation is coded. This is based on the assumption that negative plus negative results in positive. The negative words are contained in a list.[13]

Consider the following text block:

31   The boy could not stand that he was losing, so he started playing in a way that was not fair.

Programs having the facility to control for negative words (often up to a certain distance) will not assign the word 'fair' to the concept FAIR, because the word 'not' (which is in the list) immediately precedes the word. In programs not having a negation facility, the word would be coded as an occurrence of the concept.

Other prospects. There are other ways of making search entries more sophisticated. Popping (1997a) linked a dictionary to software in which users were asked to indicate their occupational title. Each occupational title was listed in the dictionary according to numerous sequences of three characters. For example, the occupational title, 'baker', was split in '__b', '_ba', 'bak', 'ake', 'ker', 'er_', 'r__', where the underscore must be read as a space. If the user entered a sequence that was listed in the dictionary, the corresponding occupational title was assigned to the user.[14] If multiple occupations were listed under a single sequence, the user was assigned the occupational title with the most matching sequences. The goal of this project was to obtain data in a setting in which user interaction was to occur as fast but as reliable as possible. Because data were input interactively, the users could indicate whether the selected title was correct or not. If not, modification or manual input was allowed. This technique not only precluded spelling errors, but also user errors such as their entering descriptions of work activities instead of their occupational titles.

An example dictionary. Given the discussion above, a dictionary can be presented and evaluated. Four concepts are used: SELF-REFERENCE, OTHER-REFERENCE, FAIR, and UNFAIR. These concepts are illustrative. In Table 4.5 the search entries are listed under concept headings. Many search entries are ones obtained directly from the texts. The search entries are not exhaustive.

In the OTHER-REFERENCE both words 'opponent' and 'opponents' are available as search entries. The word 'her' is not captured by words starting with 'he', because this would include lots of words unrelated to OTHER-REFERENCE (e.g., 'herb', 'here', 'herring'). The dictionary contains several word chains, all for the UNFAIR-concept. Table 4.6 contains the frequency of occurrence of each of the concepts in the text blocks.[15]

Text formats

Text analysis software usually requires that machine readable texts be input using a particular format. These requirements are: 1) texts usually have to be available in ASCII or ANSI format;[16] 2) Delimiters must be used to separate text blocks; and 3) identifying information may be necessary.

In the situation of thematic text analysis, but also other forms of text analysis, texts are available in a file in a computer system. The file contains only standard characters according to the ASCII or ANSI definition. Each line ends with a carriage return and a line feed character. One can type such a text by using a text editor or word processor. Note however, that in this latter case the text should probably not be saved in the standard format provided by the word processor. Hyphenation of words in texts is in most programs not allowed, for the computer programs will consider these words as two separate words.

Table 4.5 *Dictionary for the example data*

SELF	OTHER	FAIR	UNFAIR
' I '	'_he_'	'_cautious_'	'_angry_'
'_mine_'	'_her_'	'_fair_'	'_beat> head_'
'_me_'	'_him_'		'_brut>'
'_my_'	'_his_'		'_cause> crash_'
'_myself_'	'_opponent'		'_harm_'
'_our'	'_she_'		'_hiss>'
'_we_'	'_their_'		'_hit>'
'_us_'	'_they_'		'_hook>'
	'_this boy_'		'_hurt>'
			'_intimidat>'
			'_kick_'
			'_kill>_'
			'_knock> down'
			'_lying_'
			'_make> afraid'
			'_pushed_'
			'_unfair_'
			'_yell>'

Note, the underscore '_' should be read as a space in the search entry

The different text blocks that need to be analysed are separated by identifiers. These are special characters that do not appear in the real text. These identifiers consist of characters like '$', or '@', and have to be at the beginning of the block. Sometimes the identifier is on a separate line, sometimes it is the first character on a line. Some programs also demand a special character to indicate the end of a block.

The starting identifier is mostly followed by a number to indicate the text block. Some programs allow (hierarchical) dimensions of identifiers. Now one can relate, for example, the first dimension to the books, and the second one to the text blocks sampled within these books, or (if data would have been collected in that way) the first one to the sportsmen, and the second one to their sayings that are sampled. These dimensions also allow to distinguish between sampling unit and recording unit. Often a clause is used as a recording unit. In their simplest form the indicators are symbolized by ID1, ID2, and so on. The recording unit depends on the last identifier. Assume the text blocks 1 and 33:

> $ID1 He made a sliding, $ID2 and as he started too late, $ID2
> he hit me against the ankle. $ID2 I had an enormous pain.
> $ID1 She was losing the match, $ID2 therefore she became very
> angry and $ID2 started yelling at the referee.

This is considered as:

Table 4.6   *Frequency of occurrence of the concepts in the example data*

	self	other	fair	unfair			self	other	fair	unfair
1	2	3	0	1		21	0	5	0	1
2	1	0	0	1		22	1	0	1	0
3	0	2	0	2		23	0	1	0	0
4	0	0	0	1		24	0	1	0	2
5	0	1	0	2		25	0	0	0	0
6	1	0	1	0		26	2	0	0	0
7	0	1	0	0		27	2	2	0	2
8	3	0	1	1		28	1	0	0	0
9	0	0	0	0		29	1	0	0	0
10	2	0	1	0		30	1	0	0	0
11	0	1	0	1		31	0	3	0	0
12	2	1	0	1		32	1	0	0	1
13	0	3	0	1		33	0	2	0	2
14	0	0	0	0		34	0	2	0	1
15	0	0	0	0		35	0	2	0	0
16	1	1	0	2		36	2	0	0	0
17	2	3	0	2		37	0	0	1	0
18	2	0	0	0		38	0	0	0	2
19	3	0	0	0		39	2	0	0	0
20	3	0	1	0		40	2	0	0	0

ID1	ID2	Text
1	1	He made a sliding,
1	2	and as he started too late,
1	3	he hit me against the ankle.
1	4	I had an enormous pain.
33	1	She was losing the match,
33	2	therefore she became very angry and
33	3	started yelling at the referee.

Now the sampling unit is known, and within that unit the recording units. On the level of the sampling unit the 'I' in the first text block co-occurs with 'hit'. On the level of the recording unit this is no longer true, now they are part of two different recording units. This might have enormous consequences for the results of the analyses. Note, however, the 'yelling' in text block 33 does no longer co-occur with 'she', although it should. This can only be solved by adapting the clauses manually, or by using a parser.

By having this smaller recording unit the situation is better prevented that concepts are encoded as co-occurring with other concepts, while in the text these concepts are not related. See the example above. From this point of view, it is better to use small recording units, like a sentence or a clause. Here it is much more probable that co-occurring concepts are grammatically related. The total number of recording units in the example text is 89. On the other hand, however, nesting is introduced now. The sample size is inflated. This has to be taken into account during the actual analyses. A simple way to do this is by weighting the recording units within a sample unit.

Thematic concept mapping

Some investigators use word frequencies as data without aggregating them into more general concepts. In this way their analyses are strictly of manifest content, or what Weber (1984) denotes as empirical (as opposed to category-based) content. Iker and Klein (1974) were possibly the first to work exclusively with empirical content using their set of programs called WORDS. In analysing transcripts of psychiatric interviews, they applied what they called 'association analysis' in order 'to fill the need for text analytic methods that would be free from the constraints imposed by a *a priori* categorization system' (Iker, 1974: 95). They quantified the occurrence and co-occurrence of words in a squared matrix.

Association analysis begins with getting rid of all trivia. This includes the deletion of all articles, prepositions, and conjunctions, as well as words that mean little outside of their context. Certain words were deleted according to a combination of word-speech rules. Synonyms had been looked for.[17] The matrix used in the first studies was only based on the 215 most frequently appearing words.

The next step was to obtain factors or clusters in a multivariate analysis, and the final step to infer meanings for the factors or clusters. These meanings represent the relevant themes in the texts. Categories have been developed now *post hoc* in an inductive way.

Although the method has not been used for a long time, there is some renewed attention to approaches like the one by Iker and Klein. In their investigation of terrorist rhetoric Hogenraad et al. (1995) examined both empirical and category-based content. All analyses were performed using the program, Protan (Hogenraad et al., 1995). This program generates data matrices with occurrence of both concepts and words in the row. I shall discuss only their analysis of empirical content. Their data were the texts of 18 terrorist treatises. These texts comprised a time-series of texts that appeared during a period of 14 months, starting in October, 1984.

Their analyses began by transforming all inflected forms of words into uninflected forms. Word counts were calculated for these uninflected words. Words occurring 10 times or more were entered into a factor analysis. Five factors were found. Lagged Pearson's product moment correlations were computed between factor scores on each factor over the different texts. Among others, the authors found that a lag of one text the factor labelled 'Concrete utopia' predicted the factor 'Marxist ideology', and 'Socio-economic concern' predicted 'Imperialist concern'. These predictions concern the sequence of topics addressed in these terrorist treatises.

Other programs that allow special attention for the analysis of words are the set of programs VBPro (Miller, 1993) and the program Catpac. VBPro is a package that allows *concept mapping*, 'a computerized multidimensional scaling technique that generates maps of content themes based on the frequency and co-occurrence of key words' (Miller and Riechert, 1994: 3). The statistical analysis is different from the one in the study above.

First one has to choose key terms for analysis. The terms are selected by the program based on their mathematical information value. A word is indicative for a theme of a text segment to the extent that it has a relatively high frequency in that text. For example, stories on health will contain the term 'health' and related terms at a higher rate than will stories on other topics. In the program this logic is automated via a χ^2-statistic. Specifically, an expected value for occurrences of a word in a text is computed based on the percentage of that word in the combined set of all text segments. This expectation is compared with the actual number of occurrences in the text. These values are used in the usual χ^2-formula.

In an analysis of articles on pesticides in four news magazines, Miller and Riechert used their software to identify the 121 words with the highest χ^2-rank that were not substantively vacuous function words (articles, prepositions, conjunctions, and auxiliary verbs). Frequency data on these words were submitted to their concept mapping procedure, which calculates a matrix of cosine coefficients that are indicative of the degree of co-occurrence between pairs of selected words. This coefficient is described in Salton (1989: 479 ff). The largest three eigenvectors for each word are then extracted from the cosine coefficient matrix. These vectors were submitted to a cluster analysis program. The resulting clusters were examined to determine the kinds of themes they indicated.

The results suggested that environmental protection is the central issue in the pesticide debates. According to the investigators their procedure has substantive credibility as this finding makes sense, both intuitively and logically. The argumentation for the technique is that it readily addresses complex topics, like environmental problems, that include many issues and diverse points of view or frames (Miller, 1997). In particular, the method does not involve time-consuming efforts in constructing dictionaries.

Mapping the 28 non-trivial words in the example data from Chapter 3 that occurred at least three times using Miller's mapping-program did not result in a solution in which a meaning could be inferred to the eigenvectors (with Eigenvalue > 1) found, or to the results of the cluster analysis based on these eigenvectors. The analysis is repeated, not based on the words this time, but on the concepts of interest, SELF and OTHER-REFERENCE, FAIR and UNFAIR. A two-dimensional mapping is asked for, because two strong relations are expected: the one between SELF and FAIR, and the one between OTHER-REFERENCE and UNFAIR. In Table 4.7 the results of this mapping is presented.

Table 4.7   *Concept map based on words related to the concepts* SELF *and*
OTHER-REFERENCE, FAIR *and* UNFAIR

	I	II
SELF	.34	.63
OTHER	-.60	-.18
FAIR	.62	-.37
UNFAIR	-.60	.14

The first vector in the concept map shows the concepts, OTHER-REFERENCE
and UNFAIR, to occur, as do the other two concepts. These findings indicate that
these are pairs that somehow 'go together,' but nothing more than that.

Is computer assistance helpful?

It was already mentioned that in the view of several authors computer-assisted
text analysis has several advantages over the hand-coded way of working.
Several studies have investigated this claim. In these studies a hand-coded
versus computer-coded data supported text analysis is applied on the same data.
In both, the same concept scheme is used.

A main objection against using the computer to encode texts is that the
context of words or phrases might be ignored in the process, such that
linguistically complex relationships like negation, synonym, irony, or metaphor
would be ignored. Heinrich (1996) investigated how serious this all is.

His starting point is car test reports. These reports are considered as an
expression of societal discourse about cars. Heinrich investigates whether
powerful motors are uncritically supported, or whether they are critically
evaluated on references to their negative aspects. The sample is very small,
consisting of 18 car reports. Each report is split into several text units, at the
level of the sentence.

In the computer-assisted analysis an interactive approach was used, such that
during the coding process new search entries could be defined. Concepts were
ranked by a rating team along a 6-point scale ranging from very negative to
very positive motor-power evaluation (in developing the hand-coded data a 7-
point scale was used).[18] The results of the analysis are presented on the level of
the report and not of the sentences.

Considerable differences were found between the coders' and the computer's
judgement. The former gave higher scores for all reports. This variation between
coders and computer is probably due to positive impressions gleaned from
particular text passages, that would not have been taken into account in the
computer's encodings (for example 'reaches high torque with much less effort').
According to Heinrich the fundamental advantage of computer-assisted text

analysis is the intersubjectivity of the result. Personal evaluations by the coder have no effect on the results.

In their study Rosenberg et al. (1990) analysed speech samples from 71 subjects from four medical diagnostic groups. They got these samples by following the manual coding method used in Gottschalk-Gleser text analysis (Gottschalk and Gleser, 1969; the computerized method of this form of text analysis is discussed in detail in the next chapter). The transcripts of the speech samples were coded in three ways. First they were scored by hand yielding a score for each transcript on each of them on twelve Gottschalk-Gleser scales measuring psychological traits. The transcripts were also twice analysed using the General Inquirer program, once using the Dartmouth adaption of the Harvard III Psychosociological Dictionary, and once using the Harvard IV Psychosociological Dictionary. Disambiguation rules were used as both of these dictionaries were applied. Frequencies of occurrence of concepts were used to assign subjects to one of four diagnostic groups. Discriminant analyses showed the Gottschalk-Gleser scales to classify 62% of the subjects correctly, the Harvard III concept frequencies to correctly classify 80%, and those of the Harvard IV dictionary to correctly classify 85% of the subjects. Other results found the computerized methods not to be more accurate than the Gottschalk-Gleser method in placing subjects within the diagnostic groups. Still, the results suggest that the data from the computerized analyses yield more accurate diagnostic classifications than hand-scored data. In the discussion the authors also point to the fact that computerized coding is difficult and expensive.

Nacos et al. (1991: 112; 125) also compared the results of manual and computer-assisted coding of news. Their conclusion: 'Computer-assisted content analysis can make significant contributions to social science research.' Especially the speed and the consistency with which the computer programs can code large amounts of text are acknowledged. Part of the coding task was to locate specific words, that are in close proximity to modifier words. In performing this task the agreement between human and computer coding was just over 80%. When in the next step the text blocks had to be assigned to categories, agreement decreased to about 50%. This is according to the authors due to limitations of the computer-assisted procedure: 'the computer follows programmed rules and does not recognize ambiguities or problems as an attentive human coder would, in particular when instructions are not sufficiently precise, when text does not seem to fit into prescribed categories.' Earlier in this chapter it was shown that some problems of ambiguity can be overcome. The fact that coding instructions were not precise (it is not clear whether this is with respect to the human coders or to the dictionary) can also be solved. So Nacos, et al. (1991) might even have found higher agreement between hand- and machine coding.

These studies do not report about fully identical comparisons of the same data using different coding instruments, one a human, in the other situation a computer. I am not aware of such studies. But they all give us the feeling that a computer-supported text analysis does not give worse results than an analysis by human coders.

The representational approach

The instrumental approach to text analysis requires only the single theoretical perspective of the investigator. As a direct consequence of this requirement, words and phrases can be automatically classified as theme occurrences according to a theory-based dictionary that the analyst has developed for just such classification. When the representational approach is followed, units of analysis are classified according to how they were intended by the source of the message. Accordingly, total automation is not possible, because coders are needed to judge which coding is a valid reflection of the source's intentions. In a representational text analysis key word in context programs are extremely useful (if not essential) in helping the coder to identify not only idioms (remember idiomatic ambiguity) based on the word's contexts, but also to recognize from the source's standpoint when it reflects one theme versus another.

Table 4.8 *Key word in context list of the search entry ' I ' generated with FlexText*

```
Concepts    Options    View    Return
      end of a football match (1:I) always have so many blue spots on (1:my) le
                              (1:I) always have to remember it is just a game,
                              (1:I) always train alone, so you miss talking to oth
       At the end of a match (1:I) am always out of breath. It gives you a goo
                              (1:I) am always playing (3:fair).
    ) (4:hit) me in an awful way, (1:I) became dizzy, and had to consult a phy
                          If (1:I) can prevent a goal made by the others by ta
                              (1:I) don't understand why people like wrestling,
      It was wet, therefore (1:I) fell and broke (1:my) arm. (1:I) should hav
When (1:I) went down skiing (1:I) fell and broke (1:my) leg.
ter a quarter of an hour (1:I) got a ball in (1:my) stomach, which causes
it) me against the ankle. I had an enormous pain.
     (2:He) fell, and said that (1:I) had hurt him and (2:he) had a lot of pa
s just a game, therefore (1:I) have to keep it (3:fair).
                              I like a rough play, but it should be fair. If so, n
                              (1:I) like swimming, it is very good for your condit
                              (1:I) played far too long, therefore a muscle in
(1:I) fell and broke (1:my) arm. (1:I) should have been more cautious.
      It was wet, therefore (1:I) slipped on the course, and broke (1:my) arm.
              By accident (1:I) smashed the ball into the audience. Fortuna
                    When (1:I) went down skiing (1:I) fell and broke (1:my) l
rs by tackling some one, (1:I) won't do it. Sorry.
              PgUp      PgDn      Alt-H=Help      F10=Menu
                  Text Analysis Service Corporation (TASC)
```

In Table 4.3 the concordances are shown, but there is no reference to whether they are coded or not. In Table 4.8 however, it is clear (from words' enclosure in parentheses with concepts codes) which concordance has been coded and which one has not. In FlexText, a program to be used when the representative approach is to be followed, coding is performed interactively by marking and based on these concordances.

Popping (1997b) tested a help option that was added to his computer program for nominal scale agreement. Test persons, who either did or did not have access to this option, were asked to report on the results of a computation. The hypothesis to be tested was that those who were able to use the help option would write a more informed report in comparison to those who were unable to use the help option. Reports written by the test persons were analysed using FlexText. The task was to code the test persons' intentions. In their reports they might, for example, have referred to the significance of the z-value that was found. This can be done in many ways. From the instrumental point of view it would be necessary to use a search entry like 'significance z-value' (assuming that the words 'of' and 'the' were part of a trivial word list).

One concept measured whether the test person found the value of kappa in the computations to be sufficiently large. Some phrases from the texts in which this was indicated were: 'high enough', 'very beautiful', 'high', 'sufficient', 'rather high', 'sufficient agreement', 'it fits'.[19] It is very hard to put these terms in a dictionary in such a way that at the very end they are coded as they should be. When applying the representational view it is the coder who identifies such phrases on the screen, and who decides how to code them. The coder can also define them as a search entry during the coding process. The hypothesis Popping tested was not rejected, those using the help option wrote a more informed report.

The second text block in the example contains the sentence:

Fortunately nobody was hurt.

The word 'hurt' might conceivably be used as a search entry for UNFAIR. When the representational view is followed, the coder could have noticed that 'hurt' is not used here in this way. Those applying the instrumental view might not only have coded the word as UNFAIR, if they used a program that controls for negative words (and the word 'nobody' had been added to the list of negative words) it might equally inappropriately have been coded as FAIR. A similar situation is found in text block 8:

I would kick,

from the sentence 'I would feel very bad in case I would kick someone into hospital.' The person (SELF) is not behaving UNFAIR, but applying the instrumental view the part might be coded so that it is suggested from the co-occurrence of the concepts.

Looking at the word or KWIC-lists might have resulted in finding search entries like 'the players of the other team' (text block 5) and 'opponent' (text block 7) for the OTHER-REFERENCE. The last part of text block 33 is:

started yelling at the referee.

This holds for the 'she' what the complete text block is about, so this can be coded. When the representational view is followed these complex situations are more likely to be identified and coded according to the source's intention.

Differences between instrumental vs representational coding

Some differences in coding were already indicated above when the representational view instead of the instrumental view was followed. In 15 text blocks 18 differences were found (comparing coding in Flextext and Intext), twice with respect to both SELF and FAIR, three times with respect to UNFAIR, and 11 times with respect to OTHER. This suggests that the view followed during the coding process might result in completely differently coded data. These differences are due to the way the context was evaluated by the coder who followed the representational view. Table 4.9 shows the frequencies of occurrence of the four

Table 4.9   *Frequency of occurrence of concepts*

Program	Intext				VBPro				FlexText			
Concept Frequency	S	O	F	U	S	O	F	U	S	O	F	U
0	19	23	34	22	19	23	33	22	20	24	34	24
1	8	7	6	10	9	7	7	10	11	7	6	9
2	10	5	-	8	10	5	-	8	6	4	-	7
3	3	4	-	-	2	4	-	-	3	4	-	-
4	-	1	-	-	-	-	-	-	-	1	-	-
5	-	-	-	-	-	1	-	-	-	-	-	-

(S = SELF REFERENCE; O = OTHER REFERENCE; F = FAIR; U = UNFAIR)

concepts, SELF REFERENCE, OTHER REFERENCE, FAIR, and UNFAIR as found after applying the programs Intext, VBPro, and FlexText.

The differences between the programs in which coding was performed according to the instrumental view, Intext and VBPro, are due to the fact whether negative words are taken into account and to the dealing with abbreviated forms like 'I'm'. The differences with FlexText, allowing the representational view, are as mentioned before based on the evaluation of the context.

Output

Figure 3.1 in Chapter 3 shows the type of data matrix that is downloaded to allow statistical inferences within a thematic text analysis. The data matrix always contains the frequency of occurrence of each theme within each text unit. Many of the programs mentioned do this: The General Inquirer, Textpack, Intext, VBPro, Cmatrix2, FlexText. Some even provide a set-up for a program for a statistical package. VBPro and Cmatrix2 also allow downloading a matrix containing occurrence or non-occurrence data. The program Kwalitan only downloads a matrix containing the occurrence versus non-occurrence data.

Analysis

Many types of analysis can be performed on the data generated during a thematic text analysis. In general the analysis that is performed is dictated by the theoretical question that is to be answered. Below a very broad overview of possibilities is given. A more detailed overview is in Merten (1983).

In analyses concepts can be summarized, yielding answers to questions like: 'in how many of the text units did the concept occur', or 'what is the minimum, maximum, average frequency of occurrence in a text unit'. If identifiers were used referring to specific groups, it becomes possible to investigate differences between these groups. For example, Klein's (1996) study (mentioned at the beginning of this chapter) compared transcripts from four TV news-programmes. Frequency data also allow one to investigate the attention a theme has received in time. Danielson and Lasorsa (1997), for example, compare the frequency of use over time of words related to social change (e.g., the words Communism or Communist(s), agricultural words, religious or ritual words) in the New York Times and the Los Angeles Times. Their goal was to describe social and political changes in American society. Thus the flow of symbols is used here to reflect social change.

One can also investigate the co-occurrence of concepts: 'with what frequency do two concepts occur together in a text unit'. Here a warning is in order. When occurrence measures are positively correlated, these 'co-occurrences' must not be interpreted as reflecting how themes are semantically related in the texts under study. Such correlations only indicate to us that themes occur together in text units, not how they co-occur.

From occurrence measures correlations between concepts can be computed. From these correlations, more advanced techniques can be applied: cluster analysis, factor analysis, path analysis, etc. Weber (1990) contains an extended example of how structural equation models (here LISREL) can be used. Analysis based on co-occurrence of words is supposed to result in the true concept scheme of the person who created the text, the scheme is found afterwards. Other investigators start with concepts schemes. The theoretical position of investigators who perform the coding process according to the instrumental view, is represented in the coding scheme and in the search entries, so in the dictionary. An investigator applying the representational view on coding has the opportunity to include new search entries and even new concepts. In this situation the coding scheme represents only part of the theoretical position. When the investigators using coding schemes, apply multivariate statistics, these statistics are based on the concepts.

Correlations and associations can be computed between the (frequency of) occurrence of the concepts in the text blocks, but also between these concepts and contextual data obtained (independently) in another way. For example, Hogenraad et al. (1995) compared the patterns they found in their terrorist treatises with data concerning targets that had been attacked by these action groups.

In Table 4.10 correlations are presented for the comparison on the levels of sampling and recording unit, based on the analysis using Intext and FlexText and based on the coding of frequency of occurrence versus non-occurrence. Co-

Table 4.10   *Correlations between concepts*

based on sampling units (N = 40)				
	Intext		FlexText	
	FAIR	UNFAIR	FAIR	UNFAIR
SELF	.30	-.15	.42	-.51
OTHER	-.36	.54	-.34	.79

based on recording units (N = 89)				
	Intext		FlexText	
	FAIR	UNFAIR	FAIR	UNFAIR
SELF	.16	-.08	.30	-.34
OTHER	-.19	.34	-.19	.61

occurrence of the concepts, SELF and FAIR, as well as the concepts, OTHER and UNFAIR, is indicated by a sufficient high positive correlation between occurrence measures of the concepts. Such positive correlation indicates that either both or neither tend to occur in text blocks or clauses. Negative correlations indicate concepts, only one of which occurs in text blocks or clauses. The results in the table show outcomes in the direction hypothesized.[20]

Conclusion

Carley (1993: 81 ff) has listed eight choices on which the investigator must have decided before coding begins. Until now these choices have been discussed implicitly. The investigator has to decide the following:

1. The level of analysis. What constitutes a concept: a word or a phrase?
2. How to deal with irrelevant information, should it be deleted, skipped over, or used to dynamically reassess and alter the coding scheme?
3. Predefined or interactive concept choice? This is related to the instrumental and representational approach.
4. Level of generalization. One might code explicit concepts and search entries as they occur in texts, which facilitates automation. Contrasted with that,

words in texts might also be recoded in some altered form, giving more possibilities for cross text comparison (e.g., all pronouns are converted into proper nouns).
5. Creation of translation rules. Concepts in texts must be systematically generalized, therefore one needs 'rules' or a thesaurus that translates less general concepts and words into more general ones.
6. Level of implication for concepts. Should the manifest or the latent meaning presented in a text be coded?
7. Existence or frequency. Does the investigator want to know the occurrence or the frequency of occurrence of concepts in the texts?
8. Number of concepts. How many concepts should be used in the analysis?

Several of these choices are related to the use of the computer. In the computer era subsequent to Janowitz's (1969) discussion of barriers, organizational and administrative aspects have become much easier. Readily available now are machine readable texts to be analysed and text analysis software packages used for these analyses. These varied packages prescribe how texts are formatted, and also how the concepts, search entries, and trivial words are stored. Adding, deleting, editing these entries is very simple, and coding choices are made explicit when these programs are used. Selecting a specific package will depend largely on whether one opts for predefined or interactive concepts. Of course, one's software should not drive one's research strategy. The activities are more conveniently arranged than in the pre computer era, and coding, especially in the instrumental approach, is performed very systematically. Janowitz's wish to have one format is not honoured.

If the instrumental view is followed one's concepts must be derived from theory. The representational view allows concepts to be based on one's familiarity with the sources of one's data. The gap between 'theory' and 'empirical data' is not bridged. The representational view, however, allows one to code text blocks in line with the intentions of the source of the message. Another barrier that has not been solved is co-occurrence of concepts in a recording unit, which is generally interpreted as indicating a relation between these concepts. This assumption however, does not have to hold. Most of the last decades' improvements are methodological, search entries are more explicit now that the computer is used, and coding is more consistent, leading to improved reliability.

Notes

1. There are 151 words that appear only once, and are not listed in the table. The list is produced by using the program Intext. This program places the frequency before the word. In Intext dots, commas, semicolon, etc. are considered as words.
2. Here follows a long list with stop-words. Self and other references are not included, as well as separation characters (characters like !, ", #, $, %, and so on): a, about, above, after, again, against, ago, all, already, also, always, am, an, and, another,

any, are, around, as, at, be, because, been, before, being, both, but, by, can, could, did, do, does, down, each, either, even, every, far, few, for, from, further, had, has, have, hence, here, how, however, if, in, into, is, just, may, maybe, meanwhile, more, most, Mr, Mrs, much, must, neither, never, next, no, nor, not, nothing, now, of, off, on, once, ones, only, onto, or, out, over, per, perhaps, previous, should, so, some, still, such, than, that, the, then, there, these, thirteen, thirty, this, those, three, thus, to, too, towards, twelve, twenty, two, under, up, very, was, were, what, when, whence, where, whether, which, while, who, why, will, with, within, without, would, yet. Note, these are general words. In specific investigations some of these words can be very important. Note these stop-words do not appear in the list in Table 4.1. This is because the program Intext has the facility of using stop-words. VBPro or Swift would also list the stop-words.

The program Delcon, which is part of the MECA-package removes stop words from a text, so that the size of the text is reduced. Krause (1996: 86), working in the field of information retrieval remarks that a text is often reduced by 50% when these words are excluded.

3. The programs VBPro and Swift consider these combinations like 'I'm' as one word. Differences were found in the ways Intext and VBPro handled the text blocks 8 and 17, both times with respect to the coding of 'I'm'. In Intext this is converted into 'I ' m', therefore the 'I' is coded as a SELF-REFERENCE. In VBPro it is not converted, and therefore the 'I' is not read.

4. Some programs use not only key word in context lists but also key word out of context (KWOC) lists. KWIC lists consist of short concordances, often a text string containing up to 30 characters preceding and following the search entry under investigation. In KWOC lists the concordance is much longer, in general some lines. In this latter situation the concordance might contain information that does not belong to the context of the search entry any more.

5. Evans and Hornig Priest (1995: 335) argue that text analysts have developed few viable theoretical foundations of their own. These analysts apply social theories, which they seldom acknowledge. Earlier researchers such as Lasswell and Berelson were concerned and routinely engaged with social theory.

6. The Lasswell Value Dictionary and the Harvard IV Psychosocial Dictionary are available for The General Inquirer and Textpack. The program MCCA has a dictionary of its own containing 117 concepts (McTavish and Pirro, 1990: 253). See also the remarks in the appendix when MCCA is discussed.

7. The computer programs Swift and WinMAX (a qualitative code and retrieve program) allow this way of coding, which can be very useful when a dictionary is developed.

8. In the Harvard III dictionary (the predecessor of version IV) self reference is split into two concepts, corresponding to single and plural personal pronouns. Other reference has forms of the pronoun 'you' for its search entries. The pronouns 'he,' 'she,' and so on are entered into concepts MALE ROLE and FEMALE ROLE (Stone et al., 1966: 144). This example illustrates possible differences between specific and general dictionaries.

9. In this situation the search entry is a homonym. In Chapter 9 (dis-) ambiguity is considered from a linguistic point of view. There it will be explained that this type of ambiguity is known as lexical ambiguity.

10. Within The General Inquirer disambiguation routines now leave only 2% of the words assigned a wrong meaning. Before disambiguation it was 25% (Stone, 1969: 217). See also Kelly and Stone (1975).

11. The alternative might be very useful when thematic concept mapping, to be discussed later in this chapter, is applied.

12. This argument is questionable. I would expect coding takes more time as all upper case letters have to be replaced by lower case ones or reverse. Modern computers are very fast, therefore the amount of time probably is negligible.

13. The list in note 1 contains the word 'not'. This word should be moved to the list of negative words.

14. See also note 7 in Chapter 9.

15. The texts were analysed using Intext, a program that uses a list of stop words and one of negative words, and by using VBPro, that does not use any list. VBPro also does not recognize word root chains. This problem was solved here by entering crucial parts of the chain in the dictionary. Differences in coding were found for two situations. The first is with respect to text blocks 8 and 17 because VBPro did not recognize the 'I' in 'I'm', while Intext did. The other is in text block 31 where VBPro coded the word 'fair', while Intext has skipped this as the word is preceded by the word 'not' from the list of negative words.

16. The text is not allowed to contain any code symbols related to a text editor, it should be a flat text. Under the operating system MS-DOS the file containing such a text is indicated as an ASCII-file (American Standard Code for Information Interchange), under Windows it is called an ANSI-file (American National Standards Institute). This variation is due to the fact that both operating systems use different character sets. These standards might in the future be replaced by another standard Unicode (HTTP//:WWW.UNICODE.ORG).

17. If analyses are based on words, it is important that synonyms are recognized and presented under one label. This affects the frequency of co-occurrence with other words. In case this synonimization would not occur more than one frequency is found that indicates in fact the same co-occurrence. This might result in other (and wrong) outcomes of the analyses.

    The reverse is also necessary. Words having more than one meaning must be recognized, and assigned the correct meaning.

18. Heinrich evidently used six content analysis categories with exclusive search entries, although he does not mention this explicitly in his text.

19. The original texts were in Dutch.

20. It is not my intention to discuss analysis methods in detail. An extended overview of possibilities for analysis is offered by Merten (1983).

5

Semantic text analysis

In the thematic approach the investigator makes *post hoc* inferences about relations between concepts on the basis of co-occurrence patterns found among recording units. In sentences however, concepts are already related. These are grammatical relations denoted by a verb. Therefore the terminology Subject–Verb–Object relation is used. A simple example is 'John (subject) gave (verb) a picture (object).' Such relations are elaborated in the semantic approach to text analysis: not only the concepts are counted, but also the relations among these concepts. In addressing the grammatical relations, the investigator can apply syntax grammars and semantical grammars. Syntax grammars (grammatical rules for forming sentences) captures the surface structure of text into grammatical categories. The semantic grammars map the deep structure of a text (linguistic units that cut across words, sentences, paragraphs) into a finite set of functionally defined categories. Now the meaning of the object 'picture' in the example above also becomes important. The object might refer to a painting or poster, but also to a verbal description (as in 'He gave a picture of his activities'). When the exact meaning is apprehended, an unambiguous encoding can be made.

Were the sentence to have been 'John bought it,' the meaning of the anaphora 'it' also has to be made clear. This type of ambiguity is more complex than idiosyncratic ambiguity, discussed with respect to thematic text analysis. A semantic grammar identifies a general set of functionally defined (coding) concepts and provides explicit potential relationships between concepts (Franzosi, 1989, 1990). Using such a grammar allows one to concentrate on concrete relations between concepts and not on researcher-inferred relations like those used in thematic analysis. The coded data also preserve as much as possible of the original source lexicon.

More generally, the grammar is represented as a semantic triplet as in Table 5.1. The representation of such a grammatical structure is a more complicated task than counting words, as is done using programs for thematic text analysis.

The triplet, Subject–Verb–Object, usually provides the basic linguistic structure for parsing text. In the semantic grammar in Table 5.1 <subject> is made up of (or mapped as) one or more <actors>, such as students, visitors, and others, with possible <actor modifiers>. The type and number of modifiers vary

Table 5.1   *A semantic grammar*

```
<semantic triplet>   →    {<subject>}{<verb>}[{<object>}]
<subject>            →    {<actor>}[{<actor modifiers>}]
<actor>              →    I, he, the person, ...
<actor modifiers>    →    genitive, related clause
<verb>               →    {<verb phase>}[{<verb modifiers>}]
<verb phase>         →    go, do, look, ...
<verb modifiers>     →    tense, modal auxiliary
<object>             →    {<actor>}[{<actor modifiers>}]
```

with the specific substantive application.

The most important characteristic of a grammar is that all elements of the grammar are interrelated in complex ways. Not only are specific subjects related to specific verbs and objects, but sets of the semantic triplet, Subject–Verb–Object, are related to one another in ways that closely approximate the complexity of natural languages.

The grammar is also distinguished on another dimension: *phenomenal* or *generic* (Roberts, 1997c). A phenomenal grammar is used to extract phenomenon-related information from a text-population. A generic grammar yields data about the text population itself. Each grammar specifies the ways relations among concepts in texts may be encoded. Once concepts in the texts are encoded according to these relations, the encoded relations can be used as indicators of various characteristics of the phenomenon, or text population being studied. In applying a semantic grammar the investigator assumes that the texts under analysis are structured according to the grammar.

In applying a phenomenal semantic grammar the investigator assumes the phenomenon of interest is related in a specific way. For example, Markoff, Shapiro and Weitman (1974) and Shapiro and Markoff (1998) examined the *cahiers de doléances* of 1789. These are documents produced by corporate and territorial entities that were written in the course of the king's convocation of an Estates-General. The documents contain information about grievances the entities have and about what might be done about the grievance. The documents were encoded according to a syntax grammar for the phenomenon, grievance. The grievance was thus the unit of analysis in their research. Here only a simplified version is presented of the way the grievances were coded, for details see Shapiro (1997). First, there was the object of the grievance (the government, the religion, the economy, and so on). Second, there was the action demanded. These actions were encoded as 'to abolish', 'to improve', 'to modify', 'to reestablish', and so on. The king of France and his representatives always were implicitly the subjects who should act. Accordingly, the investigators only coded verb and object, in applying a Verb–Object grammar for the phenomenon, 'grievance'. In this way the investigators yielded data that have been used to make inferences about public opinion on a variety of topics just prior to the French Revolution.

Another example of a phenomenal semantic grammar is found in Franzosi's (1997) work on Italian labour disputes. Using texts of newspaper articles, Franzosi conceptualizes labour disputes as clusters of actors' actions toward each other, i.e., as S–A–O (subject–action–object) tuples as a subset of all S–V–O tuples in the texts. In this type of research (actions in) events are investigated. An event is a set of actions performed at a particular place and time by some actor(s) against or in favour of some other actor(s) (Franzosi, 1989: 276).

In a phenomenal grammar encoding is restricted to text segments with relevance to the phenomenon of interest. If one's research purpose requires one not only to analyse information about a specific phenomenon, but rather to draw inferences about *all* clauses in one's texts, it is a generic, not a phenomenal syntax grammar that is called for. Encoding texts according to a generic grammar allows the researcher to investigate the conditions under which specific concept relations occur. Such generic grammars are applied in the works of Gottschalk, Schrodt, and Roberts. Gottschalk (1995) uses entire texts to draw inferences about their author's psychological states and traits. Schrodt (1994) parsed every first sentence of 1982–1992 Reuters articles about Middle East to draw inferences about originators and targets of Middle East conflicts. Roberts (1997c) encoded a random sample of clauses from 1979 East and West Berlin radio news coverage of some military conflicts to draw inferences about sources of information cited in all East versus West news coverage of the conflicts. In all these analyses inferences are drawn about *all* clauses in a well-defined population of texts.

Generally stated, questions requiring characterizations of text populations, for example those commonly posed in cultural indicators research and media research, lend themselves more easily to applications of generic than phenomenal grammars.[1]

As will shortly be explained, investigators with an instrumental approach to coding use syntax grammars, whereas those with a representational approach use semantic grammars. However, before making this point I shall first make some general remarks regarding the nature of coding when relations among concepts are taken into account. While discussing instrumental and representational approaches to semantic text analysis, I shall then provide more detail about the types of grammars associated with each.

Clauses

Most applications of semantic text analysis involve coding clauses according to the S–V–O triplet. Just this fact already has some consequences of which investigators have to be aware. One can distinguish between main and subordinate clauses. Subordinate clauses are ordinarily those related to a main clause by conjunctions ('because', 'since', 'when'), relative pronouns ('which', 'who', 'that') or proxies. Proxy clauses replace either the subject or the object of a clause.[2] Information on these relations among clauses can also be encoded.

Subordinate clauses may be classified as adverbial, adjectival, or nominal clauses. Main clauses are not related in any of the above ways to another clause. In the coding process the subordinate clauses have to be conjuncted to the main clauses. Here the syntactic deep structure has to be taken into account.

Anaphora associated with pronouns like 'he', 'she', 'it', has to be replaced by the names of the persons or things referred. In some situations one must also take verbal anaphora into account. For example, 'does' and 'did' refer to action.

During coding also compound forms ACTOR1 and ACTOR2 have to be recognized. As an example take the sentence 'John and Mary benefited from efforts by Peter.' This sentence is to be coded as:

> JOHN <benefited from> PETER,
> MARY <benefited from> PETER.

All programs based on the semantic or the network (discussed in the next chapter) approaches build upon this basic approach to encoding texts.

The vocabulary that is used in these approaches, should only contain clearly distinct categories. This is to assure that different coders will classify words or phrases in the text in the same ways. For example, if the verbs 'to understand' and 'to recognize' were different vocabulary items, coders would be unsure how to classify the verbs in phrases such as 'I get what you mean,' 'I cannot grasp your purpose,' and the like.

The verb-part in the clause might be considered as the means that indicates the relation between subject and object. In the chapter on network analysis it will be shown that four meaning types can be distinguished for the relation: the direction, the strength, the sign, and the meaning. These types are at most implicitly used by the investigators that apply the semantic approach (a notable exception is Roberts; who however does not use these terms). Therefore these types are only considered in the next chapter.

The instrumental approach

It has already been mentioned that encoding problems associated with linguistic ambiguity are avoided when the instrumental view of coding is followed. There are several research situations in which this may be useful. Such analyses are not based on the semantic grammar, but on a syntax grammar, i.e., on surface grammatical relations. Gottschalk and the Bierschenks, from the field of psychology, and Schrodt, from political science, have all developed methods in which relations among concepts are (semi-) automatically encoded. Each considers the text as symptomatic of the phenomenon of interest, and therefore follows the instrumental approach. Gottschalk concentrates on the individual and generates an aggregated score for each text's (or transcript's) human source. His starting position is that people often betray their mental states in the ways they phrase their discourse, making the words' surface phrasing more relevant than their intended meanings in making a psychological diagnosis (Gottschalk, 1995). The Bierschenks investigate the consciousness of people. They argue that texts can be contrasted on the basis of different 'metaphysical cubes' (concepts) and their associated 'boundary conditions' (relative). Schrodt concentrates on the political event. He does not find aggregated data, but data on the level of the clause. His analyses are of a sufficiently structured domain of texts (e.g., Reuters news service articles on international conflict), such that theme relations may follow sufficiently fixed, descriptive formulae that their surface relations are nearly always unambiguous (Schrodt, 1993). Note, this unambiguity does not hold in general, it holds for Schrodt's research project.

The methods these investigators developed are discussed below. Because each method relates concepts according to syntax grammar, software for the methods could be developed with parsers that identify which of each clause's themes function as subject, verb, and object. The encoding is thus largely automated, because no coders are needed to divine clauses' intended meanings.

Gottschalk-Gleser approach

Gottschalk and co-workers have developed affect scales that measure psychological states and traits like anxiety and anger through the analysis of speech content. These measures are based on a text analysis of verbal behaviour.[3] A tape recording is made of a subject, who is asked to speak for five minutes about an interesting or dramatical personal life experience. A transcript is made of this speech. Text units (S–V–O–tuples) are assigned to affective categories. Summation of weighted scores on categories and then aggregated into a scale score.[4] These scales are used in fields like abnormal and clinical psychology, medicine, psychiatry, psychosomatics. Gottschalk et al. (1975: 237) present some examples to illustrate several shortcomings in text analyses based on single words or phrases – analyses that discard too much highly relevant information:

- [These automated projects] fail to identify who did or felt what about whom.
- They throw away the meaningful classification of referents such as 'it', 'that', 'which', 'those', 'these', and so forth, when these are easily comprehended in context by human text-analysis scorers.
- They ignore the scoring of emotionally charged words that, out of context, cannot be properly classified, such as 'get' (in 'I'll get you for that'), 'dig' (in 'I dig you'), or 'make' (in 'She's on the make').

To overcome these problems the authors focused on the meaning carried in clauses, in sentences and, eventually, in a still broader contextual framework. In doing so they identified subjects (agents) and objects of actions and emotional verbs signifying actions or states. Based upon an earlier non-computerized scoring system designed for content analysing the speech of psychiatric patients (Gottschalk and Gleser, 1969), a computerized version was developed. Anxiety scale results based on the first edition of this program are reported by Gottschalk and Bechtel (1982).

The goal of later versions of this program has been to quantify the quality and intensity of writers' and speakers' psychological states (anxiety, hostility, cognitive impairment, etc.) as made manifest in their clauses or sentences. The program uses a parser with accompanying grammar for mapping a subset of English. The grammatical clause is taken as the smallest unit of communication. The software identifies whether or not a verb is transitive and involves an object, or is intransitive and describes a state of being. Each clause is assigned a weight on the basis of its verb (or action) and the noun-phrases that function as initiators and recipients of this action. These weights are then combined into text-block-specific scores that measure the psychological states of each text/transcript's source (i.e., its author or speaker). The program generates a data matrix with each of these source's scores on the scales selected. The program can also provide data on word frequencies, on occurrences of the various psychological-state-related phrases, on average scores across text-blocks, and on the extent to which sample scores deviate from the norms for each scale. Say, the following sentence must be scored: 'The garbage man hit my dog with a belt' (Gottschalk et al. 1975: 243). First it is parsed as in Table 5.2.

Table 5.2   *Parsed sentence in the Gottschalk-Gleser approach*

```
(SENTENCE DECLARATIVE
  (NOUN-PHRASE (DETERMINER the)
    (ADJECTIVE (NOUN-PHRASE (NOUN garbage)))
    (NOUN man)
    (NUMBER SINGULAR)
  (AUXILIARY (TENSE PAST))
  (VERB-PHRASE (VERB hit)
    (NOUN-PHRASE (DETERMINER the)
      (POSSESSIVE (NOUN-PHRASE (PRONOUN I)))
      (NOUN dog)
      (NUMBER SINGULAR)
    (PREPOSITIONAL-PHRASE (PREPOSITION with)
      (NOUN-PHRASE (DETERMINER a)
        (NOUN belt)
        (NUMBER SINGULAR))))
```

To perform its task the program uses a description of a clause's syntactic deep structure.

In the parsing process 'my dog' is replaced by 'the I dog'. The main verb, subject (actor), and object (possible recipient) are isolated as in Table 5.3.

Each of these three constituents is assigned a set of semantic features:

Table 5.3   *Isolation of subject, verb, and object*

```
Main verb: hit

Subject:
     (NOUN-PHRASE (DETERMINER the)(ADJECTIVE garbage)NOUN man))
Object:
     (NOUN-PHRASE (DETERMINER the)(POSSESSIVE (NOUN-PHRASE (PRONOUN
     I)))(NOUN dog)(NUMBER SINGULAR)(PREPOSITIONAL-PHRASE (PREPOSITION
     with)(NOUN-PHRASE (DETERMINER a)(NOUN belt)(NUMBER SINGULAR))))
```

```
     Main verb:    V₁
     Subject:      (+OTHER+ANIMATE)
     Object:       (+PET+SUBHUMAN+ANIMATE)
```

The feature of the main verb is used to determine the appropriate information structure or score tree. Several such score trees have been developed. Here the tree V_1, meant for a verb referring to causing death or physical injury, applies. There are other main verbs indicating mutilation, separation, guilt, shame, and diffuse anxiety. The tree for death or injury anxiety is shown in Table 5.4.

The tree has two nodes. The first one is made up of tests for the features of the subject, the second node is composed of tests for the object. The scoring algorithm first determines which score tree to access by determining the verb type of the main verb in the clause. Next, a first level node is chosen by overlapping the features of the subject noun phrase with the features of successive first level nodes until some partial match is achieved. Finally a second level node accessible from the current first level node is chosen by overlapping the features of the object noun phrase with successive nodes until another partial match is achieved. Associated with the second level node is the score assigned to the total clause.

The score associated to the above sentence with the second level node is output IIA2. This code symbol gives the weight 2 to its thematic concept and also serves to identify the concept. In practice the scale-specific weights of all clauses are added. A correction for a text's length is made on this total weight. The correction factor for each verbal sample is as follows (Gottschalk et al., 1969: 14):

$$\frac{1}{number\ of\ words} * 100.$$

This produces the raw score. When no scorable references are found, the raw score is set to 0.5 times the correction factor. Finally, the square root of this score is taken as the final corrected score. This last step is necessary to reduce skewness.

Table 5.4   *Score tree for the type of verbs indicating causing death or physical injury*

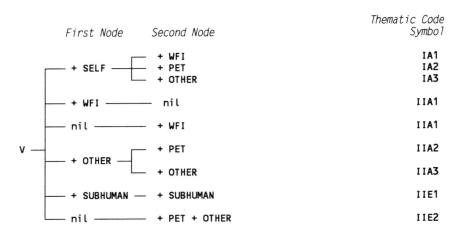

WFI = WILDLIFE + FLORA + INANIMATE

In this way many different kinds of emotions and subcategories of emotions are measured.

The results with the first version of the computer program were not very satisfying, due to limited computational linguistic knowledge and tools available at that time. Using a more elaborated version in which a linguistic parser and a knowledge based system, based on the Merriam-Webster dictionary, are employed results have been found that are comparable to those of human raters (Gottschalk and Bechtel, 1989). The program is even able to identify idioms and slang, and is capable of continuous learning.

The method is especially used in psychosocial and biomedical research but also in fields like sociology and the humanities. The validity of the method is emphasized in many studies.

Perspective text analysis

The Bierschenks (Bierschenk, 1989) have developed their perspective text analysis method, based on the observation that as the cognitive instrument in the communication of phenomena, language must be capable of expressing relations of the observer-observation kind. Texts contain intentions that can be discovered by a formal mechanism. This mechanism is based on a S–V–O relation, or in terms of the investigators, on an A–a–O (Actor–action–Object) relation. The primary component is the Agent, who controls the perspective of the text. The Agent determines what viewpoints are chosen and how they change throughout a text. Therefore, if one wants to control consciousness, one has to control the Agent.

The Bierschenk's theory for an intentionally based text analysis is based on the Kantian schema axiom (Bierschenk, 1991). In Kant's view (Kant, 1995) some knowledge, such as mathematical rules and laws of physics, is true *a priori*. That is, *a priori* knowledge refers to that that is certain without having to take experience into consideration. In contrast, *a posteriori* knowledge is experience-based knowledge, this is less certain. Closely connected to this is Kant's distinction between analytic and synthetic propositions. An analytical proposition analyses only the content of an idea; it does not add new knowledge. The synthetic proposition adds new qualities to an idea. Whereas, *a priori* knowledge is primarily analytic, *a posteriori* knowledge is synthetic. But, synthetic propositions are commonly embedded in *a priori* knowledge, for example causal propositions are elaborations of the *a priori* principle of causality in physics. Once *a priori* elements of knowledge become clear, they become the conceptual basis for discovering knowledge based on experience.

Bierschenk argued that the analytical proposition gives clauses a formal structural definition. Concepts are understood according to their denotation. When the predicate is contained (maybe in a covert way) in the subject, the analytical proposition is at hand. Take the sentence, 'A triangle is a three-sided figure.' This expression is analytic, since the term 'triangle' can be substituted with 'a three-sided figure' each time an identity relation is established within a closed system, i.e., the mechanism of symbolic logic. The problem here is that when concepts are abstracted (triangle replaced by three-sided figure, figure replaced by ..., and so on), their connotation will be lost.

The synthetic proposition uses the connotations, here meaning can only be understood in synthetic terms. A subject can be linked to a predicate based on a relation other than the equivalence relation. The predicate is neither thought to be part of the subject nor to be analysable out of the subject (Kant, 1975: 110–112). Transformed into a psychological model for the study of consciousness, Bierschenk expresses the synthetic proposition as:

$$(intent(A)) \; a \; (ort(O)).$$

The first bracketed expression denotes that the Agent A has some intention to act. Intention indicates a course of action; it is necessary to act purposefully. The action itself is indicated by (a). The second bracketed expression indicates the importance of the ability to orientate (ort) toward some object(ive) (O). In behavioural science terms, this means that psychological phenomena must be conceived as meaningful actions carried out by an Agent. Acting purposefully presupposes not only that structure can be detected but also that intentionality and orientation can be observed.

Texts can be depicted as a series of (A–a–0) relations manifesting themselves in a hierarchy. These depictions are thus of a process, such that the O part in the clause is unfolded in the next clause in the series:

$$A-a-(A-a-O).$$

Bierschenk presents the example 'Researchers (A) observed (a) that (infants (A) crawled (a) over eggs (O)).' This example is just one possible representation. The expression has a syntax that constitutes a schema, i.e., an empirical independent (A–a–0) formula.

The objective component has associated with it four modifiers that help in locating the relative position of viewpoints: figure, ground, means, and goal. The figure modifier refers to the direct object in a clause. This circumstance is syntactically identified through the absence of prepositions. The ground modifier represents the where and when. The modifier is identified by prepositions like 'in', 'on', 'under'. The means modifier represents the how, it is regarded as an explication of the action which effects the number of viewpoints in the observation. It gives expression to an optional aid by which an action is performed. Means modifiers are identified by prepositions like 'with', 'through', 'by'. The goal modifier refers to what can be perceived or conceived. It is identified with the preposition 'for'. Figure and round are sub-components of the objective component, means and goal are optional sub-components of the objective. Bierschenk does not give a theoretical justification for these four modifiers.

Especially the prepositions 'on', 'with' and 'for' represent three kinds of pointers toward structural variability. The perspective order among them is the one presented and refers to the distance from the verb. Viewpoints that are not proceeded by a proposition are next to the verb and in direct focus. In the algorithmic approach 'for' has priority over 'with', and 'with' has priority over 'on'.

This is the basis of the method called perspective text analysis. Its task is to characterize the mental model that governs language production and to foster an understanding of changes in language usage as a text proceeds.

The principles of perspective text analysis have been implemented in the computer program Pertex. The analysis starts from normal text and ends up in a topological representation of the mentality a text presents. The method uses events that appear in the clauses in produced text. The sentence 'I want to go to the town by bike to buy a present for my friend's birthday' (Helmerson, 1992: 7) is coded as in Table 5.5. The sentence contains three clauses. Actions can be coded in active voice as in the example, but also in passive voice. For the greater part coding is done automatically. In some situations the coder has to assist in finding the correct code. Dictionaries are used containing the agent, the action (in active or passive voice), and the objective (figure, ground, means, goal). In Table 5.5 the results of the coding of the clauses is shown, as well as the results after supplementation. During supplementation the 'nesting' of

Table 5.5   *Example of coding in Pertex*

```
                        after coding   after
                        clause         supplementation
        boundary               *
          Agent                I        I                          start

        clause
          action (active)    want       want
          Objective (figure)   *        I to the town by bike

        boundary             to         to
          Agent                *                                   start

        clause
          action (active)    go         go
          Objective (ground) to         to the town
          Objective (ground) the
          Objective (ground) town
          Objective (means)  by         by bike
          Objective (means)  bike
        boundary             to         to
          Agent                *        I                          start

        clause
          action (active)    buy        buy
          Objective (figure) a          a present
          Objective (figure) present
          Objective (goal)   for        for my friend's birthday
          Objective (goal)   my
          Objective (goal)   friend's
          Objective (goal)   birthday

        end                   .          .
```

clauses takes place.

Pertex does a clause-by-clause mapping of texts into matrices either with the categories of the agent in the row and categories of the object (per type) in the column, or vice versa. So in the column of the matrix might be the unique agent, and in the row the unique objectives of a particular type (e.g., 'ground'). The cells do not contain frequencies, but indications of co-occurrence. The sentence that was analysed contains only one Agent (I), which appears in three clauses. There are two objectives of type, figure. For this combination of agent and objective a 1*2 matrix will result, having a 1 in each cell because the agent is linked to each of the objectives. In a real investigation one will find larger data matrices. With the aid of cluster analysis, the number of agents or objectives in these matrices can be collapsed into empirically defined 'natural groups' (Bierschenk, 1991: 26–8). Thus, the researcher does not develop a set of meaning categories *a priori*. A cluster analysis is used to identify what one's subject- and predicate categories should be. But this leaves the researcher with the problem of 'naming' the empirically derived categories – a problem of which Bierschenk is aware. Like factor analysis, cluster analysis is a data-reduction technique that leaves problems regarding the naming of the categories. Such problems were already discussed in relation to the analysis of the empirical content within the previous chapter.

Coding event data

Another program that uses pattern recognition among subject-verb-object triplets, or better, that uses syntax grammar put among subject-action-object triplets is the Kansas Event Data System (KEDS) (Gerner et al., 1994; Schrodt et al., 1994; Schrodt and Gerner, 1997). This program is used in international relations research where journalistic descriptions of international interactions are converted to categorical data that can be analysed statistically. The program works primarily with short news articles. It codes statements regarding who has done what to whom and when. With respect to the publications referred to above the program has been tailored to capture event data from Reuters wire service leads in stories regarding the Middle East. However, it is also adopted for other topics and news sources. Savaiano and Schrodt (1997) applied KEDS in their study on environmental change and conflict in Ethiopia in 1984–85. Here they use data on food production provided by the Food and Agricultural organization (FAO) and on transboundary refugee flows provided by the United Nations High Commission on Refugees (UNHCR). Political event data were collected in a text analysis of lead sentences from news reports drawn from the Nexis archive of the Reuters news service.[5] The investigators were especially interested in conflicts between the Ethiopian government and rebels from Somalia or Sudan.

Political conflict is usually investigated in terms of violence and isolated from routine civil interactions. Bond et al. (1997) argue that mass conflict is multidimensional, therefore they take both aspects in consideration in their study. Three dimensions of conflict are defined – contentiousness, coerciveness, and change goals – and indices of the civil society that are central to mapping global trends in mass conflict. Just like Schrodt and colleagues they use the PANDA protocol (Protocol for the Assessment of Nonviolent Direct Action) for coding data about democratic transitions and escalated conflicts in several countries between 1984 and 1994. Now they were able to give profiles of these transitions and conflicts, and show the strength of civil society in this process.

The developers use in their empirical research newswire leads, which have a relatively simple grammatical structure. Therefore it is sufficient that KEDS contains a simple parser.[6] The program also employs a knowledge base of verb patterns to determine the appropriate event code. Each word in the input-text-file is checked to see if it occurs in the actor and verb dictionaries. If it is found, it is assigned to the appropriate type, otherwise it is designated as untyped. The parsing operations deal with words that are typed. Despite its lack of sophisticated natural language processing features, the program is able to classify about 90% of the leads. It also assigns 80%–90% of the same codes that a human coder would assign (Schrodt et al., 1994: 573). The program downloads subject-action-object relations ordered on a time-scale.

The investigators list some problems KEDS cannot handle (at the time of their writing). These problems have, among others, to do with passive voice, ambiguous words, and the incorrect interpretation of conjunctions.

In the investigation on Middle East occurrences an actor file was used containing proper nouns and the concepts with which they are associated. For example, the actor 'AMMAN' is associated with JORDAN. Multiple nouns can map to the same concept, both 'TEL AVIV' and 'RABIN' are all coded as ISRAEL.

Common nouns like 'electorate' and 'emigrant' are called agents. Coders are requested to assign an actor identity to all agents and to replace pronouns (he, its, they) by their referents whenever possible. Verbs are assigned numeric codes. When multiple verbs are found in a sentence, priorities are set. A subordinate code indicates that a verb is to be coded only if no other events are found. When a phrase with a subordinate code is encountered the program continues to search for other verb patterns in the sentence rather than stopping. KEDS is best used in coding descriptions of events. In the sentence 'George Bush said he rejected Syria's assertion ...' the important event is USA <rejected> SYRIA, and not USA <said> SYRIA. This is handled by replacing the pronoun 'he' and by using a subordinate code.

Both in the studies in the Middle East and in Africa, the investigators report on the level of action of one party (often a country) against another party with respect to a specific characteristic like cooperation, consultation, or conflict. These actions are all placed on a time scale, allowing one to compare, for example, how often country 1 opposed country 2 versus the frequency with which country 2 opposed country 1 over time. In these studies the investigators used the WEIS (World Events Interaction Survey) coding scheme developed by McClelland (1976) for research in the field of international relations.

The representational approach

Wittgenstein once observed, 'If language is to be a means of communication there must be agreement not only in definitions but also (queer as this may sound) in judgments' (1953, I 242). This is why sentences that are perfectly clear from a grammatical standpoint may sound ambiguous in the absence of contextual information. For example, it is unclear whether 'George is standing up' refers to a static state-of-affairs of George's standing upright (emphasis on the subject, 'George') or to a dynamic process of George's standing up (emphasis on the predicate, 'standing up'). Moreover, the sentence may involve an evaluation of 'George' (e.g., as brave enough to stand and volunteer for a dangerous mission) or of 'standing up' (e.g., as the appropriate thing to do, given that George is the King of England). Ferdinand de Saussure ([1916] 1974) was probably the first to point out how language serves not only to describe processes and states-of-affairs, but to positively or negatively judge them as well. Surface grammatical relations cannot capture these differences in the intentions behind statements (cf. Austin, [1962] 1975). Instead, there may be deeper syntactic structures that have less ambiguous ways of relating words than one finds in everyday speech (Chomsky, 1957).

This problem of ambiguity is ignored when the instrumental view, and thus syntax grammar, are applied in encoding relations among words. The representational view requires Verstehen from coders as they infer texts' intended meanings. Semantic grammars aid coders in drawing these inferences.

Semantic grammar

Linguists have argued that the intended meanings of texts are not solely captured by their surface grammatical relations. One needs a semantic grammar that allows clauses' context to be taken into account. Syntax grammar does not suffice. For example, the syntax grammar of the clause 'He is a doctor' is clear but its meaning is not. Its intention might have been to indicate that 'he helps people who are sick,' or that 'he has an academic title.' One's semantic grammar must be able to capture such distinctions.

Frege (1974 [1884]) has noted that the sentence 'x acts' contains two assertions: 'there is an x' and 'x acts.' That is, this sentence describes a state-of-affairs and a process. This is commonly expressed with the notation:

$$(x)f(x).$$

The first element in the form indicates 'There is an x.' The second element $(f(x))$ is read as '$f(\cdot)$ is a predicate involving x.' If $f(\cdot)$ predicates acting, $f(x)$ predicates x as acting. Roberts (1997a, 1997c) has shown that this interpretation is semantically ambiguous, because it has no unique semantic opposite. Therefore the form as such cannot – without modification – serve as a basis for a generic semantic grammar.

A semantic opposite differs from a logical opposite in that it is the negation of the intended meaning of a speech act, and not the literal formal meaning. For example, consider the sentence 'Ann went to school.' Applying the $(x)f(x)$ functional form, and setting x = 'Ann' and $f(\cdot)$ = 'went to school' yields 'There is Ann and Ann went to school.' In formal Aristotelian logic, the sentence is rendered as:

$$\exists(\text{Phenomenon } x)\ \exists(\text{Process } p)\ [p(x) \wedge x = \text{`Ann'} \wedge p = \text{`went to school'}]$$

This statement reads, 'There exists a phenomenon, x, such that there exists a process, p, such that p is predicated of x, x is "Ann", and p is "went to school".' The unique logical opposite is:

$$\forall(\text{Phenomenon } x) \ \forall(\text{Process } p) \ [\sim p(x) \vee x \neq \text{'Ann'} \vee p$$
$$\neq \text{'went to school'}).$$

This reads, 'For all phenomena, x, such that for all processes, p, p is not predicated of x or x is not "Ann" or p is not "went to school".' In analyses of ordinary discourse, however, the semantic opposite of the sentence's intended meaning has a much narrower scope.

Roberts argues that in ordinary discourse, the efficient functioning of natural language requires that both source and audience take much of the original Aristotelian expression's content for granted. This means, most elements of the expression will be assumed semantically invariant and thus superfluous to its intended meaning. There are four such elements:

- $\exists(\text{Phenomenon } x) \ [x=\bullet]$ – The speech act mentions physical and symbolic phenomena that are true to the audience's experiences;
- $\exists(\text{Process } p) \ [p=\bullet]$ – The speech act relates phenomena in ways that are comprehensible to an audience fluent in the language of discourse;
- $p(x)$ – The source genuinely or credibly intends to communicate a process predicated on a phenomenon;
- $\sim(x \neq \text{'Ann'} \wedge p \neq \text{'went to school'})$ – The source intends to communicate relevant information.

Thus, if the audience assumes the truth, comprehensibility, credibility, and relevance of the source's speech acts, the sentence, 'Ann went to school,' has exactly two semantic opposites:

$$\exists(\text{Phenomenon } x) \ \exists(\text{Process } p) \ [p(x) \wedge x \neq \text{'Ann'} \wedge p =$$
$$\text{'went to school'}],$$

and

$$\exists(\text{Phenomenon } x) \ \exists(\text{Process } p) \ [(p(x) \wedge x = \text{'Ann'} \wedge p \neq$$
$$\text{'went to school'}].$$

Once the domain of a generic semantic grammar is restricted to ordinary discourse, the simpler $(x)f(x)$ notation can be substituted for expressions of Aristotelian logic. Accordingly, the functional forms of the two just-mentioned semantic opposites are as follows:

$$(x)f(\sim x)$$

and

$$(x)\sim f(x).$$

When applied to the sentence, 'Ann went to school,' the first form's transformation can be read as, 'Something "other than Ann" went to school,' whereas the second transformation generates the semantic opposite, 'Ann did "something other than" go to school.'

It is because of these dual semantic opposites that all sentences fitting the $(x)f(x)$ form are ambiguous. In other words, the intended meaning of the sentence about Ann depends on whether its function was to answer the question, 'Who or what went to school?' or 'What did Ann do?' In the former case, the sentence functions to convey a description of a state-of-affairs; in the latter case, it functions to convey a description of a process.

Roberts argues that once these two descriptive forms are supplemented with two judgmental functional forms, a four-fold semantic grammar is revealed that enables the unambiguous encoding of clauses. Table 5.6 depicts this two-by-two typology of functional forms. Syntaxes for the four forms are as follows:

Table 5.6 *Representation of four unambiguous functional forms*

The intended meaning of the clause is to . . .

	Describe	Judge
a Process	Perception	Justification
a State-of-affairs	Recognition	Evaluation

description of state of affair
$(x)a(x)$ with semantic opposite $(x)a(\sim x)$.
A fit between sentence and form is read as 'There was (a schoolbound) Ann,' with semantic opposite 'There was no (schoolbound) Ann.'

description of a process
$(x)^i p(x)$ with semantic opposite $(x)^i \sim p(x)$, $i = 0, 1$.
(The i-superscript is introduced to acknowledge the optional role of the semantic subject in passive voice.) Example: 'The school was gone to,' with semantic opposite, '"Something other than" going to school happened.'[7]

judgment of a description

$(x)a(x)L_a$ with semantic opposite $(x)a(x)\bar{L}_a$.

(Here x's attribute, a, is assigned the positive qualifier, L_a; in the latter expression the same attribute is assigned the opposite, negative qualifier, $\bar{L}_a$.) In this case the sentence 'Bill makes generous contributions' has as opposite 'Bill is stingy.' (Remember, the intention conveyed in the clause is a judgment of the subject.)

judgment of a process

$(x)^i p(x)L_p$ with semantic opposite $(x)^i p(x)\bar{L}_p$, $i = 0, 1$.

(Again, the i-superscript acknowledges that a subject need not be made explicit in such speech acts.) Before, Bill was judged, now the process is negatively judged: 'Bill's making of generous contributions (e.g., to the Nazi Party) is immoral.'

When applying a generic semantic grammar to relatively unstructured texts, the coder's task is not one of identifying themes' surface grammatical relations but one of identifying each theme's role within the functional form(s) appropriate to its clause of origin. During the coding process such identifications can only be made after selecting the appropriate functional form – a selection that requires the coder to look beyond the clause. That is, the selection of functional forms requires that the coder understands both the source's intentions and the social context within which the clause appeared.

Roberts bases his generic semantic grammar on these four functional forms. The grammar is a model of text (T), according to which text is a sequence of one or more clauses (C) separated by markers (+) that indicate subordination, coordination, and sentence boundaries:

$$T = C(+C)^n, \ n > 0.$$

Each clause in this sequence can be represented within its situational context (SC) according to one or more of the four unambiguous functional forms just introduced. Differently put, intention (I) is a function that maps ($\rightarrow$) clause-context pairs into a multi-set comprised of subsets having one or more occurrences among recognition (R), perception (P), evaluation (E), and justification (J):

$$I(C_i, \ SC_{i-1}) \rightarrow MS_{\{R,P,E,J\}},$$

where MS $\neq$ {},

and $R = (x)a(x)$ with semantic opposite $(x)a(\sim x)$;

$P = (x)p(x)$ with semantic opposite $(x)\sim p(x)$;

$E = (x)a(x)L_a$ with semantic opposite $(x)a(x)\bar{L}_a$;

$J = (x)p(x)L_p$ with semantic opposite $(x)p(x)\bar{L}_p$.

The restriction that this intention function has a single situational context as an argument ensures a coherent set of assumptions made by the source regarding truth, comprehensibility, credibility, relevance, and evaluation and justification criteria, as are needed for a one-to-one mapping from clauses' surface representations to their appropriate functional forms.

Finally, situational contexts are continually updated by virtue of successive clauses' intended meanings. If SC_0 is the situational context at the beginning of a text and SC_i is the situational context after the ith clause, then situation (S) can be presented as a function that takes the current clause's intention into account in transforming one situational context to the next:

$$S(SC_{i-1}, I(C_i, SC_{i-1})) = SC_i.$$

To the extent that situational contexts (and rules for transformations among them) lack formal definition, coders' intuitions regarding these contexts and transformations will be necessary when this generic semantic grammar is used in encoding texts.

Any semantic text analysis based on this grammar takes a representative approach to texts. This is because it is solely on the basis of a clause's intended meaning that coders decide which of the four functional forms to apply. Roberts goes further than any other investigator toward offering a generic solution to the ambiguity problems in text analysis.

Valence

The S–V–O statement is often extended to a S–V–V–O statement, where the second V stands for valence. The valence indicates whether what is described in the clause is going on or not going on. For example, 'John is a salesman' or 'John is not a salesman.' The valence is generally indicated by a number in the range -1 to $+1$. The first clause is positive, and might therefore be valenced as $+1$. The other clause is negative, and might be valenced as -1. Often clauses are in between, it may hold that 'John is occasionally a salesman.' Now the clause is still positive, but the valence $+1$ is not realistic any more. John is not totally a salesman, but only occasionally. Therefore a valence of $+0.5$ (at least $0 <$ value $< +1$) is to be preferred. This is the strength of the valence.

Depending on the issue that is stated in the clause some extremes can be distinguished:

positive	negative
totally	not at all
good	bad
of great value	of no value
appropriate	inappropriate
effective	ineffective

When the representational view is applied the strength of the valence can be determined during coding by the coder.

Linguistic content analysis

The generic semantic grammar just explained is associated with a text analysis method known as linguistic content analysis (Roberts, 1989, 1997a). The method is particularly useful in the study of differences in social knowledge across temporal and social contexts. Each clause is coded according to the meaning that it was intended to convey (namely, as a description or as a judgment of a process or of a state-of-affairs). Each of the resultant types of intention (description of process, description of state-of-affairs, judgment of process, judgment of state-of-affairs) has associated with it a distinct, but unambiguous syntax, according to which coders can render S–V–V–O relations within clauses. Once a clause is encoded according to one of the four syntaxes, the computer program, PLCA (Program for Linguistic Content Analysis), reconstructs that clause by 'translating' it according to both the meaning categories into which its words fall, and its words' intended interrelations. For example,

VIETNAM's MEDIA said, 'CHINA does not DISCOURAGE/IMPEDE a VIOLENCE toward a MEDIA.'

is a PLCA translation of the following sentence from an East Berlin news report of China's invasion of Vietnam in 1979 (Roberts, 1997c: 112):

According to statements from the news agency, VNA, China does not even resist attacking foreign journalists.

Such translations allow the coder to immediately evaluate the face validity of the encoding. Note that in this case a specific source (VNA) describes a process of China's (Subject) not (Valence) resisting (Verb) violence (Object).

Once texts have been encoded, PLCA will download a data matrix listing the S–V–V–O relations in each clause, along with an indicator of which of the four types of intention the relations reflect (plus data on tense, modal auxiliary verb, subordination, question type, etc.). Such LCA data can be used to make inferences about the conditions under which texts' authors intend to communicate specific meanings to their audiences. For example, when a totalitarian regime initiates a public relations campaign to 'democratize' its image in the US press, linguistic text analysis could be used to test whether from before to after the campaign a significant increase occurred in the odds that US news stories describe (the process of) the regime acting according to the will of its citizens.

In the coding process the coder starts from one of the four types of intentions as listed in Table 5.6. Although a particular clause may appear ambiguous in a given context, its LCA encoding is necessarily unambiguous. To illustrate this point, consider the following four encodings of the sentence, 'Chris bought that camera.' (Roberts and Popping, 1996: 660):

- Description of a process

    We both went to the shop. Then Chris purchased that camera.
    <subject = Chris> <process = purchased>
    <object = that camera>[8]

- Judgment of a state-of-affairs

    Chris is a camera novice. Despite the selection of excellent cameras in the shop, Chris purchased that camera.
    <state-of-affairs = Chris's camera> <judgment = is bad>

- Description of a state-of-affairs

    I'm trying to figure out what he spent his allowance on. Aah, Chris purchased that camera!
    <state-of-affairs= Chris's camera><classification = Chris's purchase>

- Judgment of a process

    I pointed out that he might be arrested if he stole it. Fortunately, Chris purchased that camera.
    <process = Chris's buying> <object = that camera> <judgment = was appropriate>

In each sentence the surface grammar is clear, but the intended meaning is not (illocutionary ambiguity). When a clause has been encoded according to one of the four grammars, coders may still disagree about whether the appropriate grammar was applied to the clause (i.e., about whether the clause was intended to convey a description or a judgment of a process or a state-of-affairs). However, LCA ensures that no disagreements are possible regarding which type(s) of intention is (are) the one(s) according to which each clause was encoded.[9]

Four steps are involved in encoding a sentence using PLCA. Consider the sentence, 'Pete's behaviour after school was inadequate.':

- Identify   How many clauses are there in the sentence?

(Clauses are identified by inflected verbs. The sole inflected verb in the sentence is 'was'.)

- Recognize   What is each clause's intended meaning?

(Evaluation: A judgment of a state-of-affairs, namely 'Pete's behaviour.' The sentence does not contain a judgment of a process, as it would were the phrasing to have been, 'Pete's behaving after school was inadequate.' Therefore 'Pete's behaviour' is more a summation of what Pete failed to accomplish, than it is a reference to the inept manner in which he worked.)

- Simplify   What adverbial and prepositional phrases are peripheral to the clause's intended meaning?

(There is after school to simplify.)

- Assign   What concepts are used in which ways to convey the clause's intended meaning?

(The coded sentence is: The STUDENT'S BEHAVIOUR was of little value.)

When texts are coded using the PLCA-computer program's implementation of this semantic grammar, the following attributes of a clause can be encoded:

1. The type of clause, its syntactic form;
2. The tense (present, past, future);
3. Whether or not the clause is a question (if so, there is a selection of question types);
4. The valence (varies according to clause type);
5. The speaker;
6. The audience;
7. The semantic subject of the verb;
8. The modifier of the subject;
9. The verb;
10. The modal auxiliary of the verb;
11. The semantic object of the verb;
12. The modifier of the object.

Codes for these attributes are available in the data matrix that is generated when the coding task has been finished. Table 5.7 depicts a LCA data matrix. This data matrix is (in principle) 'translatable' back into some semblance of the original text.

The original text blocks were:

Table 5.7   *A data matrix generated by PLCA*

Identifying information	Clause number	Sentence number	Depth in syntactic tree	Clause type	Type of subordination	Clause tense	Question?	Clause valence	Genitive of audience	Audience of speaker	Genitive of speaker	Speaker code	Genitive of subject	Subject	Modal auxiliary	Main verb	Genitive of object	Object	Weight info.
SPRT	06	1	0	0	-9	-2	0	+	999	999	999	999	200	-9	-9	-9	999	C	1.00
SPRT	31	1	0	4	-9	-9	0	NM	999	999	999	999	203	6	90	203	14	S	0.25
SPRT	31	2	1	1	OP	-9	0	T	999	999	999	999	203	14	1	999	91	S	0.25
SPRT	31	3	1	2	T	-9	0	T	999	999	999	999	203	-9	80	999	190	S	0.25
SPRT	31	4	2	0	OR	-2	0	-	999	999	999	999	190	-9	-9	999	999	S	0.25
SPRT	11	1	0	4	-9	-9	0	T	999	999	999	999	203	-9	1	999	99	C	1.00
SPRT	24	1	0	0	-9	-9	0	T	999	999	999	999	200	7	99	999	999	S	1.00
SPRT	37	1	0	0	-9	-9	0	T	999	999	999	999	200	-9	1	999	98	S	1.00
SPRT	40	1	1	2	3	-9	0	T	999	999	999	999	999	-9	1	999	34	S	0.33
SPRT	40	2	1	2	-9	-9	0	T	999	999	999	999	200	-9	35	999	999	S	0.33
SPRT	40	3	2	1	-9	-9	0	T	999	999	999	999	200	-9	33	999	104	S	0.33
SPRT	39	1	1	2	T	-2	0	T	999	999	999	999	135	-9	17	999	999	S	0.50
SPRT	39	2	2	1	-9	-9	0	T	999	999	999	999	200	-9	1	999	105	S	0.50
SPRT	01	1	0	0	-9	-9	0	T	999	999	999	999	203	-9	37	999	999	S	0.25

6   I am always playing fair.

31   The boy could not stand that he was losing, so he started playing in a way that was not fair.

Table 5.7 (continued)

	Values across records (read left → right)
SPRT	SPRT SPRT SPRT SPRT SPRT SPRT SPRT SPRT SPRT SPRT SPRT SPRT SPRT SPRT SPRT SPRT SPRT SPRT SPRT SPRT SPRT SPRT SPRT SPRT SPRT SPRT SPRT SPRT SPRT SPRT SPRT SPRT SPRT
id	01 01 02 02 03 03 03 04 04 05 05 07 08 08 09 10 10 12 12 12 13 13 14 14 15 15 16 17 17 17 18 18 19
	3 4 1 2 1 2 3 1 2 1 1 2 1 1 2 1 1 2 1 2 1 1 2 1 1 2 1 1 2 3 4 1 2
	1 1 1 1 1 1 1 1 1 1 1 1 1 1 1 1 1 1 1 1 1 1 1 1 1 1 1 1 1 1 1 1 1
	2 3 0 1 0 1 2 0 1 0 0 1 0 0 1 0 0 1 0 1 2 3 0 1 0 1 0 1 0 0 1 2 3 0 1 0
	1 2 1 2 1 2 4 1 2 1 2 2 2 1 2 4 1 2 1 2 1 2 1 4 2 1 2 1 2 1 2 1 2
	1 3 9 1 9 6 3 1 9 6 9 1 9 1 9 3 3 1 9 1 9 1 9 1 9 1 9 3 6 3 9 1 9
	1 1 1 1 2 2 2 2 2 2 2 2 2 2 2 2 2 2 2 2 2 2 2 2 2 2 2 2 2 2 1 1 1
	0 0 0 0 0 0 2 0 0 0 0 0 2 0 2 0 0 0 0 0 0 2 0 0 0 0 0 0 2 0 0 0 0
symbol	T T T T N T T + T T T T N T T T T + T T T – T T T T T T T T T T T
	999 999 999 999 999 999 999 999 999 999 999 999 999 999 999 999 999 999 999 999 999 999 999 999 999 999 999 999 999 999 999 999 999
	999 999 999 999 999 999 999 999 999 999 999 999 999 999 999 999 999 999 999 999 999 999 999 999 999 999 999 999 999 999 999 999 999
	999 999 999 999 999 203 999 999 999 999 999 999 999 999 999 999 999 999 999 999 999 999 999 999 999 999 999 999 203 203 999 999 999
	999 999 999 999 999 999 999 999 999 999 999 999 999 999 999 999 999 999 999 999 999 999 999 999 999 999 999 999 999 999 999 999 999
	203 200 200 205 200 203 200 190 205 203 203 205 200 200 999 200 203 200 200 190 203 200 200 200 200 203 203 203 200 203 200 200 200
	-9 17 -9 -9 -9 22 5 20 -9 -9 6 -9 -9 -9 19 -9 -9 -9 -9 40 -9 -9 40 -9 22 22 -9 40 -9 40 -9 22 40 22
	999 999 999 999 999 999 999 999 999 999 999 999 999 999 999 999 999 999 999 999 999 999 999 999 999 999 999 999 999 999 999 999 999
	999 105 999 40 999 99 99 999 99 999 98 0 100 98 99 999 105 999 999 14 999 999 999 99 999 999 999 99 999 999 999
	S S S S S S S S S S C S S C S S S S S S S S S S C S S S S S C
	1.00 (×33)
prob	0.25 0.25 0.50 0.50 0.33 0.33 0.33 0.50 0.50 0.50 0.50 1.00 0.50 0.50 1.00 0.50 0.50 0.25 0.25 0.25 0.50 0.50 0.50 0.50 1.00 0.25 0.25 0.25 0.50 0.50 1.00

These are 'retranslated' (i.e., translated by the coder into the data matrix in Table 5.7, then retranslated by PLCA into the following form) as:

I am good.

THE OTHER was not able to PERMIT that [
THE OTHER was hypothetically a LOSER
],
therefore THE OTHER PLAYED a GAME (
that was lacking)

.

If NARRATOR were used instead of I as a person code in the first text block, the subject would be NARRATOR, and the speaker would also have been NARRATOR. The second text block consists of four clauses. In the data matrix the following codes are used:

the modal auxiliaries: 6 = ability, 14 = hypothetically;
the verbs: 1 = to BE, 80 = to PLAY, 90 = to PERMIT, 91 = to LOOSE;
the persons: 200 = I_SELF or NARRATOR, 203 = THE OTHER;
the thing: 190 = GAME.

The numbers −9 and 999 indicate that the corresponding attribute does not apply to the clause. So, with respect to the first text block the data matrix contains the NARRATOR as the subject, and a positive valence referring to 'good'. The three types of subordination in the data matrix are: OP for an object-proxy clause and for the 'therefore' conjunction, and OR for a clause relative to the object.

Finally, LCA encoding requires a translation, not paraphrasing of texts. For example, one might paraphrase the sentence, 'I'll stand by you.' This is paraphrased as, 'I assure you.'. This gloss accurately classifies the statement as one of assurance, but it is *not* a translation of what was actually stated. An accurate translation must convey a promise of a future assistance, such as in the sentence, 'I shall assist you.'

Coding event data

As already mentioned, Schrodt's method of coding event data is an instrumental one. When texts on event data are coded following a representational view, the semantic triplet Subject–Action–Object is again the basis for the coding. Coding is done interactively so that texts can be coded according to their intended meanings, and with minimal ambiguity. Again, codes for relations among clauses can be assigned to map the complexity of interclause relations found in natural languages. The final dictionary consists of concepts, search entries and relations as found in the texts, or as supplied verbatim by the coders. The dictionary changes, depending on the setting (time and place) and type of collective action studied.

Franzosi (1997) has used event characteristics gleaned from newspaper accounts to investigate Italian labour disputes. Applying an extensive semantic grammar, he conceptualized labour disputes (the phenomena of interest) as clusters of actors' actions towards each other (i.e., of S–V–O tuples). Franzosi's method yields numerous S–V–O tuples per newspaper article and commonly multiple newspaper articles per labour dispute (i.e., multiple text blocks per recording unit). Consequently, for Franzosi, the generation of dispute-specific indicators of whether one type of actor acted in a specific way toward another, requires a search for this information among all S–V–O tuples associated with each labour dispute.

Franzosi's computer program, PC-ACE, allows him to code the data in such a way that they can be entered into a relational database package. Such a database consists of a set of relations. Each relation contains one or more attributes, which themselves may be relations. For example, a triplet relates the attribute actor with action, but actor may have attributes like noun and modifier that are themselves related. An illustration is given in Table 5.8.

Table 5.8   *Example of relational database*

```
triplet_table
triplet_id subject_id   action_id  object_id
    1           5            2          4
    2           1            3          4
    3           2            1          1
    .           .            .          .

subject_table
subject_id    subject_label
    1              striker
    2              police
    .              .

action_table
action_id    action_label
    1             detain
    2
    3
    .             .

object_table
object_id    object_label
    1             striker
    2
    3
    .             .

(labels are fictitious)
```

Computations on the data in this database start from a relational algebra. A special language (SQL – Structured Query Language) has been developed to have these computations performed. All full triplets from Table 5.8 having 'police' as subject are found by using the SQL-statement in Table 5.9. This statement will yield a set of S–V–O triplets like the following:

Table 5.9   *SQL-statement*

```
SELECT subject_id.subject_label,  verb_id.verb_label,
       object_id.object_label
  FROM triplet_table,  subject_table,  verb_table,  object_table
 WHERE  triplet_table.subject_id  =  subject_table.subject_id
   AND  triplet_table.verb_id     =  verb_table.verb_id
   AND  triplet_table.object_id   =  object_table.object_id
   AND  subject_id.subject_label  =  'police'
```

police detain striker.

By using SQL it is also possible to get frequencies, averages, and other statistics. Details on Franzosi's use of relational databases are in Franzosi (1994). See Date (1995) for other details on relational databases.

Franzosi's (1997) results show differences between service sector conflicts and traditional industrial conflicts. These differences are illustrated using counts of subject, actions, or objects. For example he counts the frequency with which various actors from both the industrial and the service sector participate in disputes. For example employers participate in 72.4% of the disputes in the industry sector and in 43% of the disputes in the services sector, for the public these numbers are respectively 3.8% and 19%. The percentages found for both central and local government are only slightly higher in the services than in the industrial disputes. The central government and ministries are more often subject in the services disputes than in the industrial disputes. They are also more often the object. Disputes on actions like (temporary) layoff and contract agreement occur more in the industrial than in the services sector. The reverse is found with respect to disputes on actions like criticism, declaring strike or striking. Disputes can also be distinguished with respect to type of demand. The defensive demands and agreement are found slightly more in the industrial sector, the services sector has more disputes on offensive demands and contract renewal.

Analysis

Each of the semantic methods generates a data matrix that calls for a corresponding type of analysis. These modes of analysis reflect both the research questions posed and the theoretical orientation taken by the methods' originators. Gottschalk assigns scores on trait and state scales to individual persons. Bierschenk finds clusters of related concepts to be interpreted. The others methodologists end up with a data matrix similar to the one presented in Table 3.2, however. Schrodt uses such data in studying the frequency of occurrence of specific triplets over time. Franzosi does so in studying the frequency of actors or actions, among different economic sectors and types of dispute.

Several applications of linguistic content analysis are in print. For example, in his project on East and West Berlin radio news content of two military conflicts in 1979 Roberts (1997c) was able to identify differences in East versus West Berlin news regarding which quoted source described which subject as initiator of a process.[10] In comparison to the East Berlin radio station the West Berlin station mentioned disproportionally more non- East-aligned persons or organizations either as source of a quotation or as initiator of a process.

Eltinge and Roberts (1993) and Eltinge (1997) have used linguistic content analysis to assess the degree to which science was portrayed as a process of inquiry within high school biology text books.[11] The authors provided evidence that the frequency of the portrayal of science as a process of inquiry increased in the texts from 1956 to 1965. A pattern of decline was found in 1977 and in 1985. The frequency of inquiry-portrayal was higher in the introductory chapters of the text books and in chapters dealing with genetics, and lower in chapters dealing with leaf structure. The frequency of inquiry-portrayal also was higher at the beginning of chapters and paragraphs.

Udo (1998) has also applied linguistic content analysis in investigating whether an agenda setting process can be traced by using this method. She investigated how the process developed in the Netherlands with respect to policy regarding people looking for asylum. She used a stratified sample to find articles from Dutch newspapers on this issue between 1992 and 1997. By concentrating on clauses in which a judgement is given and on the use of auxiliary verbs in these editorials she could indicate the moments at which it was tried to place a topic on the agenda. Specific combinations of speaker, subject, modal verb, object, and audience refer to different types of agenda's. Her findings provide evidence that the process can be traced. However, the random sample does not allow to follow a specific issue over time. Besides newspapers only allow to capture a part of the process.

Coding the data from the example from Chapter 3 using PLCA results in 89 clauses. Five times a text block is even split in 4 clauses. Forty-one clauses contain a perception, 38 a recognition, just 2 a justification, and 8 clauses contained an evaluation.

Table 5.10 contains information with regard to the four concepts that were also investigated in the previous chapter. These results show that both SELF (which occurs only as subject of the clause) and FAIR (which occurs only as subject of the clause), and OTHER (subject) and UNFAIR (object) are associated in transcripts of the sportsmen's speech. Text block 17 contains a citation of a member of the other group ('He said I had hurt him.', or more formal: 'OTHER said: SELF was UNFAIR'). Taking this into account the relation between SELF and UNFAIR that was found once should be removed from the table.

The correlations between the concepts based on frequency of occurrence are presented in Table 5.11. In the semantic approach two concepts co-occur only when they are part of a S–V–O statement, i.e., there is really a relation between the concepts. Concepts co-occurring according to the thematic approach might

Table 5.10   *Results of analysis using PLCA – number of relations between subjects Self and Other and objects Fair and Unfair*

		object fair	object unfair
subject	self	5	1
	other	1	15

Table 5.11   *Correlations between concepts*

	based on clauses (N = 89)		based on sampling units (N = 40)	
	FAIR	UNFAIR	FAIR	UNFAIR
SELF	.18	-.37	.22	-.42
OTHER	-.10	.58	-.12	.69

really be related, but this is no requirement. This implies that several differences can be expected when the results in Table 5.11 based on the semantic approach are compared to those in Table 4.10 based on the thematic approach. When the thematic approach is applied the number of co-occurring of different concepts found is probably greater than the number of these concepts that is related. Besides the semantic approach informs about the direction of the relation, i.e., concept X as subject can be related to concept Y as object and reverse.

Conclusion

The main difference between the thematic and the semantic approach is that only in the latter approach are relations among concepts encoded. In the thematic approach subjective inferences are made by investigators such that meanings are assigned to relations between concepts that co-occur in a text unit. In the semantic approach concept relations are explicitly encoded, allowing hypotheses about these relations to be tested directly in statistical analyses of one's data matrix. One can avoid importing the ambiguities of natural language into one's data matrix by using the generic semantic grammar developed in conjunction with the linguistic content analysis.

Returning to Janowitz's (1969) barriers as listed in Chapter 1 changes are found with respect to the organizational and administrative aspects of the analysis in the semantic compared to the thematic text analysis. Again, the important ingredients to be used in a semantic text analysis are available in files on a computer system, just as it was with respect to thematic analysis. In semantic analysis the organizational task has expanded, the coder has to make more decisions than if coding would have been according to the thematic approach. Therefore explication of the coding rules, and the training of the coders will be more intensive. Here again, however, the point of the formats is not solved.

The substantive barriers related to the time span covered in studies have not changed. A methodological barrier has disappeared. The relations that are investigated, are based on the grammatical relations evident in clauses. They are no longer relations subjectively inferred based on co-occurrences in a block of text.

Janowitz has also pointed to the gap between 'theory' and 'empirical data'. In the semantic approach relations between concepts are made explicit. The grammar that is used indicates the relations that can be found. Specific S–V–O relations can be related to theoretical notions. This is an improvement.

Notes

1. Computer programs are available for all these applications in which phenomenal and generic grammars are used.

   Yet even when computer-assisted text analysis as a method for data collection from texts is very labour intensive and therefore costly. This is especially true when the representative approach is used. Therefore the method should be applied as efficiently as possible. Franzosi (1995) gives suggestions for increasing this efficiency in case semantic text analysis is applied.

2. The term, proxy clause, originated with its use in the PLCA text analysis software program. As an example of a proxy clause, in the sentence 'The man believes that the earth is square.', the object of the man's belief is the clause 'the earth is square.' In the sentence 'You are the person, who has to do it.' the noun 'the person' is modified by the relative clause 'who has to do it.'

3. Other methods to measure these psychological states and traits are based on self-report scales or on behavioural rating scales. Gottschalk (1997: 120 ff) argues that by enhancing validity content analysis has an important advantage over the other measurement techniques.

4. More detail can be found in Gottschalk et al. (1969).

5. The archives and services are searched using wild-card search entries like 'israel*', 'jordan*', or 'palest*'. The * is the wild-card character that matches any word beginning with the preceding letters; so 'jordan*' picks up 'jordans', 'jordanese', and so on.

6. For this reason it would be less appropriate to use KEDS in analysing texts that use a complex sentence structure like for example political speeches. It would only provide superficial coding of such non-descriptive texts.

7. To illustrate an instance of passive voice, it is assumed here that the semantic subject, Ann, was not named in the sentence being encoded.
8. Although not the case here, PLCA renders perceptions with missing subjects in passive voice. Whereas the syntax (e.g., 'Chris purchases a camera'), that for a perception in active voice is 'The <Subject> <Verb>s an <Object>' the syntax for one in passive voice is 'The <Object> is <Verb>ed' (e.g., 'The camera is purchased').
9. For example, an encoding of the sentence about Chris's purchase according to Franzosi's semantic grammar would yield, <subject = Chris> <action = bought> <object = that camera>. In contrast, Roberts's method requires that the coder encode clauses according to that grammar which most closely represents its intended meaning. Depending on the coder's intuitions regarding the sentence's context, the clause might be encoded according to one or more of the four renderings of the sentence as illustrated above. In the former case, the researcher's interests in event-analysis (i.e., in descriptions of processes) release the coder from having to judge each clause's illocutionary force; in the latter case, the researcher's interests in the intended meaning of each clause require just such judgments from the coder.
10. The two conflicts were the Chinese invasion of Vietnam and the Sandinista Revolution in Nicaragua. A stratified random sample of 400 clauses was drawn out of 1923 clauses about the two conflicts, 100 from each station by each conflict. In the analysis the source could be East-aligned, not East-aligned, neutral or none. This also holds for the subject, but here a category, 'other' (a place or a thing), was also possible.
11. Indicators for expressing science as inquiry were found in literature. A series of textbooks was analysed (bringing in a longitudinal component) with respect to three subject areas: background material (i.e., the introductory chapter), genetics, and leaf structure and function. From text blocks dealing with these areas a random sample of 20% of the sentences was selected. Such a large sample allows for large expected cell frequencies, necessary in the types of discrete data analysis (here logistic regression, in the previous study log-linear models) suited to analyse LCA data. In the analysis were 813 sentences, containing 1350 clauses. In 49% of these clauses science was depicted as inquiry.

6

Network text analysis

Network text analysis originated with the observation that after one has encoded semantic links among concepts, one can proceed to construct *networks* of semantically linked concepts. When concepts are depicted as conceptual networks, one is afforded more information than the frequency at which specific concepts are linked in each block of text; one is also able to characterize concepts and/or linkages according to their position within the network.[1]

The two main contemporary approaches to network text analysis arose from empirical problems. The approaches were already briefly introduced in Chapter 3. Investigators following the NET-approach wished to analyse newspaper content and map-comparison investigators wished to construct mental maps. The methods and associated software developed in conjunction with these approaches take a representational view of texts.[2] There are other programs for constructing network representations of text (e.g., Inspiration [Helfgott and Nakell, 1992] and Semnet [Miller et al., 1991]). Although insight gained from such software could be used in conjunction with findings from the NET and map-comparison approaches, these alternative programs do not generate a data matrix suitable for statistical inference.

Quantitative research in network text analysis is restricted to work by the two groups of investigators mentioned above. For example, Van Cuilenburg et al. (1986, 1988) investigate how newspapers might evaluate the taking over of power in Iran by Khomeini at the end of the seventies. (This example will be elaborated later in the chapter.) Kleinnijenhuis et al. (1997) provide evidence of a decline in Keynesianism in the Dutch press between 1968 and 1984.

Kathleen Carley is the strongest proponent of the map-comparison[3] approach. For example, Carley (1986) examined differences in student's views of what they wanted in a tutor. Her sampling units are not blocks of texts, but (sayings by) students. The students were interviewed several times during the decision making process. Each interview was coded separately. A set of maps was constructed, each map was a representation of a student's concept of tutor at that point in time. These maps were then contrasted to see how conceptions changed over time and differed across students. Carley used four categories of concepts: aspects of the tutoring job, requirements of the tutoring job, facts about tutor candidates, qualities of tutor candidates.

The map comparison method (Carley, 1986) affords not only graphic descriptions of individuals' mental models, but also comparisons among models maintained by various social groups. The programs facilitate the parsing of texts into clauses and the assignment of words and phrases to meaning concepts.

The union of all statements uttered by members of a group comprise the group's total knowledge on a particular topic. Statements that intersect among the mental models of all members in a group, comprise the knowledge about which group members hold a consensus. For example, among residents of a M.I.T. dormitory Carley (1986: 166–9) found the concept of 'ideal dormitory supervisor' was consensually associated with concepts such as 'genuine', 'honest', and 'not artificial' for one group of residents (the 'heads') but with concepts such as 'analytic', 'mature', and 'gets high grades' for another (the 'gnerds'). This type of text analysis is particularly useful for drawing inferences about group consensus (when the frequency of maps containing the same proposition approaches the number of group members) and group dissension (when this frequency approaches zero).

Like blocks of text that are considered as embodying a propositional logic, texts that are considered symptomatic of cognitive maps can also be 'filled in.' In the former case (implemented in the NET approach) propositions are inferred from propositions explicitly stated in texts, in the latter case (implemented in the map-comparison approach) conceptual relations are inferred by extending the source's explicit statements based on knowledge of their social context. For example, given a social context in which 'gnerds are antisocial', a resident's statement that a dormitory supervisor 'should not be a gnerd' would imply that the ideal dormitory supervisor is not antisocial. The SKI computer program (Carley, 1988) includes an inference engine that 'fills in' the manifest propositional logic of texts with the logic of contextually inferred propositions such as this.

Palmquist (1990) applied the map-comparison method in an examination of differences in learning in two classrooms in which 'research writing' was taught. By interviewing the instructor Palmquist was able to create a representation of the expert's knowledge about research writing. He also interviewed the students in each of the classrooms several times throughout the term. The instructor's and students' maps were then contrasted to see whether students' maps were increasingly intersecting with the instructor's map. Student maps were also contrasted to see whether students were becoming more similar over time.

There are two important steps required when one encodes networks from texts. First, one must specify the concepts that are to be linked within networks. The second step in network encoding involves the assignment of relations between pairs of concepts. Constraints relevant to the development of conceptual categories are similar to those discussed in the previous two chapters; constraints on relations are different. Again, concepts may originate with one's theory or with the texts themselves (i.e., with themes that are empirically recurrent). Encoding involves the classification of texts' words/phrases as occurrences of these concepts.

Relations

A relationship links two concepts. A statement consists of two concepts and the relation between them. This relation does not necessarily have to be a S–V–O relation. Consider the sentence 'John and Mary are in love.' From this sentence the following statements can be derived: 'John – is in love' and 'Mary – is in love.' Formulated as S–V–O relations it would be 'John loves Mary' and 'Mary loves John,' where the verb 'to love' is defined as unidirectional. Note that a relation can indicate more than that there is merely an association between two concepts; it can also symbolize a specific meaning. Carley (1993: 94 ff) distinguishes four classes of meaning associated with relations:

1. directionality (unidirectional or bidirectional);
2. strength (intensity, certainty, frequency, and so on);
3. sign (positive, negative);
4. meaning (the content, such as 'is friends with').

As mentioned in Chapter 3, instances of these classes can be used for representation (what is the meaning of two concepts' relation), and for inference (what can be inferred from the relation). Inferential relations are generally made visible in figures by arrows. I will use the term arrow to refer to a direct inference relation between two concepts, and will reserve the term link for a series of inference relations between the two concepts. Links are thus sets of two or more arrows. Although there is only one 'is friends with' relation, there can be many links using it.

The notion that concepts and their relations can be represented as networks is not new. Many different formulations of this insight have been developed. A difference in these formulations is often one of focus. Investigators interested in dynamics of action have referred to their networks as scripts (Schank and Abelson, 1977) and schemata (Rumelhart, 1975). Investigators using frames (Minsky, 1975) have used network representations as a technique for concept representation, meaning depiction and description.

Directionality

The relation between two concepts can be bidirectional or unidirectional. Concept A might have some one-sided relation to concept B, like 'influence', 'implies', 'has meaning for', 'loves' (as in the above example), and so on. Such relations indicate a direction from A to B. In case it is only known that a relation between two concepts exists, or the investigator does not consider it as relevant, the relation is bidirectional. It is both from A to B, and from B to A. It also holds when there is a reversibility relation between the two concepts, as for example in definitions like 'a cascade is a waterfall.'

The unidirectional relation between concepts A and B is pictured by a one-headed arrow,

$$A \longrightarrow B;$$

the bidirectional relation with a two-headed arrow

$$A \longleftrightarrow B.$$

Although the relation,

$$A \Longleftrightarrow B,$$

is at times considered bidirectional, it is treated here as being directional, from A to B and from B to A, because there are two arrows. The unidirectional relation in a network is generally more informative than the bidirectional one.

Strength

The strength of a relation refers to intensity, quality, frequency, and so on. The quality 'is' is stronger than the quality 'resembles'. The statement, 'A bike is convenient transportation,' is not as strong as 'A bike is very convenient transportation.' Adverbs like 'perhaps' and 'sometimes' suggest a degree of uncertainty. In most computer programs strength is quantified using numbers. In her study of student's views regarding a tutor, Carley (1986) used a range of 1 to 3 to denote the strength with which a relationship is either implied in a text, stated explicitly, or emphasized. Often strength is referred to as 'weight', and consists of a number in the range, 0 to 1.

Also the inclusiveness of a reference can be quantified in terms of strength, again on a 0 to 1 scale (e.g., 'part of the house'). Investigators have to be aware of the difference between intensity and inclusiveness. The statement, 'He looks a little bit like his brother,' is inclusive, but its intensity is less than 1. However, the statement 'The cups have the same ear' is not an inclusive reference to cups that are identical but the reference does have maximum intensity.

Sign

The strength of a relation does not contain all possible relations connected to that strength. Take the extremes: 'John adores Mary' and 'Paul despises Ann.' In both situations the strength is very high, but the type of relation is different. This issue is captured by introducing a sign. The first sentence is positive, and might therefore be assigned a score of +1. The other sentence is very negative, and might be scored as −1. Note that the term, 'valence,' is sometimes used instead of the combination of sign and strength (see also Chapter 5). Evaluative links are often encoded on a three-point (minus-neutral-positive) scale.

Meaning

Meaning refers to the content of a relation. Meaning expressions can be derived for a specific investigation, but they can also be presented in general ways. Popping and Roberts (1997: 382–3) provide the following partial list of general classes of meaning:

- Similarity – indicates that one concept is identical with or looks like (a part of) another. This relation is symmetric (abbreviations: ALIke, SIMilarity, EQUal, EQuiValent). An example: 'The boy resembles his brother';
- Causal – indicates a cause-effect relation. The relation is asymmetric and transitive. In all methods using networks based on text the causal relation is read as 'might' cause (CAUses; is Caused BY). An example: 'Car driving causes pollution';
- Relation – indicates an ASSociation, an ORDering, an EVAluation, or a REAlization. In the first case the relation is symmetric; in the other three it is asymmetric. An example of a realization: 'The number of students has increased';
- Classification – indicates a genus-species relation. The relation is transitive (is A Kind Of, Has As Kind), asymmetric (Is Property Of), or symmetric (INConsistent with or contradicts, DIStinct). An example: 'A bike is a vehicle';
- Structure – indicates a part-whole relation. The relation is transitive (is PARt of, Has As Part). An example: 'The roof is a part of the house';
- Affective – indicates a judgment of the subject about the object. The relation is asymmetric (AFFective, WILL). An example: 'In my opinion, Joe has a bad relationship with his boss.'

These groups are found in computer programs for NET and map-comparison network analysis.[4] Implicitly in their use of verb and valence indicators, these meanings are also used by investigators who apply the semantic approach.

Constructing networks

In the NET approach networks are based on information explicitly stated in texts; in the map-approach, networks are based on knowledge gleaned from the speech and writings emanating from social groups. Software implementations of these techniques have correspondingly different methods for constructing network from available data. Procedures required by these implementations are discussed in this section.

In the NET approach sentences are interactively parsed into clauses, that are then coded as S–V–V–O statements. Figure 6.1 pictures the window used for this purpose in the computer program CETA. In the window the sentence 'I always play fair,' is encoded.

```
                                              ┌──6: 1 of 1──┐
┌──────────────────────────────────────────┐ │             │
│ I always play fair.                        └─┘             │
└───┐ ┌───Info    Copy   X→y    Del    Jump+   List   Restore──┐ ┌─┘
    │ │ Source      :  --No quote--                             │ │
    │ │ Subject     :  self                                     │ │
    │ │ Connection:    play                                     │ │
    │ │                Type:   REA          Value:  +1.0        │ │
    │ │ Object      :  fair                                     │ │
    └─┴─────────────────────────────────────────────────────────┴─┘

      altF1: covering; PgDn/PgUp: next
```

Figure 6.1   *CETA's coding window*

When there is a clear source of the message it is possible to code this source as the speaker. The sentence's subject and object parts consist of some of its words or phrases unless these are replaced by concepts in an on-line dictionary. CETA's dictionary includes a reference, SELF, as proxy for I, me, my, mine, and so on.

Complex sentences having several nouns in an 'and' (or 'or') relation are generally unravelled. For example, the sentence: 'In the 1960s the Russians and the Chinese were the enemies of the Americans and Western Europeans', becomes:

1.   In the 1960s the Russians were the enemies of the Americans;
2.   In the 1960s the Chinese were the enemies of the Americans;
3.   In the 1960s the Russians were the enemies of Western Europeans;
4.   In the 1960s the Chinese were the enemies of Western Europeans.

Note that this splitting cannot be used to infer that the Russians and Chinese were allies.

As in the semantic encoding the coder has to identify the subject and object. These may be readily apparent ('John supports Peter.'), implicit ('Peter will be supported' [by John], and 'He [anaphora for John] supports Peter.'), or even pseudonomed ('Washington [= Bill] will not give Sadam very much help.'). All semantic and network text analysis methods encode the semantic (i.e., not always the grammatical) subject as the clause's object. For example, 'John is supported by Peter.' is a sentence in passive voice. When the sentence is encoded Peter is the semantic subject and John the object, not the reverse.

The verb-part of the clause is encoded according to its 'connection' and 'type'. The connection is the word or phrase that is used to relate subject and object. (Recall the various meaning classes described in the previous section.) A verb's type is its meaning class. CETA uses four main classes of meaning links (similarity [SIM], causal [CAU], affective [AFF], and association [ASS]), which are further subdivided into 15 types of connections that may be associated with a positive (did) or negative (did not) valence. CETA also allows for user-defined meaning classes.

Two special-purpose concepts are hard-wired into CETA. These are related to the distinction made in the NET-approach between 'attitude objects', words with no fixed evaluative meaning, and 'common meaning terms,' words that have a common evaluative among reasonably sophisticated users of the language. In CETA, the user can encode a statement as a positive (is good) or negative (is bad) evaluation of a concept by relating it to the abstract concept, 'Ideal.' For example, the statement 'the man is friendly' is reformulated into 'the man has a good relationship with the Ideal (of the statement's source).' By connecting a concept to the concept, 'Real', the user can encode a statement as an affirmation that a concept's referent exists (is) or does not exist (is not). The statement 'unrest is rampant' is abbreviated within CETA as, 'Reality shows a high level of unrest.' This implies that a concept can also be encoded in an abstract way. The 15 meaning types are listed in the middle column of Table 6.1.

Table 6.1   *Meaning types used in CETA*

description	coding	transformation to basis type
evaluative	x EVA I	x ASS I
affection	x AFF y	x AFF y
will		x WIL yx AFF y
causal	x CAU y	x CAU y
causal/realization	x CAR y	x CAU y, R ASS x, R ASS y
action	x ACT y	x CAU y, R ASS y
action/will	x ACW y	x CAU y, x AFF y, R ASS y
touch	x TCH y	x ASS y
order	x ORD y	x ASS (variable chance: x ASS y) I
realization	x REA y	R ASS y
equivalent	x EQV y	x SIM y, y SIM x
is a kind of	x AKO y	x SIM y, y SIM x
has as kind	x HAK y	x SIM y, y SIM x
is property of	x IPO y	{x} SIM y, y SIM {x}*
has as property	x HAP y	x SIM {y}, {y} SIM x

* {x} denotes the set of concepts with quality x.

Source: De Ridder (1994: 81)

The last five types listed in Table 6.1 are similarity relations. With respect to the last four of these types the enclosiveness of subject or object is less 1. The enumeration below contains examples, partly derived from the CETA manual, of each of the 15 types.

EVA   Carl is excellent;

AFF   The socialists are in a strained relation with the government;

WILL   The government is willing to fight against unemployment;

CAU   Certainly, the high public spending will increase unemployment;

CAR   Unemployment has been increased by high public spending:
> the statement is coded as three sentences:
>> public spending /CAU/ unemployment;
>> R /REA/ unemployment
>> R /REA/ public spending;

ACT   The president has decreased public spending;

ACW   The president's aim to decrease public spending, has been reached:
> Sentences of this type are interpreted as two sentences:
>> The president /CAU/ public spending;
>> R /REA/ public spending.
>
> In this situation of ACW CETA supposes still another sentence:
>> The president /AFF/ public spending;

TCH   Vandalism is especially troubling for small shopkeepers;

ORD   The government has to decrease the public spending:
> CETA interprets a sentence of type ORD as the sentence:
>> government acts very well
>
> in combination with the condition:
>> if the government decreases the public spending;

REA   (=> REALITY shows) Unemployment rose again this year;

EQV   Peter is the very image of his brother John;

AKO   'Tit for tat' is an important part of governments' policy;

HAK   Criminality also includes vandalism;

IPO   That movie is violent;

HAP   Peter is happy.

A statement about two concepts might be relativized by a condition attached to it, such as the sentence, 'If unemployment decreases, the socialists will support the government.' The sentence might be read as 'The socialists support the government [ACT] if unemployment is decreased [REA].' Texts often contain conditional evaluative statements. The sentence, 'The government should reduce the budget deficit,' may be interpreted as 'The government acts very well [EVA] if the government reduces the budget deficit [REA].'

A 'quality' is a numerical value assigned to a statement. The quality of a relation is interpreted differently, depending on the type of relation to which it applies. In an evaluation (EVA) quality indicates how 'good' someone or something is. But if an intention (WILL) is expressed, quality indicates the degree of willingness.

Statements conveying what should happen are coded as 'duty statements', i.e., as conditional evaluative statements. The statement, 'The government should reduce the budget deficit,' might thus be interpreted as, 'If the government will reduce the budget deficit *then* the government will act very well.'[5]

Carley's set of programs, MECA, contains a set-up program to define the number of categories of concepts to be used (so the investigator has to know this in advance) and the concepts already known to fit in each category. In addition, the program allows the user to enter information about classes of meaning for encoding relations between these concepts. The CODEMAP program can then be used to facilitate coding by guiding the user through a series of prompts regarding the two concepts to be coded and their relation, maintenance of the list of concepts, and storage of coded statements. The program automatically adjusts its prompts and storage format to fit information that was output to a set-up file when the set-up program was run. See also Carley and Palmquist (1992: 617), they discuss several of the programs that are part of MECA. One of these programs generates a so-called 'concept circle.' This is a heuristic device that has been developed for presenting the data. A simple example is in Figure 6.2. The circle helps in investigating which pairs of concepts are related according to the interviewee.

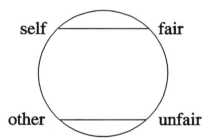

Figure 6.2   *Concept circle*

Texts and transcripts are produced within social contexts about which an investigator can obtain expertise. Using such expert knowledge it becomes possible to 'fill in' mental maps with concepts and relations beyond those explicitly stated in the texts under analysis. Carley (1988) has developed an expert system (SKI – Social Knowledge Interpreter) for filling in maps based on an expert's knowledge. The basic idea behind SKI is that when individuals use certain concepts, other concepts and relations are implied. Much of this implied information is social knowledge shared by speakers (or writers) and audiences (or readers). In a study on robots Palmquist et al. (1997: 174) illustrate how SKI operates. If one assumes the expert knowledge that 'if something has ears then it can hear,' and if a map file contains the statement, 'a robot has ears,' SKI would add to this the following two statements:

- if a robot has ears then a robot can hear; and
- a robot can hear.

Note how SKI adds concepts and statements that explicate the expert's knowledge. Insofar an expert on texts' sociolinguistic environment can explicate their expertise, SKI can be enlisted for interpreting texts emanating from this environment.

Applications of SKI can lead to enormous extensions of the original map, however Carley (1988: 177) presents the following example: 'If a student uses the phrase *Aaron is a hacker*, unless one knows what a *hacker* is, there is too much uncertainty to interpret the phrase. If you know that in the micro-world in question a *hacker is someone who does things other than studying*, then the phrase has the interpretation *Aaron is a hacker and therefore does things other than studying*.' Carley continues by explaining that further background information about the university at which Aaron is a student and the dormitory in which he lives provides richer and more detailed extensions of the phrase. As it turns out, the term, hacker is defined as entailing 22 concepts and over 60 relations (Carley, 1988: 179).

If SKI is used, one must be prepared to defend the accuracy of its knowledge base. Of course, many investigators are only interested in comparing texts' explicit information. However, for those interested in filling in maps with implicit knowledge, it is worth keeping in mind how much of one's data was manifest in one's texts, and how much was generated by the expert system. Carley defends the use of SKI as a means of eliminating loose ends due to anaphora whereby clarity is added to the mental maps being analysed. SKI can also reduce the degree to which the investigator needs to train coders, and can increase the reliability and validity of the encoded texts. Yet it is one's objective to find evidence of consensus, supplementing maps with knowledge that an expert deems *a priori* to be consensual seems tautological at best. Unfortunately Carley never warns of this problem, nor hints at a solution.

Before the actual coding starts, the investigator has to choose which meaning class(es) of relations will be admitted to his or her project, and which values or types are allowed within a class. This choice results in what might be called a 'network grammar' to texts. If the network represents a 'mental model' the relations must be defined consistently as relations of identity (as in Carley [1986]). If it represents the 'logical structure' of a debate the relations must be coded as relations of causality (as in Kleinnijenhuis, et al. [1997]). After all, it is only insofar as one understands how concepts are linked within a network that one can meaningfully interpret measures of the 'positions' that specific concepts or links hold within it. The investigator needs to develop 'relevance rules' for deciding which statements in the texts do indicate identity relations among concepts (e.g., 'the government's fiscal policy is the reduction of spending'), and which do not (possibly, 'the government's fiscal policy has resulted in the reduction of spending'). Only statements (i.e., concept-relations) relevant to the grammar of the network under construction are then encoded according to this grammar.

To my knowledge no network text analyst has specified the relevance rules applied in constructing her or his networks. As a consequence, there is no precedent for outlining how one might resolve the 'relevance ambiguity' (i.e., the relevance of some, but not all concept-relations) that will inevitably arise as these rules are applied to samples of texts. Whatever the method of its resolution, relevance ambiguity further complicates the researcher's encoding task by adding to the previously discussed problems of resolving idiomatic and illocutionary ambiguities in the texts under analysis.

Analysing networks

Networks have a wide range of attributes that lend themselves to analysis. The investigator can compare individual concepts, pairs of concepts, and relations between concepts across networks. However, the most powerful of network attributes are ones that characterize many, if not all of each network's concepts and relations. The next sections provide illustrations of these various types of attributes.

First however, the term, path, must be introduced. A path is a finite series of statements, in which the end (or object) concept of each statement is identical to the first (or subject) concept of the next statement. Paths can be used in locating the position of a concept in a network.

Concepts in a network

References to a concept's position in a network are usually characterized as some form of centrality, or relatedness to other concepts in the network. Freeman (1978) distinguished three properties of centrality within (undirected) networks. This number is extended with a fourth one by Hoede (1978):

1. adjacency – the number of concepts to which the concept is related.[6] Concepts having a high degree, have high communication potential activity;
2. betweenness – the frequency of location of a concept on the most direct paths between pairs of other concepts. It indicates the potential to withhold or distort information in a communication network;
3. distance – the number of arrows along the most direct path to each other concept. When a concept has a short distance to other concepts it is less dependent on intermediary concepts to 'communicate' with them;
4. influence – the overall connection directly, indirectly, redundantly, or by shortest distance.

Many indices based on one or more of these properties have been proposed. (For an overview see Wasserman and Faust [1994: 169 ff]). The indices are used to measure whether a concept belongs to the 'centre' or 'periphery' of a centrality just discussed. She applies these dimensions to a local and extended network domain. In the local domain all concepts directly related to the concept under investigation are used in index computation. In the extended situation indirect relationships are incorporated in the measures. Local density refers to the number of adjacent concepts. Local conductivity denotes the number of two-step paths through the concept under investigation, and thus is closely related to betweenness. Local intensity is determined by the proportion of statements in which the concept under investigation is contained with greater than average strength. This can be considered as a special case of influence. For a discussion of the extended domain, see Carley (1997: 86).

Based on her three centrality dimensions Carley builds a general taxonomy of concepts that 'derives its power as a classification scheme by simultaneously "typing" concepts and providing a framework within which the evolution of concepts, and hence knowledge, relative to a specific task can be analysed' (Carley, 1997: 87). She distinguished eight types. The taxonomy is presented in Table 6.2.

Table 6.2 *Taxonomy of concepts according to Carley*

type	density	conductivity	intensity	
1.	−	−	−	*Ordinary concepts.* These are isolated concepts;
2.	+	−	−	*Prototypes.* These have an elaborate meaning that is not highly agreed to;
3.	−	+	−	*Buzzwords.* These are highly utilized by individuals, but have little meaning;
4.	−	−	+	*Factoids.* These have a narrowly ascribed meaning that is nonetheless highly salient or accepted;
5.	+	+	−	*Place-holders.* These are highly utilized, they admit the construction of consensus;
6.	+	−	+	*Stereotypes.* These represent historical saliency or consensus to regularities perceived by members of the social unit;
7.	−	+	+	*Emblems.* These are useful communication tools as they admit instant identification;
8.	+	+	+	*Symbols.* These are the sociocultural antithesis of ordinary concepts. (Carley mentions 'social roles' as an example of a symbol.)

− denotes 'low', + denotes 'high'

Carley argues that it is useful to locate individual concepts' positions among these three dimensions. Additional complexity is introduced when one develops measures appropriate to pairs of concepts. In such cases the number of parallel links between the concept pair is investigated or the distance. The development of concept-pair indexes requires taking the directionality of their relation into account.

Relations

Networks and statistical models based on networks become richer and more interesting as the relational variables exhibit more general measurement properties. The most important relational variable is the adjacency, indicating whether there is a relation or not from one concept to another. Other relational variables that have been mentioned are directionality, strength, sign, and meaning. To be added is the multiplicity of the adjacency. The directionality is in fact already indicated by the adjacency.[7]

A network containing just signs is a so-called signed network. Such a network informs whether the relations are judged in a positive or negative way. These networks allow to investigate structural balance. When strength or meaning is investigated each arrow receives a numeric value. These values allow an ordering of relations. A network having such values is a valued network. The analysis will answer questions like 'how often does that type of relation occur,' or 'how is a specific relation valued on the average.' Again, associated indices can be computed using statistical packages for network analysis. In the literature on network analysis the types of network mentioned here are elaborated under those names.

In the analysis phase investigators often count the number of (characteristics of) relations in a network. However, relations connected to a given concept are not independent of each other. Therefore analysis of variance or the Kruskal-Wallis procedure can not be applied to these data. Carley and Banks (1993) proposed two non-parametric analyses that take the row-column dependency structure in the adjacency matrix into account.

Complete networks

One can also speak of the centrality of a complete network. Freeman (1978) contrasts the extent to which a network is compact with the extent to which it has a distinct centre. A network's centrality is one of compactness when distances between its concepts are short. A network is centred when it contains a single concept that is more central than all its other concepts. Based on this latter definition of centrality, Freeman distinguishes network centrality in terms of its degree, betweenness and distance.

Starting from distance as the basic relation between concepts (disregarding betweenness) Hoivik and Gleditsch (1970) postulate three related types of network centrality, namely, integration, unipolarity, and centralization. A highly integrated network is one in which, on the average, distances between concepts are small; a unipolar network is one in which a single concept has a small distance to all others, whereas all other concepts have long distances to each other; centralization means that there are great differences between the centralities of the separate concepts. Hoivik and Gleditsch's integration is similar to Freeman's compactness. Freeman's conception of a network centrality is split into two aspects by Hoivik and Gleditsch, namely the existence of a central concept (unipolarity) and the spread of centralities of distinct concepts (centralization).

Many networks have no clear 'centre', or have several 'centres'. Therefore there may be used for an index measuring the dispersion of centralities of the distinct concepts without direct reference to the most central concept(s). Snijders (1981) has introduced just such a heterogeneity measure based on the variance of the degrees of a network's concepts.

Aggregation within networks

Network construction nearly always involves 'simplifying' some of the relations (or links) between concepts in the text to which it corresponds.

1. Multiple links from one concept to an adjacent concept might be combined into one unidirectional link, i.e., one arrow. Thus two directional arrows between the concepts A and B

$$A \Longrightarrow B$$

might be replaced by only one arrow

$$A \longrightarrow B.$$

2. Intermediate concepts might be omitted in a chain, i.e., a series of finite links between adjacent concepts where the end concept of one arrow coincides with the begin concept of the next arrow. Chains must be elementary, such that no one concept in the network is intermediate more than once. Thus a chain of causal arrows

$$A \longrightarrow B \longrightarrow C$$

might be replaced by the causal arrow

$$A \longrightarrow C.$$

The transitivity axiom is the conceptual basis for constructing chains.

3. Subsets of concepts might be condensed or aggregated into new concepts. Such aggregation could result in relations from one concept to itself making

it necessary to specify rules for replacing links. This concerns links between concepts in the original subset, but also links with concepts that do not belong to the subset.

4. Links between concepts might be induced, i.e., directly connected by an arrow if they are adjacent to the same concept.

The three methods mentioned first are used most. A bundle is an aggregation that incorporates all three of these methods. The bundle between two concepts is the collection of all direct relations between these two concepts. All but the simplest networks contain a large number of possible chains. Although only a small portion of these possible chains is manifest in texts, their manifest number might still be innumerably large. Accordingly, one will usually be less interested in separate chains between two concepts, than in the bundle of all chains.

A better understanding of the meaning of arrow, link, chain and bundle can be gained from Figure 6.3. Three concepts are distinguished in the figure, namely A, B, and C. A positive valued relation exists from A to C, a negative valued relation from A to B, and two negative valued relations from B to C. The four arrows are shown in the left-most arrow network. In the link network the two arrows from B to C are reduced to one. In the chain network chain A–B–C is reduced to A–C. Finally, the two relations between A and C are combined in the bundle network.

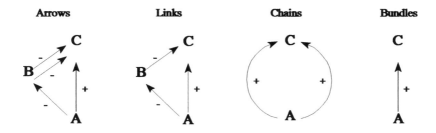

Figure 6.3   *Network aggregations*

To determine the bundle's connection (i.e., its overall value), chains are combined in exactly the same way as arrows are combined to determine the link's connection. So, roughly speaking the connection of a bundle is the mean of the connections of its constituent chains.

These operations are allowed in a number of situations. The first two operations are based on a path-algebra. A path-algebra is a set P equipped with two binary operations $\oplus$ (join operation) and $\otimes$ (multiplication operation) which have the following properties (Carré, 1979: 84–5):

1. The $\oplus$ operation is idempotent, commutative and associative:

$$\forall\ x \in P \qquad x \oplus x = x$$
$$\forall\ x,y \in P \qquad x \oplus y = y \oplus x$$
$$\forall\ x,y,z \in P \quad (x \oplus y) \oplus z = x \oplus (y \oplus z)$$

2. The $\otimes$ operation is associative and distributive over $\oplus$:

$$\forall\ x,y,z \in P \quad (x \otimes y) \otimes z = x \otimes (y \otimes z)$$
$$\forall\ x,y,z \in P \quad x \otimes (y \oplus z) = (x \otimes y) \oplus (y \otimes z)$$
$$\forall\ x,y,z \in P \quad (x \oplus y) \otimes z = (x \otimes z) \oplus (y \otimes z)$$

3. The set P contains a zero element $\varnothing$ such that:

$$\forall\ x \in P \qquad \varnothing \oplus x = x$$
$$\forall\ x \in P \qquad \varnothing \otimes x = \varnothing$$

4. The set P contains a unit element 1 such that:

$$\forall\ x \in P \qquad 1 \otimes x = x \otimes 1 = x$$

This allows operations to be performed on arrows. Arrows can be 'summed' based on the (classes of) meaning associated with them. The types might also be 'multiplied'. All possibilities that are available in CETA are presented in Table 6.3. Let us repeat the examples mentioned earlier in this chapter. Say one

Table 6.3 *The $\oplus$ (join) and the $\otimes$ (multiplication) operation in the NET-method*

The $\oplus$ (join) operation				The $\otimes$ (multiplication) operation			
	SIM	*CAU*	*AFF*	*ASS*	*SIM*	*CAU*	*AFF*	*ASS*
SIM	SIM	SIM	SIM	SIM	SIM	CAU	AFF	ASS
CAU		CAU	CAU	CAU		CAU	ASS	ASS
AFF			AFF	AFF			AFF	ASS
ASS				ASS				ASS

of the two arrows between concepts A and B below is of type similarity, and the other arrow is of type causality,

$$A \xrightarrow[\text{cau}]{\text{sim}} B.$$

The arrows might be replaced by only one arrow, this arrow is of type similarity now, because the arrows are joined.

$$A \xrightarrow{\text{sim}} B.$$

If the arrows below between concepts A and B and between concepts B and C are respectively of types similarity and causality

$$A \xrightarrow{\quad sim \quad} B \xrightarrow{\quad cau \quad} C,$$

they might be replaced by the causal arrow, because the arrows are multiplied.

$$A \xrightarrow{\quad cau \quad} C.$$

The arrows 'might be replaced', and *not* 'are replaced', this is because the transformation is not possible or realistic in all situations. The investigator will have to consider the content of the sentences. De Ridder (1994: 64) presents the following example:

- Boredom leads to vandalism.
- Vandalism is punishable.

Multiplying the sentences would yield: 'Boredom is punishable.' The issue is not whether boredom is punishable, but whether the negative common meaning 'punishable' is transmitted by an argument to 'boredom'.

In CETA, relations are characterized by the type of connection (meaning) and the four quantities of base (b), quality (q), ambivalence (a) and divergence (d). Type has already been introduced. Quality has been introduced as indicating strength of an arrow, but now we are confronted with links and bundles. I turn to base and quality.[8]

The base is an indication for the degree in which a sentence is indicative for the image of a concept as it is presented in a text. A clause's subject base, b_s, is the inclusiveness of the subject in that clause divided by the out-degree of the subject, i.e., by the number of concepts the concept is linked to. Calculation of the object base, b_o, requires division by the in-degree of the object, i.e., by the number of concepts that refer to the concept. The base indicates how important a particular arrow is, viewed in light of the whole text. Quality denotes in general the strength of a relation.[9] The quality, q, of a link is the weighted mean of the arrow's quality, weighted by the bases of constituent arrows.

Thus far I have described two quantities for describing relations between the concepts in a network:

b is the base ($0 \leq b \leq 1$);
q is the quality ($-1 \leq q \leq 1$).

The link between two concepts consists of all arrows between the concepts. This can be done bottom-up, with the subject-base as a starting point, or top-down, with the object-base as a starting point. In the formulas that follow only the b will be presented, which can be read either as b_s or b_o.

The base of the relation between concepts X and Y, given source s, is

$$B_l \ (s: \ x,y) \ = \ \sum_{i=1}^{n} b_i \ (s: \ x,y).$$

The quality of this connection is

$$Q_l \ (S: \ x,y) \ = \ \frac{\sum_{i=1}^{n} b_i \ (s: \ x,y) \ * \ q_i \ (s: \ x,y)}{B_l \ (s: \ x,y)}.$$

In going from link to chain, direct relationships (links) and indirect relationships are combined into bundles. So, to create bundles, first links have to be 'chained'. Links 'lying' beside each other are combined by multiplication.

The base of a chain is the product of the bases of the links

$$B_j \ (s: \ x,y) \ = \ \prod_{i=1}^{m} B_l \ (s: \ x_{i-1},x_i),$$

with $x_0 = x$ and $x_m = y$. A chain's base can never be larger than the base of its 'weakest' link. The quality of a chain is the product of the qualities of the links:

$$Q_j \ (s: \ x,y) \ = \ \prod_{i=1}^{m} Q_i \ (s: \ x_{i-1},x_i),$$

with $x_0 = x$ and $x_m = y$.

To create bundles, chains are combined in the same way as arrows are combined to make links. The base of the relation of a bundle is the sum of the bases of the relations of enclosed chains:

$$B_t \ (s: \ x,y) \ = \ \sum_{j=1}^{n} B_j \ (s: \ x,y).$$

The quality of the relation of a bundle is the sum of the weighed qualities of the enclosed chains:

$$Q_t \ = \frac{\sum_{j=1}^{n} B_j \ (s: \ x,y) \ * \ Q_j \ (s: \ x,y)}{B_t \ (s: \ x,y)}.$$

Let us refer again to text block 31:

> This boy could not stand that he was losing, so he started playing in a way that is not fair.

The block is coded in three parts. This is shown in Table 6.5. The boy, denoted as the 'Other', can not stand to lose. This means he is far from the ideal situation, which is encoded as a negative evaluation.

Other / could not stand losing (EVA; −1.0) / Ideal.

In Table 6.4 this is indicated by the first relation between Other and Ideal. Reality is that the boy is a loser.

Reality / was losing (EQV; −1.0) / The boy.

This is indicated by the second relation in Table 6.5, the one between Reality and Other. Finally, the boy started playing in an unfair way, again encoded as a negative evaluation.

Other / started playing not fair (EVA; −1.0) / Ideal.

This coding is shown in the third relation in Table 6.4. There are two links, as is shown in Table 6.5. The two relations between Other and Ideal are combined, as both were negative the result remains negative. The bundles that result are shown in Table 6.6. The relations between Other and Ideal and Reality and Other were already known. New is the bundle based on the relations Reality − Other and Other − Ideal. Multiplication leads to a positive relation between Reality and Ideal. These are all measurements within one network. Later in this chapter a larger text block will be analysed.

Comparing networks

Networks might be compared at two levels:

• similarities and differences in concepts;
• similarities and differences in statements (i.e., concept-relation-concept tuples).

With respect to the concepts one can count:

− the number of concepts occurring in at least one of the networks (the union);
− the number of concepts occurring in all networks (the intersection);

− the number of concepts that occur only in at least one within a subset of networks (union minus intersection).

To allow better comparisons these numbers might also be presented as percentage of the total number of concepts. Assuming there can only be one

Table 6.4 *Report nuclear sentences*

SOURCE	SUBJECT	-1————0————+1	OBJECT
φ	Other	*	Ideal
φ	Reality	*	Other
φ	Other	*	Ideal

Table 6.5 *Report links*

SOURCE	SUBJECT	-1————0————+1	OBJECT
φ	Reality	*	Other
φ	Other	*	Ideal

Table 6.6 *Report bundles*

SOURCE	SUBJECT	-1————0————+1	OBJECT
φ	Reality	*	Ideal
φ	Reality	*	Other
φ	Other	*	Ideal

statement between a pair of concepts, one can similarly count statements as a percentage of the maximal possible number of statements. Figure 6.4 pictures two simple networks (X, A) and (Y, B), where X and Y refer to the points and A and B to the lines. To avoid confusion the second point set is denoted by Y, but is identical to X. Let $X_{ij} = 1$ denote that points i and j are incident in the first network, and $X_{ij} = 0$ denote that these points are not incident. For the second network the terms Y_{ij} are used. Given n points, and assuming a point cannot be incident with itself, the number of possible incidence relations in a directed simple network is $n(n-1)$. Take this number as the number of observations, and check whether for each observation there is an incident relation or not. Table 6.7 lists results generated from the networks from Figure 6.4 (where 1 refers to an incidence relation, and 0 to the absence of such a relation).

A comparison of points is not interesting here, because they are identical in both networks. The number of statements is different in both networks. The first one contains 8 statements, the second one shows 10 statements. The number of relations that occur in both networks is 8. The indegree and outdegree (which are equal in this situation) of each of the points shows where the differences are to be found: at points 3 and 5. In the first network they are 2 respectively 1 for concepts C and E, in the second network they are 3 respectively 2 for these concepts.

Comparisons of concepts allows the investigator to contrast results obtained by network analysis with those obtained by a thematic or semantic analysis.

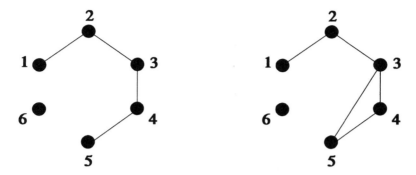

Figure 6.4 *Two networks to be compared*

Table 6.7 *Classification of incidence relations between two networks having the same points*

		Graph (Y, B) 1	Graph (Y, B) 0	
Graph (X, A)	1	8	0	8
	0	2	20	22
		10	20	30

However, frequency of occurrences in the thematic approach is not identical to frequency of occurrence as subject or object in the network approach. Comparisons of statements allow investigators to move beyond an analysis of shared concepts to an analysis of shared meaning. Comparisons of networks enable the analysis of entire constellations of concepts among texts.

Combination of results

It is possible to combine results of network analyses in CETA. An addition operation is performed that is similar to the addition of arrows into links, or chains into bundles. Links or bundles are weighted to their base. The formula below shows how links are combined. The base of a set of combined links is the mean base of the enclosed links:

$$B_{lt} \ (s: \ x,y) \ = \ \frac{1}{n} \ * \ \sum_{i=1}^{n} B_{lt(i)} \ (s: \ x,y).$$

The quality of a set of combined links is the sum of the qualities of the enclosed links; the base is the weighing factor:

$$Q_{lt} \ (s: \ x,y) \ = \ \frac{\displaystyle\sum_{i=1}^{n} B_{lt(i)} \ (s: \ x,y) \ * \ Q_{lt(i)} \ (s: \ x,y)}{\displaystyle\sum_{i=1}^{n} B_{lt(i)} \ (s: \ x,y)}.$$

The next section contains illustrative results, some of which will help clarify the meaning of this type of combination and will become clear.

Analysis

First, an example will be presented here in which a text is coded, after which it can be presented as a network. Next, more general comments will follow.

The example from Chapter 3 with sayings by sportsmen would contain 40 different small networks. As this is not informative a factious text is used referring to a situation in the beginning of the 1980s: Iran under the leadership of Khomeini has sent away the Sjah and is at war with neighbour Iraq (Van Cuilenburg et al., 1988: 88; Van Cuilenburg, 1991: 76–7). The sentences are numbered:

1. The dictatorial power of the Sjah of Iran has been broken by Khomeini.
2. The Iranian terrorist revolution and its leader Khomeini were welcomed by most Arab leaders, except of course, the Iraqi leader Saddam Hussein.
3. There has always been tremendous rivalry between Iraq and Iran.
4. So, the Iraqi position towards revolutionary terrorism in Iran is only based on opportunistic arguments.
5. Only the USA so far has taken a firm position against Khomeini's dangerous religious fanatism.
6. As president Carter has rightly said: 'We don't negotiate with political and religious terrorists.'

In the first sentence of the text two concepts, Khomeini and the Sjah, are evaluated. The Sjah has dictatorial power. This is a common meaning term having a negative evaluation. Therefore the relation has a negative valence. Khomeini is awarded by the author, he is dissociated ('has ... broken') from the Sjah, who was judged negatively by the author. Therefore the relation between

Sjah and Komeini is valenced negative. The sentences are split into 14 nuclear sentences, these are coded as follows:

sentence
nuclear sentence

1	1	Khomeini / has broken dicta-torial power of / the Sjah	(s: Iran /act −1 / Sjah)
1	2	the Sjah / has dictatorial power / the Ideal	(s: Sjah /eva −1 / I)
2	1	Iran / commits terroristic revol-ution / the Ideal	(s: Iran /eva −1 / I)
2	2	Iraq / does not welcome / Iran	(s: Iraq /aff −1 / Iran)
3	1	Iran / is in tremendous rivalry with / Iraq	(s: Iran /aff −1 / Iraq)
3	2	Iraq / is in tremendous rivalry with / Iran	(s: Iraq /aff −1 / Iran)
4	1	Iraq / rejects the revolutionary terrorism in / Iran	(s: Iraq /aff −1 / Iran)
4	2	Iraqs / rejection of the revol-utionary terrorism in Iran is in fact based on opportunism / the Ideal	(s: Iraq /eva −.3 / I)
4	3	Iran / commits revolutionary terrorism / the Ideal	(s: Iran /eva −1 / I)
5	1	USA / has taken firm position against dangerous religious fanatism of / Khomeini	(s: USA /act −1 / Iran)
5	2	Khomeini / distinguished him-self by dangerous religious fanatism / the Ideal	(s: Iran /eva −1 / I)
6	1	Carter / has rightly said / the Ideal	(s: USA /eva +.5 / I)
6	2	Carter: Iran / is political terror-ism / the Ideal	(s: USA: Iran /eva −1 / I)
6	3	Carter: Iran / is religious terror-ism / the Ideal	(s: USA: Iran /eva −1 / I)

Note that Khomeini is coded as Iran, and Carter as USA; now four concepts have been used. The I stands for the Ideal. The result of the coding process can be represented in a network of concepts. First however, the arrows have to be combined into links. There are 11 links. Three times a relation exists between Iran and the Ideal, therefore the three arrows are taken together as one link. In this way nine of the links are explained.[10] One of these relations has a specific source, the USA. Table 6.8 shows the values for base and quality after linking. The most important causal link is the negative valued one (quality −1.00) from the USA to Iran (base 0.50). Looking at the concepts (Reality and Ideal excluded) it turns out that only the bases have changed compared to the network based on all arrows. Figure 6.5 shows how the various concepts are related by the author of the text. The relation with the USA as source is not included, neither are the relations having Reality as subject. The numbers denote the quality, i.e., the valence of the intensity of the relation between the linked concepts. The figure shows that the USA is judged in a positive way by the

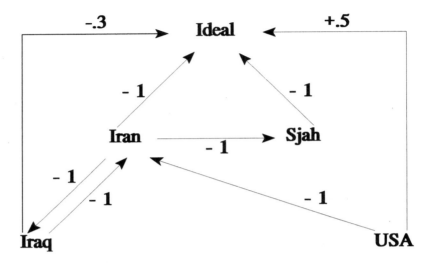

Figure 6.5   *Network based on controversy Iraq – Iran*

author of the text on which the network is based (quality to Ideal is valenced +0.5), while all other concepts received a negative quality. With respect to centrality of the distinct concept it is found that the Ideal has the highest indegree (4), and Iran has the highest outdegree (3), and Ideal also the highest score on the Hoede status index (1.88). In the network the concept Iran has the most central position. The density of the complete network, i.e., the ratio of the actual number of relations to the possible number of relation n (n − 1), where n the number of relations, is 8/20 or 0.4. Hoivik and Gleditsch's (1970) cohesion indices based on the indegree are:

Unipolarity, maximum indegree: 4.00;
Integration, sum of indegrees: 8.00;
Centralization, spread of indegrees[11]: 12.00.

The bundle contains some interesting relations. Positive valenced relations (qualities; see Table 6.9) exist between the USA and both the Sjah and Iraq, and also between Iraq and the Sjah. These qualities are an artifact of the multiplication (the first mentioned one: USA negative about Iran multiplied with Iran negative about the Sjah). You can conclude for yourself whether the author of the text had here also positively valenced qualities in mind. Creating a bundle is in general not problematic when the relations are valenced positive, or in the

Table 6.8 *Links and related indices based on text controversy Iraq – Iran*

source	subject	object	freq	type	base	quality
	Reality	– Iran	1	ass	0.50	-1.00
	Reality	– Sjah	1	ass	0.50	-1.00
	Iran	– Ideal	3	ass	0.60	-1.00
	Iran	– Iraq	1	aff	0.20	-1.00
	Iran	– Sjah	1	cau	0.20	-1.00
	Iraq	– Ideal	1	ass	0.25	-0.25
	Iraq	– Iran	3	aff	0.75	-1.00
	Sjah	– Ideal	1	ass	1.00	-1.00
	USA	– Ideal	1	ass	0.50	0.50
	USA	– Iran	1	cau	0.50	-1.00
USA	Iran	– Ideal	2	ass	1.00	-1.00

Table 6.9 *Bundles and related indices based on text controversy Iraq – Iran*

source	subject	object	freq	type	base	quality
	Reality	– Ideal	1.85	ass	0.93	0.75
	Reality	– Iran	1	ass	0.50	-1.00
	Reality	– Iraq	0.20	ass	0.10	1.00
	Reality	– Sjah	1.20	ass	0.60	-0.67
	Iran	– Ideal	4.25	ass	0.85	-0.45
	Iran	– Iraq	1	aff	0.20	-1.00
	Iran	– Sjah	1	cau	0.20	-1.00
	Iraq	– Ideal	3.40	ass	0.85	0.26
	Iraq	– Iran	3	aff	0.75	-1.00
	Iraq	– Sjah	0.60	ass	0.15	1.00
	Sjah	– Ideal	1	ass	1.00	-1.00
	USA	– Ideal	3.55	ass	0.89	0.47
	USA	– Iran	3	ass	0.75	-1.00
	USA	– Iraq	0.60	ass	0.15	1.00
	USA	– Sjah	0.60	ass	0.15	1.00
USA	Iran	– Ideal	2	ass	1.00	-1.00

situation of two relations, when at least one of the two relations is positive. But in the situation of two negatively valenced relations, the multiplication might give a result that is questionable. In all situations information will get lost.

Table 6.9 shows that most bundles denote an association. The only causal bundle is between Iran and the Sjah, but this relation is in the network not such an important one (base 0.20). More important are the bundles of type association between Iraq and Iran and between USA and Iran, both with base 0.75. Reality and Ideal are not considered here. The results presented here are results found for one network.

Given the quantitative nature of their methodologies, both network evaluation and map analysis require the development of a data matrix in anticipation of statistical analysis. When based on networks, the columns of this data matrix

Table 6.10   *Data matrices created when the network approach is used*

	concept pair 1	concept pair 2	..
network 1			
network 2			
..			

	concept pair
pair 1 network 1	
pair 2 network 1	
..	
network 2	

will typically contain information about where concepts or concept-pairs are located in the networks listed as discrete units of analysis in the matrix's rows. The type of information listed in the cells of this matrix depends on the research question to be answered.

In studying the decision process in selecting a new tutor, Carley first needed to know the social structure among the students who had to elect a new tutor. Next she needed to know the relationship between this structure and the way in which the students formulate what they wanted in a tutor. She applied a method of concept representation, i.e., for representing the way in which an individual thinks about or defines a concept relative to other concepts in his vocabulary (Carley, 1986: 148). She created individual maps (or knowledge bases) and a social knowledge base, the latter of which contains facts shared by a majority of the students in the living group. The knowledge bases correspond to individuals' maps, which can be analysed directly. Individual maps were extended with the aid of SKI. Finally she used an evaluation expert, CODESF, which utilizes social background information to assist in coding and then evaluating specific maps. These specific maps are based on information about how an individual feels about a particular alternative (in Carleys project the tutor candidate). Based on this information a ranking of alternatives can be made, here a preference order of candidate tutors.

Palmquist et al. (1997) report on two investigations. In the first, depictions of robots are explored in 27 works of science fiction. The second one explores the growth of shared knowledge about writing among students in an introductory college composition classroom. The second study includes texts and transcripts, whereas the first one restricts its analyses to text.

The first study is in fact a thematic analysis in which coding according to a tree structure is applied. The relations denote main concepts (groups of characteristics, e.g., the robot does action), and within these concepts specifications follow (e.g., the action is 'fight' or 'hear'). SKI detected many features that were not in the original maps of the robots, therefore using MECA was very useful.[12]

The study about the writing classroom started in the same way. Students were interviewed, and had to submit hand-written journals in which they discuss key concepts in the course. This occurred both at the beginning and at the end of the semester. Frequently occurring words and phrases in these interviews were added to the concept list as well as words and phrases that were used in at least three classroom sessions and key words and phrases used in textbooks. Students' maps were constructed based on transcripts of the interviews and on the journals. A cognitive mental map was also constructed for the instructor based on interviews, the textbooks used, and notes from classroom observation. The analysis compares the intersection between the student mental maps and the instructor mental map at the beginning and the end of the semester on the level of the concepts and on the level of the statements. A similar comparison was made for the intersections of the student mental map and the classmates' mental maps. Comparisons are of pairs of concepts that are related (although, unfortunately, not in any specified way). The difference in frequency of intersecting concept pairs between the beginning and end of the semester is tested using t-tests. Concept pairs that received much more attention at the end of the semester are, among others, 'analysis – summary', 'author – paper', and 'problem – writing'. Less attention received: 'notes – research', 'paper – topic', 'paper – research'.[13]

In all of these studies, individuals' cognitive maps are constructed. These maps are compared to each other or to some standard map, depending on the study's design. The individual is the sampling unit as well as the unit of analysis in each case.

The NET approach has been used to tackle quite different problems. Most notably, the approach has been used to investigate how political topics and parties are presented in the media. The earliest applications of the method examined the way in which the government was evaluated in the national media. Subsequent research compared the election campaigns of the various Dutch political parties.

Kleinnijenhuis et al.'s (1995) analysis of the campaign preceding the Dutch parliamentary election in 1994 is a case in point. The central research question was: 'Which political party with what kind of electoral program received what kind of news coverage via which medium and reached which voter to what effect?' (1994: 187). The sample consisted of pre-election articles from the first section of the five largest Dutch newspapers, and of transcribed prime time news broadcasts from both public and commercial TV stations regarding local affairs and macro economic developments. The texts of these articles were analysed with respect to several topics:

• *Support and criticism.* Here they investigated which parties, politicians (of own or other party), media, or social groups supported or criticised which politicians or parties;
• *Issues.* The positions taken by parties or politicians with respect to several issues according to the newspapers or broadcasting companies;

- *Success and failure*. The parties and politicians that are doing well compared to the ones that appear to be losing.

Links, chains, and bundles were created to reduce the huge amount of relations between pairs of concepts. In these analyses an important question was whether 'transparency axioms' already have to be incorporated in the links or not. Within a (primary) network there might be other (secondary) networks (e.g., networks of quoted or paraphrased actors). Transparency might consist between the secondary and the primary network. It is also possible that information from the secondary network provides information about the secondary network. In reverse relations from the primary network it might be necessary to interpret the secondary network. (Here is some relation with SKI as used by Carley.) Another decision to be taken was whether the transitivity rules were allowed. Problems connected to using such rules were discussed before. As far as the substance of the project is concerned, the authors claim that they were able to determine how Dutch voters respond to developments in the news during an election campaign. They found that the increasing effect of the news-coverage on voters and their voting behaviour is accounted for by the decreasing importance of structural factors.

Kleinnijenhuis and De Ridder (1998) even have extended the above analysis to a comparison of the media effects in the Netherlands with the effects of the election campaign in Germany where people also could vote in 1994. These are two rather similar countries, in both countries the Christian Democrats were the main party in the government coalition. In Germany the coalition led by Chancellor Kohl could continue, in the Netherlands the strongest political landslide ever took place. These different results could be explained by applying theories of issue voting to the media coverage of issues. The issue ownership theory predicts that a party will win at elections whenever the issues it owns dominate the news. This occurred with respect to the CDU/CSU in Germany, and not with respect to the CDA in the Netherlands. Proximity and directional theory take into account the issue positions attributed to parties in the news. Issues in the Dutch news were owned by or covered by the Social Democrats and the Liberals, and not by the CDA. In Germany this was the reverse.

Conclusion

In the semantic approach, concepts and the relations between them are investigated. One might say dyads are analysed. In the network approach not only dyads, but complete networks are examined. When dyads are analysed, information contained in each of the statements can be examined. That is, statements' information is investigated separately. Network text analyses enable such information to be merged across statements, with the development of indices for links, chains and bundles. A link that consists of several arrows taken together condenses the information in each of the original arrows (and thus the corresponding clauses in one's texts). It is fair to ask what information may be lost with such aggregation.

When coding texts, researchers need to have the ability to stay close to the text and to go back and forth between original and coded material; to handle large quantities of data, not only many texts, but long texts, and texts from many sources; to combine or contrast data drawn from various sources; to tailor analyses to research questions; to retain records sufficient for other researchers to replicate analyses; and to aggregate and disaggregate textual data. This suggests the need for flexible analysis routines that can be adapted by the researcher to the current project and so promote research-oriented analysis, tools that generate or force the researcher to generate records of behaviour and coding choices and so promote self-documenting research, and tools that facilitate text modification, reduction, and display. Computer-assisted tools can be designed so as to meet these needs. The MECA package is a step in this direction.

In the networks new relations are added by using SKI, other relations are transformed by creating links and bundles. Little is known about the consequences of these operations. More research is needed to find out whether other results will be found, and whether these are correct representations of the population that is investigated.

Statistics for analysing the various networks, that are the units of analysis, are hardly available.

The network approach also must be considered from the perspective of Janowitz (1969). The issues mentioned with respect to the semantic approach also hold when the network approach is applied. One main difference in organizational and administrative aspects of the analysis in the network compared to the thematic and semantic text analysis is that the texts to be coded do not have to be available in files on a computer system. As in the semantic analysis the coder has to make more decisions than if coding would have been according to the thematic approach. Therefore explication of the coding rules, and the training of the coders will be more intensive.

Janowitz's second point concerned the substance, and the third point was the gap between 'theory' and 'empirical data'. In the network approach relations between concepts are made explicit, just as in the semantic approach. The relation types are specified in different ways by the investigators. These specific relations can be related to theoretical notions. Besides the network is a representation of the whole text block, not of clauses within the text block.

Notes

1. In conventional network theory, concepts are referred to as points or nodes, and relations as lines, arcs or vertices. I do not use this terminology here, but follow the terminology used in the main texts on network text analysis.
2. Danowski (1993) has argued that his program, Wordlink, uses networks. In fact it is a program for instrumental thematic analysis that contains a network-like facility.

Wordlink generates a co-occurrence matrix (or network, using Danowski's terminology) based on words appearing within a certain 'distance', i.e., a certain number of words apart. Pairs of words are assigned directionality based on word-order. A so-called travelling salesman algorithm is then applied to the matrix, such that a sequence of words is found by most efficiently 'travelling' among the matrix's cells. Danowski claims that this word sequence has theoretical appeal for the model of communication vehicles and optimal message creation (1993: 212).

3. Maps can be contrasted with frames. A frame is a representation of a focused network of concepts, where the focus is the concept of interest for the individual under investigation. The frame contains everything known about this focus. A map is a similar, albeit simpler representation, it contains only part of what is known about the focus.

4. Rahmstorf (1983) provides an extended overview of meaning expressions for relations derived from a linguistic point of view. He names some relations differently, extends others, and adds a few that are not listed by Popping and Roberts (1997). For example, in addition to PAR (is part of) Rahmstorf also lists inclusion (INC) and element (ELM) relations. These relations are close to but slightly different from the 'part of' relation. Additional relations, for example refer to time (TEMporal; X takes place at time Y) and to place (LOCation; A is located in B).

5. Within a generic semantic text analysis (e.g., in which PLCA is used) such conditional relations among clauses can be encoded using the modal auxiliary verbs, 'should', 'would', 'could', or 'might.'

6. In the situation of a directed network one has to distinguish between the indegree and outdegree of the concept, i.e., the number of concepts toward versus leaving the concept. Parallels might be drawn here to Carley's (1997: 85) local evokability and local imageability, which together constitute a network's local density.

7. If one finds in the adjacency matrix a relation from concept a to concept b, and one from concept b to concept a, the relation is bi-directional. If there is only a relation from concept a to concept b, the relation is one-directional.

8. Some variance measures with dubious statistical foundation have been developed, these are based on divergence and ambivalence. The width of the interval of the arrow's qualities is denoted as the divergence, d, which is the 'variance' among the qualities of arrows. Divergence can only be established by combining arrows. The divergence of one arrow is 0 by definition. The ambivalence of a link is the weighted combination of these variances (within). These variances (divergence and ambivalence) as used in CETA are based on *ad hoc* definitions. They need to be replaced by better ones. I will not discuss them.

In general, little is known about variances in networks based on text analysis. Some first investigations have appeared however. The issue will be discussed at the end of Chapter 7.

9. Quality must not be confused with covering. Assume the sentence: 'Ann sometimes agrees with Jane.' The sentence is completely covered: all issues are possible, no one is excluded. The quality on the other hand is less than 1, for they *sometimes* agree. The quality of the sentence 'Ann perfectly agrees with Jane on parts of the project,' is 1: they *perfectly* agree. The degree of covering however, is less than 1, for they do not agree on *all* parts of the plan.

10. When linking CETA transforms the meaning type action into two meaning types: causality and association (see also Table 6.1). I will not use this second transform-

ation in the representation of the network, but in fact there are two new links: Reality related to Iran, and Reality related to the Sjah. Both relations are valenced −1.

11. This spread is defined here as the sum of differences between the indegree of a concept and the maximum observed indegree. All these indices might also have been based on the outdegree.

12. In this study on robots the data were first grouped in order to be able to investigate whether attitudes towards the robots changed over time. Next a concept list and relation types were defined. Having these, maps could be created for the robots, the maps were adapted by using SKI. Features (concepts) of robots by period are presented. It turned out that in time more features are entered and that SKI-modified maps contain more features than unmodified maps. The relations denote groups of characteristics: 'does action', 'has emotion', 'has feature', 'is of type'. Some of the possible actions are: 'hear', 'reason', 'talk', 'think', 'walk'. Based on frequency of occurrence of concepts trends are distinguished. The trends are mirrored by statistical analyses (here analysis of variance).

13. By only coding that there is 'some' relation between pairs of concepts, precious little is gained beyond an awareness of concepts' co-occurrence, leaving one information limited to what might be gained using the thematic approach.

7

Sampling, reliability and validity

This chapter contains issues on sampling, reliability, and validity. These issues are presented just here because they are related to the above distinction in thematic, semantic and network analysis. The reader is now familiar with these types of analysis. Several of these issues have not been solved yet, nevertheless they should be mentioned. This holds especially for data obtained by using the network approach. At the end of the chapter follow some remarks on sampling characteristics. Earlier in the text it was indicated that at several places no such characteristics are available, especially with respect to the network approach. In this chapter this lack is considered in the context of validity. Some impulses for solutions have been given, these will be treated.

Sampling and units of analysis

The first methodological consideration in a well-defined research project, where hypotheses and objectives have been formulated, concerns the text material to be analysed. This material is collected in the sampling phase of the investigation. There are two main questions involved in this first phase in the investigation. The questions concern: 'What to sample,' and 'How to sample.' At times these questions are hard to separate. I assume that availability of texts is no problem. First the investigator needs to decide what kind of data should be taken into account given the research purpose. He has to ask about the kind of texts to be collected, the relevant issues, whether specific senders or receivers of messages must be incorporated. Also a time period might be of interest. These conclusions are dependent on the research question. They determine the kind of answers that can be found later in the analysis phase of the study. Next decisions have to be made on how to sample. This is complicated because researchers aim at inferences, depictions or conclusions that are explicitly or implicitly relevant to a larger communication body or textual basis than the sample that has been analysed. The investigator has to realize that the sample is representative for the population under study, but he also has to take care of an adequate covering of all what is to be sampled.

In most investigations the researcher should not apply random sampling. It would imply that there is a population of sampling units (text blocks), any unit can be selected and the selected unit is judged. By simply looking at a newspaper it becomes apparent that this way of working is not realistic. Say the population consists of a volume of a newspaper. A text block can be selected at random. This text block can be an article or an advertisement that does not have to be of interest to the investigator, because it does not fulfil some criteria. Investigators are usually interested in specific articles depending on the goal of the investigation, e.g., on foreign news, home news, sports, economics, editorials, letters to the editor, etc.

Therefore one will use a stratified sample: first the issue is selected, next the text block in the issue. Restrictions will be posed on this text block, it must be related to the topic of the investigation for which the text blocks are sampled. In case a medium is to be followed over time the investigator will use time intervals. Within fixed intervals one or more issues of the newspaper will be selected at random. Multistage sampling indicates that several samples are drawn sequentially. Continuing with the previous example, an issue of the newspaper is selected in the interval, in that issue a page, and on that page a text block. More details on sampling for text analysis studies are among others found in Krippendorff (1980: 65ff).

Every investigator has to consider the following points at the moment decisions have to be made about the sampling design. Multistage sampling, or more generally a complex sampling design, can dampen the power of the statistical inferences. This should not be underestimated. The other point is that in the analysis phase of an investigation often the unit of analysis used does not coincide with the sampling unit. These two units should not be confused. More specific problems to be solved follow below.

Problems during sampling

In the 'how to sample' process the investigator runs into several problems. The most relevant ones follow.

Selection of the units. Which newspaper or which broadcasting company is to be selected? Papers differ in: morning or evening paper, national or local orientation, political preference, tabloid or serious, and so on. For broadcasting companies also such a list can be made. In all situations the investigator has to make a decision depending on the objective of the investigation. An additional problem is mentioned by Kaufman et al. (1993), who show that one must be careful in using results of on-line searches of newspapers, as all data bases do not provide the same access to information.

Next, it is possible that in a random sample not all characteristics necessary for the investigation are represented in a correct way. Especially when developments over time have to be investigated, all time-periods must be represented in the sample. In such situations a stratified sample is used. First the universe is determined from which it is to be sampled. Next the time periods are selected, and in each period a random sample is drawn. This way of sampling can also be applied to assure that for example all groups that are investigated are represented in a sample.

Several studies have been performed by a group of investigators dealing with best sampling strategies when broadcast news, daily or weekly newspapers are to be sampled either simple or stratified (Lacy et al., 1995; Riffe et al., 1996a; Riffe et al., 1996b). Given that specific topics (stories, photographs) must be included, the authors do some recommendations for how to sample to get representative data. These recommendations are based on normal curve, critical values and standard errors. The important issue is that investigators who have to start sampling take this variability into account.

Selection of the issues. Papers and broadcastings may contain regularities that are repeated. For example newspapers on Monday contain in most countries a lot of information about sports, those of Saturday contain opinion articles. There might be fixed days on which issues related to art, health or economics get attention. A systematic sample, e.g., only Monday issues, might cause some bias.

Selection of parts of the content. The parts to be selected depend on the research question. In case the content of advertisements is investigated, one will not consider the editorials. Popping and Roberts (1998) analyse editorials. The selection of issues is based on a stratified sample. With respect to the issue itself they first determined which part constitutes the basic paper. This basic paper excludes any extra pages dedicated to a particular topic. The remaining pages are the ones that contain editorials that are suited for their purposes. One of these pages is selected at random. Within the page an editorial is selected according to some strict rules. If this editorial fulfils the criteria of an appropriate editorial for the study it is selected, otherwise the procedure is repeated for that issue of the newspaper.

Sometimes only parts of text blocks are analysed. This is when blocks are too long (especially when human coding is applied), or some parts do not contain relevant information. In editorials, for example, the point the author wants to make is generally mentioned at the beginning or at the end. Explicit rules are necessary for deciding which parts are analysed and which parts are not. An alternative way was followed by Udo (1998) in her study on agenda setting in the field of dealing with refugees, she used summaries of the text blocks to overcome the problem of length. Another choice might be to use only a specific paragraph or sentence. In the situation of transcriptions of speech, one usually uses the speech uttered in a specific time interval. Remember Gottschalk and colleagues who ask a person to speak for five minutes.[1] With respect to newspapers the 'basic space unit' (BSU) is often used. This is a standardized text segment. The width of the text to be analysed is one column, and the length

0.05 column. For more details about these sampling problems, see Budd, Thorp and Donohew (1967: 23ff).

It is not possible to solve these problems here, they are different for each project in which text analysis is used. The investigator however has to be aware of the problem and has to come up with solutions.

Reliability

The term 'reliability' as used with respect to coding in text analysis refers most to coder consistency and not, as commonly, to data consistency. According to Holsti (1969: 135): 'Reliability is a function of coders' skill, insight, and experience, clarity of categories and coding rules which guide their use, and the degree of ambiguity in the data'. The term reliability points to three different issues: stability, agreement, and accuracy.

When an instrumental text analysis is performed by using some computer program, and the dictionaries, the trivial-words-list and the lists of negative words are not changed, the second analysis will come up with the same results as the first one.[2] This refers to stability, in a next analysis the same results are found. In the situation where the coding is performed by some human coder following the representational view, one also hopes to find no real differences between the first and the second coding. Differences that might be found should only be due to random errors. When the amount of differences is significant, there is some problem. One cannot assume these differences to be due to randomness. The investigator has to find out why the coder is not performing in a stable way.

When coding is performed by humans there are usually several coders. It should not matter now which coder does which coding, all coders come up with the same results. This holds under the conditions that the categories and the coding instructions are clear, and that the coders have been trained. In case small differences are found these are based on chance. Indices are available to test whether there are really differences between coders, or whether categories are hard to distinguish. In case there are really differences, this is often due to ambiguous or inconsistent coding rules, or to cognitive factors like abstraction mismatches. In case specific categories are often exchanged, it might be that these categories are hard to distinguish, or not exclusive. The reliability that is considered here is sometimes denoted as reproducibility and often as agreement.

Agreement is very often considered as a special kind of association. There are differences however. It is important to determine the similarity of the content of behaviour (in a broad sense) between coders in general with the degree of identity of this behaviour. The behaviour of one coder does not have to be predicted from that of the other. In the case of association one investigates the strength of the linear relationship between variables. Here the goal is to predict the values of one variable from those of the other. With regard to agreement, most important is the similarity of the content of behaviour between coders, with the goal of determining the degree of identity of this behaviour (see Popping [1985], about the same reasoning is followed by Krippendorff [1987]). The basic idea of an agreement index is looking at the fraction of units on which coders agree in assigning to a category.

Accuracy is investigated when a coder is compared to a standard that has been established in some way. This often occurred previously or was done by an expert. In the situation of agreement it is allowed that coders agree on an assignment, nevertheless the assignment is not correct. In the situation of accuracy it is known how the assignment should be. Now deviation from a norm can be investigated. Sometimes a slightly different definition of accuracy is used. In this situation it is meant that the coder codes as if s/he were an expert (Krippendorff, 1980: 131). To give an example: someone very familiar with a specific field will be more accurate in encoding utterances from that field than a novice coder with less expertise.[3]

Consensus is growing among investigators who use indices for reliability in their research that the preferred index should be of the type,

$$I = \frac{O - E}{M - E},$$

where O stands for observed, E for expected of chance, and M for maximum agreement (Galtung, 1979). The index computes the proportion of agreement after chance agreement is removed from consideration. The index has to suffice several quality criteria (Popping, 1985, 1992b). Two very important ones are that the maximum value of the index should be 1, no matter the number of coders, units (that what is judged) or categories, and that in the case of statistical independence between the assignments by the coders the index has to take the value 0. Even in this extreme situation of independence the coders will agree on the classification of some units, purely by chance. The correction for such chance agreement has played an important role in the literature.

Different views

Several agreement indices of the above type are known. They differ in their definition of chance agreement. Scott (1955) has proposed an index for comparing the assignments by two coders based on the idea that an equality relation exists between these coders, they are drawn from one universe. Therefore the computation of the expected agreement should be based on one stochastic variable, referring to the mean distribution over the categories across all coders.[4] He proposed an index, called pi, π. This view is criticized by Cohen, 'one source of disagreement between a pair of judges is precisely their proclivity to distribute their judgments different over the categories' (Cohen, 1960: 41). Therefore for each coder a stochastic variable exists, containing the distribution over the categories according to that coder. Cohen proposed a slightly different index, called kappa, κ. Confusion increased when Fleiss (1971) proposed an extension to the situation where assignments by more than two coders were pairwise compared. He based himself on Cohen, denoted the index also as kappa, but followed Scott in the computation of chance expected agreement.

The different starting positions between these two authors can easily be understood from their field of application. Scott, doing text analysis, needed many coders to analyse the answers on open-ended questions used in survey research. He was just interested in 'check-coding': if one part of the data was judged by one coder, and another part by another coder, would that make a difference? Cohen, in the field of clinical psychology, had all units classified by all coders, these coders had their qualifications that should be taken into account. In case text analysis is applied the view as initially expressed by Scott is the one generally to be preferred. This view is followed below in Table 7.1 and in the extensions. In the training-phase, however, especially when coders are compared to a standard, I would use the index according to Cohen.

Basics

The basic idea of agreement is explained by using a 2*2 table, containing proportions of occurrences.

Table 7.1   *Example of 2 * 2 table*

```
                      rater 2

        rater 1 ┌─────────────┐
                │ a       b   │  p₁
                │ c       d   │  1-p₁
                └─────────────┘

                  p₂    1-p₂
```

In the situation of perfect agreement all units would fall on the diagonal. This makes the M-part in the formula equal by definition 1.[5] The observed agreement is the proportion $O = a + d$. The investigator's theoretical position is that the mean distribution over the categories across all coders is identical, one expects here that $p_1 = p_2$. This does not always occur, a good estimator is

$$p = (p_1 + p_2) / 2.$$

Now the E-part in the formula, referring to the proportion of agreement expected under the conditions of chance, i.e., coders do not even look at the units they are categorizing, is $E = p^2 + (1 - p^2)$. This is the view first proposed by Scott.

Extensions

The index is extended into several directions, taking into account more than two categories, more than two coders, seriousness of disagreement. In the situation of more than two coders three views on agreement are allowed. One might consider the mean agreement between all pairs of coders (pairwise agreement), but it is also possible to take the position that agreement exists only in case all coders agree in assigning a unit to the same category (simultaneous agreement). In the third view at least h out of m judgements per unit should be in the same category (majority agreement). The first view is used most. A general formula for this situation, even allowing that units are coded different numbers of times, is presented by Schouten (1986).[6]

Say the number of units is N, each unit is coded at most m times. The number of times unit s is assigned to category i is denoted by n_{si}; and the frequency with which that category is used by the coders is n_i, the sum over s of all n_{si}. There are c categories. The seriousness of disagreement between categories i and j is denoted by w_{ij} ($0 \leq w_{ij} \leq 1$). Usually the extremes are used, 1 indicates agreement, and 0 indicates disagreement. Define for the situation where not all units are coded the same number of times:

$$n_{s.} = \sum_{i=1}^{c} n_{si};$$

otherwise:

$$n_{s.} = m.$$

$$p_{ii} = \sum_{s=1}^{N} n_{si} (n_{si} - 1) / [N \, n_{s.} (n_{s.} - 1)];$$

for all $i \neq j$

$$p_{ij} = \sum_{s=1}^{N} n_{si} \, n_{sj} / [N \, n_{s.} (n_{s.} - 1)],$$

$$p_{i} = \sum_{s=1}^{N} n_{si} / N \, n_{s.}.$$

Now observed and expected agreement can be computed:[7]

$$O = \sum_{i=1}^{c} \sum_{j=1}^{c} w_{ij} \, p_{ij};$$

$$E = \sum_{i=1}^{c} \sum_{j=1}^{c} w_{ij} \, p_i \, p_j.$$

It is also possible to investigate the amount of agreement per category. This is not discussed here. The same holds for the situation where the number of text units that are analysed is very small.

Two specific views on seriousness of disagreements exist. Cicchetti (1972) proposed to use in the situation of data at an ordinal level of measurement the weight

$$w_{ij} = 1 - |i - j| \, / \, (c - 1),$$

and in case of an interval level of measurement the weight

$$w_{ij} = 1 - (i - j)^2 \, / \, (c - 1)^2.$$

The level of agreement that is suitable in a text analysis study depends on how important the data need to be with respect to (policy) implications based on results found in the study. For simplicity assume that only the O-part (the proportion of observed agreement) constitutes the index. The value 0.7 now means that on 70% of the units the coders agree in assigning to the same category, while this is *not* true for 30% of the units. It means that 30% of the units is for whatever reason not classified by the coders in an identical way. Note, there is normally no standard telling what is the correct way of coding, the exception being the situation where accuracy is investigated. In the actual research situation it is to the investigator to decide which value of the agreement index is acceptable. When the correction for chance is made the index indicates the agreement above what chance would yield. Ordinarily the value that is found now is less than the proportion of observed agreement, actually this proportion is biased upwards. The chance corrected index is more severe. Again it is to the investigator to decide which level of agreement is still acceptable. Rules of thumb are mentioned at some places (e.g., Landis and Koch, 1977: 165). These rules should not be followed strictly, the acceptable level of agreement depends on the actual research situation.

The group of investigators active with respect to sampling procedures has also considered the reliability issue. Lacy and Riffe (1996) report that in many text analyses, only an arbitrary sample of all coded units is judged by multiple coders. This sub-sample can be considered as drawn from a population of units, which is actually the original sample. Lacy and Riffe are referring here to the sampling units, but a sample of recording units is also possible. This sample needs to have reliability estimates representing the real population. Therefore the size of the sub-sample has to permit a known degree of confidence that the agreement in this sub-sample is representative of the pattern that would occur if all units are coded by all coders. Therefore investigators need to estimate the size for the sub-sample required for valid reliability assessments. The authors provide a formula for this goal. Similar formulas for more extended research situations have been proposed by Flack et al. (1988).[8]

Elaboration

In the situation where the computer-assisted text analysis is applied according to the instrumental view, computing reliability is not necessary because all the rules are dictated by the dictionary, the trivial- and the negative-words lists. In the situation of the representational view (and hand-coding) the situation is different.

The following is stated in terms of the thematic approach, but for a considerable part it also holds for the other approaches. Reliability is computed on the level of the unit of analysis. In case the investigator looks at occurrence or non-occurrence of the concept in each text unit two categories are used. When the frequency of occurrence is investigated the data are on an interval scale. Agreement can be computed on the level of the category, now the occurrence or non-occurrence is in fact investigated.

In the representational coding process the coder uses 'Verstehen' to encode the texts according to the meanings their sources intended. The issue is not 'how' to encode text (instrumental approach), but 'whether' one chooses to apply one's own theory or one's sources' theories to the texts under analysis. Moreover the coder might want to code implicit concepts (Carley, 1994: 726), i.e., words or phrases that occur in the text only by implication. At issue then, is what level of implication is allowed. Explicit concept analysis locates which words or phrases are explicitly in the text, this type of analysis is easy to automate. Implicit concept analysis requires the investigator to develop some defensible procedure for appending one's manifest content by inserting latent content that is contextually implied in some way. As has been shown, such procedures are available in several text analysis software packages.

To illustrate the distinction between manifest versus inferred propositions, consider the following two statements that Bill Clinton made during his 1992 presidential campaign: 'George Bush has increased unemployment in this country.... Our current high level of unemployment is not only unwanted, but unnecessary.' The propositions 'Bush caused unemployment' and 'Unemployment is bad' are manifest in Clinton's speech. Yet taken together one can infer from them that 'Bush caused something bad.' Moreover, such inferred propositions comprise data of legitimacy no different from that of the manifest propositions upon which they are based.

In the situation where the dictionary was developed during the coding process, the coders might end with different categories. For this situation also reliability indices are available (Popping, 1983, 1992b). In these indices the amounts of observed and expected agreement are not the basis for the analysis, but the observed, expected and maximum amount of assignments of pairs of units to identical or different categories as utilized by each of the coders. As the coders ended up with different sets of categories, it is the task of the investigator to decrease these to only one set of categories. Popping (1992a) has proposed an algorithm to realize this, this algorithm is based on a discussion between the coders, and eventually the investigator.

Once the categories are (in principle) definite, low agreement between the coders is still possible. Such low agreement is a consequence of the coders being not well enough trained and the categories being not sufficiently distinctionable. If this omission turns out in the pilot phase of the investigation, adaptions are still possible.

The new approaches to text analysis, the semantic and the network approach, demand in part other types of reliability indices. In the semantic approach the clause is the basic unit for coding. Let us assume that the coders all distinguished and analysed the same clauses.[9] In this clause several characteristics are distinguished. As an example, look at all the attributes that are judged when PLCA is used. Eltinge and Roberts (1993: 73-4) compute kappa for each of these attributes. They might have taken into account that a dependence relation exists between some of the attributes, for example the way valence is coded depends on the clause type. Here, computing a conditional agreement is preferred: given the clause type selected, a specific valence type is coded. This conditional agreement is addressed by Krippendorff (1980: 151 ff).

Another problem, for which no solution is known, deals with the fact that different coders might have selected different numbers of clauses. This becomes especially apparent when complex sentences have to be coded. An example is my sentence 31 about the boy who could not stand losing, which was coded in four clauses when the semantic approach was followed, and in three clauses when the network approach was applied. This problem is only solved by providing clear coding instructions. Experience and training are also relevant. The number of clauses that is finally used might also be related to possibilities a program offers.

To investigate the correspondence between the structure of networks one can build on methods for comparing graphs (Katz and Powell, 1953; Wasserman, 1987; Frank, 1991). See also Figure 6.3 and Table 6.8 in the previous chapter. In the most simple situation, when the networks have identical concepts and only the fact whether there is a relation between pairs of points is counted (as in the table) it is even possible to compute the kappa as mentioned before.

Measurement error denotes the discrepancy between the 'true' score of a category and the score assigned to that category. Such errors might have substantial implications on the results of an investigation. The more complex the coding procedures are, the more likely these errors occur. It is to the investigator to be well aware of this detail.

In his description of reliability Holsti (1969: 135) had mentioned three aspects:

- Coders' skill, insight, and experience;
- Clarity of categories and coding rules which guide their use;
- The degree of ambiguity in the data.

The first point refers to errors made by the coders. Such errors are reduced by better training or by using a computer-aided coding. Especially when the instrumental view is followed the computer-aided coding is very reliable. In training programs attention should be given to the following:

- Coders should be aware of the goal of the investigation;
- Coders should exactly know the meaning of the categories used (also part of the second point);
- Coders should be trained in identifying the target behaviour. In case they have to code different categories at once, they should be trained in which category to look first at;
- In case there are reasons to assign different categories to a text unit, they should know which category is to be preferred in which situation, and why.

Furthermore, coders should be trained in being clear about their assignments. If coding is performed by using a computer program, this program will only allow the coders to indicate whether a specific category applies or not. In paper and pencil coding they can colour a square grey, to indicate that they have to reconsider the assignment. When a computer program is used, it should be allowed to reconsider an assignment, the coder must have made notes about questionable assignments.

In the semantic and network approach issues on the relation between concepts are to be added. Therefore, the coder must be able to identify the clause itself, and must be familiar with the grammar used. So, if PLCA is used, the coder has to be familiar with the four functional forms as distinguished by Roberts, or, if CETA is used, with the relational meaning types as used in CETA.

If categories or coding-rules are not clear one might be confronted with procedure-errors. It implies that it must be clear to the coder which words or phrases refer to which specific category. The decision rules in complex situations must also be clear. In the pilot phase of a study, the researcher might investigate the frequency with which different categories used for assigning specific units, i.e., he looks at the non-diagonal cells of the agreement table. A high frequency in such a cell might indicate that the disagreement perhaps is not due to the coders, but to indistinctness of the categories. One way to solve such a problem is adapting or merging the categories.

The coding process can be structured for human coders with the aid of computer programs that guides their correct application of coding rules. Now reliability will increase as words or phrases will only be coded in existing categories. In the situation where statements are coded, this also holds for the relations.

It was stressed that ambiguity of language is at present at many places. Investigators have to be aware of it, computer-aided methods can assist in finding the ambiguity, especially when the representational view is followed. There are no tools (yet), like expert systems, to validly explicate linguistic relations in texts.

Validity

Validity deals with the question whether the findings in the investigation represent real events. The investigator is especially confronted with the issue when the categories and search entries are developed and applied. In the development phase the main issue is first of all whether the categories that are defined are the relevant ones for this research question. Next comes the question whether the correct method of text analysis is applied. In case the thematic approach will be followed, the investigator has to wonder whether the correct search entries are used.

The questions about the categories and the search entries can also be posed in the coding phase, especially when the representational view is followed. To be added is the question whether the search entries are used in a correct way.

Three different interpretations exist of the requirement that the results of a measurement should be about 'what it is intended to measure'. These are based on different meanings of 'realism' (Andrén, 1981: 51):

1. The realism of a certain set of data consists of its *correspondence* to some facts, i.e., its truth.
2. The realism of a certain set of data consists of its *connection* with some significant problem or with the purpose of the study, i.e., its relevancy.
3. The realism of a certain set of data consists of its *correspondence* with precisely those facts that are *connected* with some real problem or the purpose of the study, i.e., truth and relevancy.

The meaning of the term 'validity' often oscillates between the choices (2) and (3). The first choice refers to reliability, in particular, to the view of accuracy.

Face validity or content validity is a means that is generally used first, but often this is not sufficient. It refers to the way things are considered at first glance. It is estimated by judging how well the instrument represents a whole class of situations, knowledge domains or skills about which conclusions are drawn. In the development phase of the instrumental investigation one constantly has to wonder: 'are these the relevant categories and search entries?', in the coding phase the question is: 'are these the correct search entries and are they used in a correct way?' Face validity gives an impression, but just that.

The computer program PLCA reconstructs a clause by 'translating' it according to both the meaning categories into which its words fall, and its words' intended interrelations (Roberts, 1989). For example,

> The LITERATURE will be OBLIGATED to DESCRIBE [how it is that NATIONAL SOCIALISM's ACTING is socially appropriate].

is the program's translation of the following sentence from the 1927 preface to the Nazi party platform:

> These pamphlets should give a uniform and complete picture of how National Socialism relates to the various tasks of our public life.

Such translations allow the coder to evaluate the face validity of the encoding. In this case, note how the main clause in the sentence describes the future process of as-yet-unwritten pamphlets' description of how (in the subordinate clause) National Socialist actions are to be judged positively.

Validity is often split in internal and external validity. Internal validity then is equal to reliability. It investigates whether research findings have anything to do with the data at hand. One must be careful however, a high reliability does not mean there is validity. Campbell and Fiske (1959: 83) note that 'Reliability is the agreement between two efforts to measure the same trait through maximally similar methods. Validity is represented in the agreement between two attempts to measure the same trait through maximally different methods.'

Before going into external validity, it must be emphasized that in many researches the investigator wants to generalize the results that were found. In that case the validity is to be claimed for a larger class of characteristics than just the coders. Cone (1977: 414 ff) depicted the characteristics in which an investigator performing an observational study is most interested. Rephrased for a text analysis study, these characteristics are:

1. The *coder*, it should not matter who performed the coding, see before;
2. The *variable*, does the variable measure what it is supposed to measure (this can be investigated by considering the internal consistency or by correlating the variable to another variable measuring the same characteristic although measured in another way);
3. The *time*, this has to do with the extent to which data based on text dating from one point of time are representative of data from texts written at other points of time;

4. The *setting*, here the question is whether data collected in one setting are representative for those obtainable in another setting;
5. The *method*, here this would mean whether data collected in a text analysis are comparable to data collected in another way; and
6. The *medium*, this concerns the comparability of data based on two or more different media. This refers especially to speech versus text. I would also consider text versus text, for texts from different media might vary in length and level of complexity.

These aspects come back in at least one type of external validity that follows.

The external validity measures the correspondence between variations inside the process of analysis and variation outside that process. Moreover, it indicates whether findings represent the real phenomena in the context of the data as claimed. This includes many aspects. Krippendorff (1980: 158) distinguishes three aspects for which validity is to be considered. The first aspect is related to the data: semantic validity and sampling validity; the second is related to pragmatics: correlational validity and predictive validity; and the third one is process oriented: construct validity.

Semantic validity. A meaning category is said to have semantic validity if there is consensus among persons familiar with the language and texts under study that the words or phrases judged into this category do reflect the category's meaning (Krippendorff, 1980: 159–62). Assurance of semantic validity requires more than a face validity check for similarities among words' meanings when taken out of context. It is for semantic validity that coders use KWIC software to verify that words are used in ways that are appropriate to their respective meaning categories.[10] Overcoming the types of ambiguity that have been distinguished so far, idiomatic, illocutionary, and relevance ambiguity, falls under the semantic validity. This type of validity is necessary to secure that results of studies are realistic in the second sense as indicated by Andrén. The aspects mentioned by Cone that get most attention concern the coder and the variable.

Sampling validity. Assesses the degree to which available data are either an unbiased sample for a universe of interest or sufficiently similar to another sample from the same sample so that the data can be taken as statistically representative of that universe. This also fits in the second sense as indicated by Andrén. Remarks on sampling earlier in this chapter are connected to this type of validity. This type of validity precedes for the greater part the aspects mentioned by Cone; time, setting and eventually dimension, however, can be relevant.

Correlational validity. The degree to which findings obtained by one method correlate with findings obtained by another and thus justify their substitutability. This relates to the method as mentioned by Cone. This type of validity also fits in the second sense according to Andrén.

Validity studies in text analysis are hardly performed. A scarce and good example of a study on correlational validity is one performed by Saris-Gallhofer et al. (1978). They compared the method prescribed by Holsti with the semantic differential technique by Osgood et al. (1957) and an own method. They concluded that at the level of the dictionary, Holsti's scores for evaluation, as well as for potency scores, are valid. This does not hold for the scores for activity. Also the assumptions regarding the theme scores are valid.

Predictive validity. This type of validity refers to the ability of an instrument to predict events for which evidence can only be found at a later point of time. After World War II, when investigators had access to Nazi documents the accuracy of inferences on Axis behaviour could be assessed (George, 1959a: 253–84). Carley (1986, 1988) made cognitive maps of her respondents, based on these maps she predicted how they would vote when the new tutor is to be elected. After the elections she could verify whether her predictions were correct. The results can be used in a prediction, but it is required that this prediction holds. This fits in the third sense as indicated by Andrén, both truth and relevancy are required. The main aspects according to Cone that deserve attention are time and setting.

Closely related to predictive validity is *concurrent validity*. Here it is judged how much the results correspond to criterium data that are available at the same time.

Construct validity. Investigates the qualities measured by a test, it 'is not only concerned with validating the measure, but also the theory underlying the measure' (Holsti, 1969: 148). So, the validity is on the results of an investigation and the theory in which the problems behind the investigation are represented. This again seems to fit in the second sense as indicated by Andrén.

An interesting study in which construct validity is put forward is one by Klingemann et al. (1982). They replicated by using computerized thematic text analysis Sorokin's study on the comparative influence and popularity of different systems of truth and knowledge in several cultures from 580 B.C. to 1920 A.D. (Sorokin, 1937). Sorokin provided quantitative empirical evidence in answering questions on, among others, whether the relative importance of different systems of truth and knowledge is constant or variable over time. Klingemann et al. could show that Sorokin's data have both construct and face validity. The investigators found some differences compared to Sorokin however. Contrary to Sorokin they found since 1500 a linear trend, indicating an increasing rationalization of Western societies and culture. Also a cyclical trend was found, this occurred in all categories of truth. The average length of the cycli was 148 years.

Andrén (1981: 54) proposes to identify the reliability of raw data with their truth and the validity of raw data with their relevancy. The truth deals with the first sense of realism. This is actually the reliability. Relevancy deals with the second sense of realism, this is the validity. When these are combined they cover the third sense of realism.

Semantic and network text analysis do not only use concepts, but also relations between concepts. To investigate the meaningfulness of the relations that have been mapped among concepts coherence validity is to be investigated. For example, Schrodt and Gerner (1997) have linked actions in the Middle East. These should be activities that existed. Coherence validity is best estimated by someone who is familiar with the language and texts under analysis.

In some network analyses maps are 'filled in', i.e., conceptual relations are inferred by extending the source's explicit statements based on knowledge of their social context. This is done by using the SKI (Social Knowledge Interpreter) program (Carley, 1988). In other analyses arrows are taken together in links, and links are combined into bundles. Investigators using these methods claim it is allowed, but there has to my knowledge not been any systematic research on the effects of such transformations. The only discussion on this type of problem I am aware of is in Kleinnijenhuis et al. (1995). This is the discussion also mentioned in the previous chapter on whether it is allowed to incorporate transparency axioms in links.

This book is on computer-assisted text analysis. Relevant dictionaries are often only available in English. Programs for semantic text analysis demand that the texts are in English. For this reason it might occur that text blocks have to be translated into English. In cross-cultural research it might even be from several different languages into English. The way a text is translated depends on circumstances in which the text was produced: who said it, when, and in relation to what. Here is a clear relation to the representational view on coding. After being translated a text should still indicate what it said before the translation. One has to be careful of typical expressions, which can not be translated directly.

Text can also be considered from a specific point of view, which has consequences for the translation. Temple (1997: 615) presents two translations of one sentence from Polish into English:

'Women can organize everything, but they cannot lead,'

and

'Women are allowed to organize everything but to take the lead on nothing.'

The first translation is from the perspective of women's abilities to lead. Women tried to become the same as men. They had ended up doubling their workload, but not changing their status. The second translation is from the position that there are different expectations of the roles suitable for men and women, and differences in definitions of what 'leadership' is and therefore in what successful leadership is.

Coders well familiar with the two languages involved, and applying the representational way of coding might even be able to code the texts in one language, e.g., Polish, directly in the other language, e.g., English. Translating programs are on their way, it is questionable whether such programs are sufficiently specific to capture details like the ones in the example above.

Sampling characteristics

When the analysis of the data generated in a text analysis starts, the investigator has to be aware of the level on which this analysis is performed. Typically the analysis is performed on the level of the sampling unit. The texts however, are coded on the level of the recording unit, and sampling and recording unit do not have to coincide. The sampling unit usually consists of several recording units. Therefore the recording units that belong to one sampling unit are usually weighted by 1/x, where x is the number of recording units within that sampling unit. Per sampling unit, this weight can be different. Roberts (1997c) solved the problem in his study on East and West Berlin radio news coverage by concentrating on clauses. He drew a random sample of clauses within each of the relevant groups he distinguished. In this way he had four samples of the same size and he did not have to worry about differences between sampling units.

In the analyses by different investigators attention was given to the networks that have been created. These networks have been interpreted in an *ad hoc* way, often only based on countings of relations. Statistics in which the variance in and between the networks is investigated are hardly developed up to now. To do this one can take two positions. Both start from the position that for each item (block of text, person) a graph is constructed, these graphs form the unit of analysis.

In the first approach the investigator starts from a fixed structure of the network. Now one can take an average graph as starting point and compute the distance to all the separate graphs. For this approach one needs a fixed set of points. So, when some points are not available in a graph, it is to be assumed that they exist as isolated points. Some articles dealing with this approach have recently appeared (Banks and Carley, 1994, 1996). Close to these approaches come the probability models for networks that change over time (Sanil et al., 1995).

The second approach starts from the development of categories. One should try to make a classification of categories that occur many times, and next try to define indices for each category. Categories can for instance be based on balance or transitivity. Even distance indices can be very useful. They might indicate many differences at once. Such indices might be dependent on the density in the graphs, therefore a correction might be necessary. Now you might get indices like the Matching coefficient or the coefficient of Jaccard.[11]

In case, nevertheless, categories or pairs of linked categories are taken as the unit of analysis, these variables are likely to be correlated among units of analysis within the same text block. This is a violation of the fundamental statistical assumption that the units for each variable are statistically independent of each other. Now one should use complicated statistical techniques to model the correlated errors among one's units.

Notes

1. In case the investigator wishes to analyse according to performers' mental models (or conceptual frameworks) s/he will begin by dividing the texts into blocks associated with each performer. On the other hand, if the investigator wishes to analyse the narratives (or story-lines) depicted on programs, one has to begin with dividing the texts into blocks associated with each program. Performers are likely to appear in more than one program, and programs will involve many performers. As a result, the researcher's inferences will differ, depending on this initial division of the text-population.

2. In case the second analysis is performed by using another computer program this program must have at its disposal the same dictionaries, trivial- and negative-word-lists. This requirement means that analysis by some other programs will not yield identical results. Results found by using Textpack and Intext, having these lists, might be different from the results by using VBPro, which uses only a dictionary.

3. Investigations often contain a training phase for the coders. Here they all code the same texts. Afterwards their assignments are compared, here they learn how to code in a specific situation. At the end it is assumed that all coders will do the task in the same way, so it does not matter which coder codes which texts. Agreement is used when the assignments are compared.

4. Krippendorff (1987) introduced also the term 'equity'. The term indicates that the expected use of all categories is equal, i.e., in the situation of two categories, it is 0.5. This distribution, but not the name, was introduced by Bennett et al. (1954), and was rejected by Scott (1955) because the assumption of equity is not realistic.

5. Some investigators state that the maximum amount of agreement should be based on the marginals. If corresponding marginals are unequal the maximum amount of agreement possible is determined by the smallest of these marginals. So, in this situation it is possible to find a value 1 for the index while there is no perfect agreement among the raters. These critics on kappa should not be accepted; for these discussions see Brennan and Prediger (1981), Umesh et al. (1989).

6. For the other situations, denoted as simultaneous and majority agreement, see Popping (1992b: 75ff). All the indices can be computed in the AGREE software package (Popping, 1995).

7. The computation of the p_i is based on the principle of replacement. In the coefficient alpha this principle is not followed (Krippendorff, 1980: 142).

8. Their formula is implemented in the AGREE-package.

   Krippendorff (1980: 146) takes the position that 'all categories of analysis, all decisions specified by various forms of instructions, are indeed represented in the reliability data regardless of how frequently they may occur in actual data.' It is questionable whether all this is needed in the sub-sample. Situations that hardly ever occur might receive too much weight. The problem is solved in part by taking a larger sub-sample.

9. In case this has not occurred, clauses that were not distinguished by the coders, or in different ways, have to be left out of the analysis. I know about efforts where an algorithm has been developed to locate time intervals in observation studies which were scored differently by the coders. A comparable situation is met here. Time intervals might have different lengths, clauses might have different deep structures. The results with respect to the time intervals were not too successful.

10. Likewise, it was to improve semantic validity in word-count measures that a preprocessor was added to the General Inquirer program to correctly classify various usages of the same word (Kelly and Stone, 1975).
11. For the 2*2 table presented earlier in this chapter, Table 7.1, the Matching coefficient is defined as a/(a+b+c+d), and the coefficient of Jaccard as a/(a+b+c).

8

Relation to qualitative research

The label 'text analysis' is used for many approaches as was also indicated in the first chapter of this book. These approaches have one element in common: there is some analysis of the content of text material or of some other medium that can be transcribed into text. So far, the type of text analysis was especially emphasized in which a data matrix is generated and downloaded on which statistical inferences can be performed. Another group of approaches is denoted by the general label 'qualitative (text) analysis' or qualitative research. These approaches are especially used in case a topic is to be described in detail or if concepts are to be developed. According to Barton and Lazarsfeld qualitative research is a part of theory construction, very useful, but not a goal in itself. Qualitative research is an (explorative) phase in the empirical cyclus. 'Qualitative materials are particulary suitable for this exploratory phase of research; their wealth of detailed descriptive elements gives the analyst the maximum opportunity to find clues and suggestions. For testing hypotheses, on the other hand, the ideal model would be the controlled experiment with precise measurements on a limited number of preselected variables' (Barton and Lazarsfeld 1982: 279).

I am most of all interested in this type of qualitative research. In a project where text analysis will be used, this phase will give the investigator insight in the usefulness of concept categories. The origin of the concept categories has hardly received attention so far. They are derived from theory, or they are based on the texts that are being analysed, i.e., on empirical data. An explorative study is valuable to investigate whether the theoretical concepts can be employed in ongoing empirical research, and how these concepts might be adapted if necessary. The study can also be used to find concepts available in the data but not covered by the theory. The concepts that result will be used in the final coding. The study can also be used to find relation types in case the investigator wants to use other ones than those listed in the chapter on network text analysis.

Qualitative research can be considered as a collective noun for various approaches. These approaches are related to different aspects of the research procedure. Tesch (1990: 77) distinguishes 26 different approaches in qualitative research. To structure these approaches, she presents an 'outline' format (Tesch, 1990: 78). Overlap between components is allowed:

1. The characteristics of language
   a. as communication
      i. with regard to its content
      ii. with regard to its process
   b. as its mirror culture
      i. in terms of the cognitive structure
      ii. in terms of the interactive process
2. The discovery of regularities
   a. as the identification and categorization of elements and the establishment of their connections
   b. as the identification of patterns
3. The comprehension of the meaning of text or action
   a. through the discovery of themes
   b. through interpretation
4. Reflection

From the top to the bottom in this outline the approaches to research become less structured and less formal. Tesch considers text analysis as was denoted so far as a kind of qualitative research, for one attaches codes to text. In the outline this type of analysis belongs to the component denoted as 'characteristics of language.' The explorative study can be part of both the first and the second component. The elaboration of field notes is part of the second component, this elaboration is applied most in descriptive studies or case-studies (Pfaffenberger, 1988). Techniques as the grounded theory approach and event structure analysis to discover regularities also belong to this component. The identification of patterns is found in action research and in ethnography. Phenomenology is listed under the third component.

Nowadays qualitative research is frequently considered as part of the grounded theory approach (Glaser and Strauss, 1967), as mentioned part of the second component. This is a method to find structure in texts with the purpose to describe specific developments with regard to some issue and even to find possible explanations. It is used as a method for theory construction and hypothesis testing in an inductive way. An essential point in this theory construction is to find concepts that fit the data. The concepts should not be derived from theory. The early 1990s saw the publication of a torrent of books and articles on qualitative text analysis based on grounded theory and related computer programs. I will shortly go into this approach as the computerized part of it can be used in qualitative (exploratory) research.

The starting position of research as described in the previous chapters, which I will for the moment mark as quantitative research (although the research has strong qualitative parts), and qualitative research is at least different in three perspectives: the research question and therefore the research design is different, coding is performed from a different perspective, and text blocks are used in another way.

In the quantitative research the goal is to test hypotheses, the research goal is formulated in a logico-deductive way. These hypotheses are statements about the relations between certain concept categories. Exact rules are applied that lead to the decision on whether a hypothesis can be accepted or must be rejected. These hypotheses are generally about a well-defined population. The investigator has a sample of text blocks (sampling units – eventually divided into recording units) available that are representative for that population. These text blocks are defined in advance, and they are exclusive. Besides concept categories representing phenomena are available. If the instrumental view on coding will be followed, these categories are known before the actual coding starts (*a priori*), in the situation of the representational view some categories might be added as they are found in the data. Text blocks are assigned to the concept categories. These concept categories are mutually exclusive, for they represent clearly defined empirical events.

In the exploratory phase of a research project the same research question holds. The best would be to have a different sample of text blocks from the same population. The categories are subject to change. They are tested, and might be adapted.

In qualitative research, mainly based on the grounded theory approach, strategies are developed by which systematic theories can be derived from research. The way of working is inductive. Notions and theories are not formulated in advance in a logico-deductive way, but have to rise during the research process from the reality that is investigated. Important in this process are the comparative analysis, the constant comparison of social situations, and the theoretical sampling, the joint collection, coding, and analysis of data based on constant comparison. The investigator starts with emphasizing concepts. When these are confronted with the data the investigator meets regularities that can be coded into categories. Categories, and relations between them, arise in an inductive process. The total of categories and relations shapes a theory. Categories are not used to condense relevant information, but are used as heuristic tools for theory building. The way grounded theory has influenced computer-assisted qualitative data analysis is elaborated by Lonkila (1995).

In qualitative research one often speaks of 'codes' instead of concept categories. Codes are used in two ways. A code might refer to a text passage containing specific information to allow its retrieval – referential coding, or it denotes a fact – factual coding (Seidel and Kelle, 1995: 52; Richards and Richards (1995: 83 ff). Referring to this first meaning Mergenthaler (1996: 8) considers the codes as 'markers'. The codes can be compared to an index in a book. The investigator knows in which text blocks to find which specific information. Inspection of codes allows him or her to find text blocks with similar content. The content of these text blocks can be compared. The second meaning comes close to the way I use the term concept. Now a match indicates that the text block contains a specific phenomenon. There is a difference in interpretation between code and concept. Seidel and Kelle (1995: 52–3) demonstrate this in the following example. A text block where someone expresses his predilection for the Liberal Party can be denoted by the code *Liberal Party affiliation*. The researcher can draw on the information that the person is an adherent of the Liberal Party without even looking at the original text. From the quantitative perspective one can investigate whether a text block (unit of analysis) refers to a political event that was defined, and which attitudes towards this event the person expresses (affirmation, disapproval). The two functions of coding can be used very well together in a qualitative investigation (Richards and Richards, 1995: 83 ff). The functions should not be confused, however. It is conceivable that in an investigation the referential coding refers to male or female speech, and the factual coding refers to the facts that are distinguished in that speech. Using a hierarchy of codes one finds which facts are found for the men and which for the women.[1] The codes are not known in advance.

In qualitative analysis a text block is a part of a text body that contains specific information or a reference to a fact. As such a text block might be determined by the coder, and therefore is not fixed, I will indicate it as a text segment. Text segments might be overlapping, one segment might even be nested in another segment.

Three phases are distinguished in the coding process in qualitative research (Strauss and Corbin, 1990):

1. Open coding – 'the analytic process by which concepts are identified and developed in terms of their properties and dimensions. The basic analytic procedures by which this is accomplished are: the asking of questions about data; and the making of comparisons for similarities and differences between each incident, event, and other instances of phenomena. Similar events and incidents are labelled and grouped to form categories' (1990: 74). This is the part where new concepts are generated.

2. Axial coding – here the concepts are specified in terms of the conditions that give rise to them, the context, action and interactional strategies and consequences.

3. Selective coding – the most central concept is adopted, the investigator tries to orient the investigation around this concept by specifying and validating the relationships it has with other concepts.

Qualitative research usually includes more than analysing texts. The investigator has to assemble texts, often field notes that are written down. A detailed overview of qualitative data analysis, including writing and assembling text, is given by Miles and Huberman. They also indicate where software can be used in this kind of research (Miles and Huberman, 1994: 44):

1. Making notes in the field;
2. Writing up or transcribing field notes;
3. Editing: correcting, extending or revising field notes;
4. Coding: attaching key words or tags to segments of text to permit later retrieval;
5. Storage: keeping text in an organized database;

6. Search and retrieval: locating relevant segments of text and making them available for inspection;
7. Data 'linking': connecting relevant data segments with each other, forming categories, clusters or networks of information;
8. Memoing: writing reflective commentaries on some aspect of the data, as a basis for deeper analysis;
9. Content analysis: counting frequencies, sequence or locations of words and phrases;
10. Data display: placing selected or reduced data in a condensed, organized format, such as a matrix or network, for inspection;
11. Conclusion drawing and verification: aiding the analyst to interpret displayed data and to test or confirm findings;
12. Theory building: developing systematic, conceptually coherent explanations or findings, testing hypotheses;
13. Graphic mapping: creating diagrams that depict findings or theories;
14. Preparing interim and final reports.

The quantitative research fits especially under points 9 and 10 in this list.

The use of computers for qualitative research started only in the early 1980s. This is because it is really necessary to have text on screen, where the coder can indicate (by using the cursor or the mouse) the beginning and the end of a text segment to be coded. As the meaning of text is to be understood or the intentions of the sender of the message (representational view), the coding can not be computerized. It is not an algorithmic process. Some tasks, however, can be performed by the computer. The most important one is the management of data material. A researcher performing qualitative research usually has huge amounts of unstructured textual data, which can result in 'data overload', there is too much material to have at hand in an arranged way.[2] A second task of these programs is that they keep records of which codes are assigned to which text segments, and where these segments begin and end. Around these tasks techniques have been developed.

Several of these techniques have many details in common. This is used for grouping the programs. Up until now programs for qualitative analysis are grouped under a heading that (although roughly) describes the main objective of the programs: text base managers, code and retrieve programs for descriptive and interpretative analysis and theory builders. Sometimes text retrievers are also considered as programs for qualitative analysis. These programs allow you only to search for words or phrases in a text. Text retrievers are not listed here.

The groups of programs are discussed later. Individual programs will be mentioned as examples, but they are not dealt with in detail. Many programs for qualitative research are discussed in Weitzman and Miles (1995), Prein et al. (1995), and Tesch (1990).

Text base managers

Text base managers became first available. These are special purpose data-base programs that do not use predefined fields of fixed length (like common data bases[3]), but that allow information of 'unlimited' length to be entered. This is a requirement because the length of text is not defined in advance. Text base managers are especially useful in descriptive (case-) studies. They assist the investigator in organizing, sorting and making subsets of text (text segments) in a systematic way. They have facilities for search and retrieval. The programs differ from text retrievers in their specialized capabilities for managing and organizing data, and particularly for creating different subsets of data for further analysis. They search for and retrieve various combinations of words, phrases, and coded segments. Examples of text base managers are the programs askSam and TACT.

Code and retrieve programs

Code and retrieve programs for descriptive and interpretative analysis enable the user to attach codes to segments of text, and to search for (and assemble) text-segments that have been coded in a certain way. A detailed treatment of these topics is presented by Tesch (1990: 150 ff). These programs take over the marking up, sorting, reorganizing of especially note cards as was previously done. Several code and retrieve programs also have facilities for making annotations and for memo writing (writing reflective commentaries on some aspect of the data, as a basis for deeper analysis [Glaser and Strauss, 1967: 107–8]), and to present the text segments grouped on basis of the codes. The programs are used in studies where the goal is to describe a specific something, but they can also be used to generate concept categories.

The codes that are used are either previously developed or are developed *ad hoc*. Text segments connected to identical codes are reexamined and if necessary recoded (first in the axial coding phase, later in the selective coding phase). This replaces the cut and paste procedure. A more detailed coding is attached to the segments. Several codes can be attached to one text segment. This process is repeated several times. Finally, a list of concept categories remains that can be transposed into a theory. During this coding memos are used to support the *why* of attaching a specific code to a certain text segment, or to make it recognizable for other coders. Any program that allows coding in the representative way should possess a memo facility, in quantitative research this *why* question is also relevant. Now it informs about *why* assign this concept, and not about *why* develop this concept.

Examples of code and retrieve programs are WinMAX, Kwalitan (remember the program can download a data matrix based on occurrences, moreover it uses text blocks), and The Ethnograph.

The methods used in the code and retrieve programs might be used in the exploratory phase of a quantitative study to find the concept categories. When the program permits this, the text segments can coincide with the search entries (the program WinMAX for example allows this). When this is not possible, notes have to be made. The memo facility can be used for this purpose. Of course the facility is also used to motivate categories.

Retrieve facilities are not available in the programs used in the thematic approach, or one should consider the KWIC-facility as such.

Theory builders

These are programs primarily for building theories, in general based on conceptions from grounded theory construction. These programs usually have the same capabilities as code and retrieve programs. On top they offer extra facilities. The programs allow the investigator to explore relationships between concepts or text segments.[4] Therefore they allow building a conceptual structure. A few programs have facilities to formulate and test hypotheses. Axial coding actually also involves relating concepts. The code and retrieve programs do not allow this, but theory builders do.

Due to the possibilities the computer offers, knowledge representation methods are developed now for representing grounded theory construction, in which a hybrid approach of fuzzy set theory and semantic networks is applied (Yuen and Richards, 1994).

Examples of theory builders are Aquad, Atlas/ti, HyperRESEARCH, and NUD•IST.

Weitzman and Miles (1995) discuss what they call conceptual network builders. These programs help one formulate and represent conceptual schemes through a network of nodes and links. Some theory builders have facilities that makes them network builders. In Atlas/ti one can build a real network, in NUD•IST it is more a hierarchical network. Weitzman and Miles also mention programs having strong network drawing capabilities under this heading.

A type of program that will receive more and more attention in the years to come are programs that use hypertext[5]. The core feature of hypertext is breaking up the linearity of information by linking portions of information together. Hypertexts are set up as networks. Links between points (concepts) are possible, but also links between segments of text. Most of the existing hypertext systems provide graphical overviews of the hypertext network. For details on hypertext, see Conklin (1987) or McAleese (1993).

Concept categories

For the development of concept categories for text analysis in quantitative research two 'ideal' types may be distinguished:

- A set of concept categories is developed *a priori*, based on theory underpinning the research project. These categories are an operationalization of theoretical notions.
- The concept categories are 'data-driven', i.e., they are constructed *a posteriori*, based on words or phrases in the texts that are analysed. It is possible they were developed in the exploratory phase of a project.

Combinations of both types are found frequently. The investigator starts with theoretically derived concepts, and adds data-driven ones.

When the categories are to be found in the data, the investigator might use technical methods to generate from the available text blocks those categories that are relevant for the analysis. Now the investigator will at first look at the frequency of occurring words or phrases. Later clusters of words or phrases become relevant. These are found by applying statistical procedures as cluster or factor analysis.[6] Now thematic concept mapping might be applied, but the clusters can also reveal the categories that need to be used.

Deriving data driven concept categories might start from the frequency of occurrence of words or phrases, this is not sufficient. One should also consider why and how certain words or phrases occur, especially in relation to the research question at hand. In this consideration process resulting in concept categories the investigator might rely on qualitative research, because it is more explicit on how codes are developed. Besides corresponding computer programs contain more useful tools. In this process the investigator might also use indicative schemes that have been developed.

Contas (1992: 256) differentiates two domains for developing concept categories: components of categorization and temporal designation. The components of the categorization process are most relevant. These components are discussed according to three procedural elements: 1) origination, 2) verification, and 3) nomination.

Origination refers to the locus of category construction: 'Where does the responsibility or authority for the creation of categories reside?' Contas distinguishes five loci: participants (as opposed to investigator – I interpret this as to whether the representational or instrumental view must be followed), programs (categories are sets of goals or objectives), investigative (personal interests, investigative perspective – intellectual constructions of the investigator), literature (based on statements or conclusion from literature), interpretative (based on data).

Verification details the strategies used to support the creation and application of categories: 'On what grounds can one justify the creation or existence of a given set of categories?' Here Contas distinguishes sources of justification: external (panel of experts), rational (relies on logic and reasoning), referential (uses existing research findings or theoretical arguments to justify categories), empirical (examines the coverage and distinctiveness reflected by categories), technical (borrows procedures from quantitative methods to answer verification questions) and participative (participants must get the opportunity to modify codings).

Nomination, finally, is concerned with the naming of categories: 'What is the source of a name used to identify a given category?' Here the same sources are met as under categorization.

Concerning the temporal design Contas remarks that categories are developed at three moments: *a priori*, i.e., before the data are actually collected; *a posteriori*, i.e., after the data are collected; or iterative, at various points in time during the research process. If the instrumental view is followed the categories are developed *a priori*. If the representational view is followed, all three moments are allowed.

Apart from using such questions investigators might start with general phenomena that are not content specific but point to general domains. One such scheme is presented by Lofland (1971: 14–5). The phenomena are sorted from microscopic to macroscopic:

1. *Acts*. Action in a situation that is temporally brief, consuming only a few seconds, minutes or hours.
2. *Activities*. Action in a setting of more major duration – days, weeks, months – constituting significant elements of persons' involvements.
3. *Meanings*. The verbal productions of participants that define and direct action.
4. *Participation*. Persons' holistic involvement in or adaption to a situation or setting under study.
5. *Relationships*. Interrelationships among several persons considered simultaneously.
6. *Settings*. The entire setting under study conceived as the unit of analysis.

Using the schemes by Lofland and Contas, one can now ask:

*   What are the characteristics of acts, activities, meanings, participation, relationships, and settings?
*   Which forms do they assume?
*   Which variations do they display?
*   From which perspective should the corresponding concept categories be created?
*   What justifies these categories?
*   From which perspective is the name of the category derived?

This gives a handle to start developing concept categories.

Another general accounting scheme is provided by Bogdan and Biklen (1992: 167 ff). Their scheme is more extended than the one by Lofland:

*   *Settings/context*; general information on the setting, topic, or subject, that allows the investigator to put the study in a larger context.

- *Definition of the situation codes*; how subjects define the setting or particular topics.
- *Perspectives held by subjects*; ways of thinking shared by subjects about their setting.
- *Subject's ways of thinking about people and objects*; understanding of each other, of outsiders, of objects in their world.
- *Process codes*; coding words and phrases that facilitate categorization sequences of events, changes over time, transitions from one type of status to another.
- *Activity codes*; regularly occurring kinds of behaviour.
- *Event codes*; specific activities occurring in the setting or in the lives of the subjects.
- *Strategy codes*; subjects' tactics, methods, techniques for meeting their needs; ways of accomplishing things.
- *Relationships and social structure codes*; patterns of behaviour among subjects that are unofficial, such as cliques, coalitions, romances, friendships, enemies.
- *Method codes*; material pertinent to research procedures, problems, joys, dilemmas.

Again, combined with Contas' questions, this is a handle. The schemes only help the investigator think about categories, they might be useful as a starting point.

In qualitative research, concept categories are developed as part of theory construction. The explorative part of a quantitative study might be performed using the tools and computer programs developed for qualitative research to develop the concept categories (and search entries) to be used in the final project. The facility to write memos is always useful. Programs for text analysis that allow representative coding should contain such a facility, for during this coding process many decisions are made that need to be remembered.

Once the categories have been developed, coding can start. Not surprisingly, a coder coding according to the representational view performs several tasks that can be compared to the tasks performed by a coder in qualitative research. With respect to the concept categories the following tasks are to be performed:

- The coder interprets a text block – in quantitative research a text block is at least on the level of a unit of analysis, in qualitative research the coder can take a text segment in a text block;
- The coder assigns the phenomena in this block to existing concept categories taking into account the context in which these phenomena occur – in the quantitative research the category is a factual code, in the qualitative research it might also be a referential code;
- If, according to the coder a phenomenon should be assigned to a category that does not exist, he or she adds this category (possibly after consulting the investigator) – in qualitative research the categories might also be changed or refined, etc.;

- If a search entry for a specific category does not exist, it is added – in qualitative research search entries are not relevant. In the open coding phase they might have served as codes.

When the semantic or network approach to text analysis is followed, the number of tasks is extended:

- The coder has to distinguish clauses – this is not relevant in qualitative research;
- Next the concepts in the clauses about which something is said must be identified and coded – as before;
- Finally the relation between the concepts is specified and coded – in qualitative research this is performed when theory builders are used. The concepts are not restricted to a clause. Not only the relation between concepts, but also the relation between text segments might be coded.

This listing shows that coding in qualitative research and coding in quantitative research according to the representational view have much in common. This is despite the fact that the goal in both types of research is different. At several places cooperation is possible. Fielding and Lee (1998) picture their project CAQDAS (Computer Assisted Qualitative Data Analysis Software) for investigating the software available for qualitative research. In the chapter on managing data they present lots of details on the way concept categories are developed and on the way coding is performed, both in an individual setting and as in teams.

Network analysis

The programs for building and representing networks that fit under the umbrella of qualitative research can serve very different goals. The ones mentioned before are especially suited for theory building. Other programs are used for problem solving or representing the state of art in some field.

The process of problem solving is among others supported in the program, Cope (Cropper et al., 1990). This program is designed to hold knowledge encoded using the cognitive mapping technique. The program only permits causal relations between concepts. The program is designed to assist in the delineation of causally related classes of phenomena. It accomplishes this goal by making it easy for the user to redefine concepts as additional causal data arise. Cope is for representing facts.

Another approach is known as knowledge graphing. Knowledge graphing methodology was originally developed to describe the state of the art in some scientific field. It results in a network representing empirically tested facts. The methodology begins with a researcher's explicit choice of a relatively few types of relations (James, 1992: 98). These are even fewer types than used in CETA.

The method then proceeds to the *text analysis* step, in which a list of concepts is generated. An 'author graph' is then constructed with each node corresponding to a specific concept as found in the text (publication), and with each link of one of the chosen types.

In the next, *concept identification* step, the author graphs are compiled into a single graph by combining their corresponding nodes. During this process linguistic ambiguities are eliminated as synonyms across author graphs are combined, and as homonyms are not. The resulting 'compiled graph' is further refined by alternating between *concept integration* and *link integration* steps. In the first refinement step, theoretically interesting substructures are identified; in the second, new links are inferred from those already encoded.[7] This 'integrated graph' can then be further refined (i.e., further 'integrated') with the initiation of another concept integration step. By superimposing various frame relations on the graph, this step identifies further knowledge structure. Each frame relation generalizes several concepts and relations as a single concept. Additional link integration is then possible as inferences are made based on these concepts newly added to the graph.

Popping and Strijker (1997) have applied knowledge graphs to represent sociological theories about labour markets. The graphs are based on empirical results found in theses from a research school. In the integrated graph hardly any connections between the original graphs were found. This is because in each thesis a different part of the 'theory about labour markets' was investigated. Therefore, a graph was constructed based on theories, i.e., notions about which issues (concepts) are assumed to be related but for which no empirical evidence is available yet. This is a graph at another level. It has now turned out that the graphs on the empirical level are in principle related. The linking parts however, still needed to be proofed.

The above example shows that graphs can been constructed at different levels. Malrieu (1994) has proposed to indicate these by using different colours when they are represented on the computer screen. The notion of coloured graphs might be applied for several purposes:

- To indicate different levels;
- To indicate different types of relations;
- To indicate graphs constructed by different coders.

This all is useful when the network is represented on the computer screen. In the explorative phase of a project such a representation is informative with respect to the choice of concepts and relation types that are by that time under construction.

Notes

1. In the quantitative research the distinction addressed in the referential code is part of the design of the study. See for example Sly (1991), who compared male and female speech.
2. The investigator doing qualitative research has in my view structured material, because this investigator uses a well-defined sample of text blocks.
3. Many forms of data base programs exist. These can be programs that handle only flat files, i.e., each table is separate. Exchange of data between two tables is not possible (only by using tricks). It can also be a relational data base, where one table is related to another. See also the remarks in the chapter on semantic text analysis.
4. The two situations are distinguished in Figure 3.2. This figure shows a relationship between the concepts p and r. These concepts represent (a quality found in) the text blocks A and X. One can image that the text blocks are also related, as for example one contains the answer to a question posed in the other block.

    The program Atlas/ti has five specific types to indicate text–text relations. The first one CRIT (criticises) is asymmetric, the other ones are transitive. They are: SUP (supports), DISC (discusses), JUST (justifies), and EXPL (explains).
5. One also meets the term 'hypermedia'. The different 'media' in here support graphics, texts, pictures, audio and video, whereas hypertext only relates to the textual content.
6. A thematic analysis, where the concept categories are found, might serve as a phase in the research preceding the semantic or the network approach.
7. Bakker's (1987) KISS (Knowledge Integration and Structuring System) program has powerful procedures for concept and link integration.

9

Relation to linguistics and information retrieval

The cooperation between the fields of text analysis on the one hand, and linguistics and information retrieval on the other is not that close. There is certainly no systematic cooperation. Nevertheless, these are both fields of research that are closely related to text analysis. This includes also qualitative research. In this chapter linguistics and information retrieval are shortly introduced and related to text analysis. The places where text analysis *might* benefit from each of the two will be indicated. Anyway, I believe that parsers are very useful in preparing a text for analysis. Several issues mentioned in this chapter have been discussed in previous chapters, but from another point of view.

When the context in which text is uttered is also the subject of the investigation, more information than just the text is needed. Such information might be collected from interviews or observation. Therefore some remarks are made about these issues at the end of the chapter.

Linguistics

The following citation is very illustrative for the relation between text analysis and linguistics: "'Content analysis" is a form of language analysis and "language analysis" usually is a form of linguistics. The word "automated" refers to the computer as a tool in any kind of human activity. Nevertheless, the word 'automated content analysis' however does not refer to computational linguistics' (Boot, 1978). First general remarks on linguistics will be made, after that the relevance for text analysis is emphasized.

Linguistics is a collective noun for several kinds of research dealing with language. Strictly speaking linguists analyse sentences within a language. Pure linguists even neglect all questions about pieces of language bigger than a single sentence. Language is a system of rules referring to sounds and sound symbols that is followed by humans in communicating ideas, feelings, desires, and so on. Within this system the humans produce and understand an unlimited number of utterances. Grishman (1986: 12) defines language as 'a set of sentences, where each sentence is a string of one or more symbols (words) from the vocabulary of the language.' It is a representation of an internalized grammar. Therefore, Grishman proceeds: 'A grammar is a finite, formal specification of this set.' Most grammars related to syntax have a phrase structure. Such a structure contains four components. (1) Terminal vocabulary, the words or symbols of the language that are defined. (2) Non-terminal vocabulary, the symbols (distinct from the terminal vocabulary) that are used in specifying the grammar. (3) A set of productions (of the form a → b, the relation between [parts of] two vocabularies). (4) A start symbol (a member of the non-terminal vocabulary).

A grammar, however, is not just restricted to syntax, but refers to the complete mental system that allows humans to form and interpret words and sentences of their language. In the grammar different levels or sub-disciplines are distinguished:

- *Syntax* lays the rules of proper (grammatically correct) sentence formation;
- *Semantics* studies the meaning of words, sentences, and discourse in general;
- *Pragmatics* deals with the use of language in context;
- *Morphology* deals with the formation of words;
- *Phonology* studies how sounds and intonation are used;
- *Phonetics* studies the articulation and perception of speech sounds.

The levels interact to some content, the first ones have already been mentioned before in this text. The chapter on semantic text analysis is mainly about semantic, but also syntactic grammars are used for text analysis. Still, let us consider the grammars in some more detail. For an extended introduction the reader is referred to the text book edited by O'Grady et al. (1997).[1]

Syntax lays the rules of proper sentence construction, it is concerned with the use of characters, words and sentence construction in texts. It is a strategy for describing text structure. A generative grammar was first developed by Chomsky (1957). This grammar describes sentences by giving rules to construct them rather than by listing the sentences or their structures. Take the rules in Table 9.1. Word categories used here are: noun, verb, and determiner. In general lexical categories are distinguished (noun, verb, adjective, preposition, and adverb), and non-lexical or functional categories (determiner, degree word, qualifier, auxiliary, conjunction) (O'Grady et al., 1997: 182). The first group is most important in sentence formation. Nouns name entities as individuals and objects, verbs indicate actions, sensations, and states. The determiner specifies the noun. Table 9.2 shows the sentence 'The man loves the woman' that is generated.

Functional categories are harder to define than lexical ones. With respect to our type of analysis these categories are very informative. The qualifier (e.g., always, often) specifies a verb, and the degree word (e.g., very, quite) is a specifier of an adjective or a preposition. Auxiliaries indicate differences in strength. The sentence, 'The government must do that,' expresses a much stronger position than the sentence, 'The government should do that.'

Table 9.1   *Example of a grammar*

sentence :=	noun phrase + verb phrase
noun phrase :=	determiner + noun
verb phrase :=	verb + noun phrase
determiner :=	the
noun :=	man
noun :=	woman
verb :=	loves

Table 9.2   *Example of a generative grammar*

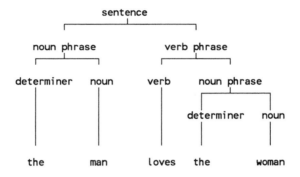

Rules like these have become standard in linguistics. They are also used in computer applications. By using a finite set of rules, one can describe an infinite number of sentences. Chomsky has distinguished four types of grammar:

0.   Unrestricted phrase structure grammars;
1.   Context sensitive grammars;
2.   Context free grammars;
3.   Regular grammars.

These types of grammar are not explicated here. For a short introduction, see Grishman (1986: 16 ff). In semantic text analysis as presented in the fifth chapter context free grammars are used. Context free grammars have productions where the left side is a single non-terminal, and the right side is a non-empty combination of terminals and non-terminals.

Semantics studies the meaning of words or sentences. The distinction between denotation and connotation is basic. The denotation points to the fixed relation between a word and the object it refers to; the connotation indicates what a word is suggested to refer to. The term semantic composition is the combining of meanings of words to form the meanings of phrases and sentences. Such a composition is often represented as logical formulas. One often found within computer languages is:

loves (john, mary)

which represents the S–V–O-relation in the sentence 'John loves Mary.' Such formulas provide a representation for the meanings of words and phrases as well as whole sentences. Formal languages as predicate and propositional logic are used for the representation of meaning. Given that:

All men are mortal
Socrates is a man
we may conclude *Socrates is mortal*;
or with respect to propositional logic, given that
If it is raining you will get wet
It is raining
we may conclude *You will get wet.*

The relevance of semantics for text analysis is in the removal of all kinds of ambiguity. The types found most in linguistics are lexical, structural and referent ambiguity. The first one to be removed is lexical ambiguity. This type of ambiguity is especially caused by polysemy and homonymy. Polysemy occurs when a word has two or more related meanings, consider the word 'bright' in 'The moon is bright,' and in 'The girl is bright.' In both sentences 'bright' refers to a quality that is judged as good. Homonymy exists when a word has two or more completely distinct meanings, e.g., a 'bank' might be a financial institution, a row of cylinders in an engine, but also a strand. As a verb it refers to banking a fire.[2]

The reverse situation is when different words refer to the same something. Synonyms are words or expressions that have the same meanings in some or all contexts, e.g., 'car' and 'automobile'. They do not contribute to ambiguity, but if such words are not recognized, one might get two concepts having the same meaning. In this way they can contribute to confusion.

Phrases, whose meaning is not predictable from the meanings of the parts, are called idioms. Idioms are non-compositional. An example is 'kick the bucket', which means 'die'. Such idioms have to be replaced in the type of text analysis that is considered here. Investigators who do not want to consider phrases, but only single words, have to be aware of multiple word strings (e.g., United Kingdom). These words form one unit.

Other issues related to meaning and relevant in the discussion about lexical ambiguity, e.g., extension versus intentions, have been discussed in the first chapter of the book.

Structural ambiguity is that the meaning of component words in a sentence can be combined in more than one way. 'Bright boys and girls' might be read as,

> 'bright boys' and 'bright girls,'[3]

or as,

> 'bright boys' and 'girls' (that are not [necessarily] bright).

Referent ambiguity is found when a pronoun is found that might refer to several nouns. An example is in the following sentence: 'The girls married the boys and *they* became pregnant.' It should be clear that it is the girls who became pregnant. In most situations, where the context is known, these types of ambiguity can be solved. I return to this issue when pragmatics is discussed.

For a better syntactic and semantic interpretation of a sentence the investigator might try to determine the so-called thematic roles or syntactic components that are found in a sentence. These components are used to describe the part played by a particular entity in an event. The following ones have already been mentioned:

- *Agency* the initiator of an activity;
- *Position*   the position regarding the agency's activity;
- *Action* the activity under consideration (also indicated as *theme*);
- *Object* the target of this activity.

Depending on what is investigated one might add:

- *Source* the starting point of a movement;
- *Goal*   the end point of a movement;
- *Location*   the place where an action occurs.

The first four components are used by among others Roberts (1997c) and Franzosi (1989), who also uses the final three components.

Syntax grammars map the surface structure of texts into grammatical categories, semantic grammars map the deep structure of a text into a limited set of functionally defined categories. The S–V–O-relation as addressed in the chapter on semantic text analysis is one way of representing a semantic grammar. Genres of texts are characterized according to their sequence of functional forms. The grammars underlying such sequences have been referred to as narrative grammars (Griemas, 1984), text grammars (Van Dijk, 1972) or story grammars (Rumelhart, 1975).

In linguistics syntax and semantics are used to investigate issues like style and emotion as used by certain persons, e.g., in the prose of authors (Whissell, 1994), or at specific occasions (comparison of speeches). In text analysis, as viewed in this book, these are instruments for finding which concepts are related to each other in which way.

Pragmatics concerns the use of language in context, it deals with the relation between a text and its users. Whereas syntax and semantics study sentences, pragmatics studies speech acts and the situations in which language is used.[4]

Schank has emphasized the relevance of foreknowledge when texts have to be interpreted. Schank (1973: 189–90) distinguishes several mechanisms that cause expectations by readers of texts. He mentions the already known syntax, semantics, and context. He indicates pragmatics as 'conversational'; indicating the mechanism that people talk and write with a specific goal (pragmatics), and that some texts can only be understood in the context of this goal. Here one uses an *individual memory model*, indicating personal opinions people have regarding the situation that is described. The *cultural memory model* refers to common knowledge that is shared in a specific culture. Within this cultural memory model one might even distinguish between *semantic memory*, referring to notions that are common in a community of language, and *episodic memory*, notions that are not common, generalizations to time and place are questionable.

An important concept in pragmatics is implicature. The implicature of a sentence comprises information that is not part of its meaning, but would nonetheless be inferred by a reasonable hearer. Actually, Carley's SKI program (Carley, 1988) takes care of such implicature. Another important concept is presupposition. This refers to the things that must be true in order for a statement to be either true or false.

Morphology is word formation. Every language knows two kinds of word formation processes:

• Inflection, provides the various forms of any single word;
• Derivation, invents new words from old ones.

Examples of inflection are the singular 'man' and its plural 'men', and the present form 'goes' and its past 'gone'. An example of a derivational process is the creation of 'writer' from 'write', and '-er'. The suffix '-er' is added to a verb to form a noun with the meaning 'one that does X' (here 'work'). One might not only investigate suffixes, but also prefixes and infixes. Especially inflection is very useful for dictionary construction. Sometimes all inflected forms of words in the text blocks to be analysed are replaced by their basic word (Hogenraad, et al., 1995). This is the process of lemmatization: different word forms belonging to one word root are taken together as one word. Stone, et al. (1966: 89) describe a suffix editing procedure that can be used. Dictionaries may contain all inflected forms of a word. Most dictionaries, however, use wild card like search entries as were presented in the chapter on thematic text analysis. When using such entries ambiguity might remain.

Phonology studies of how sounds are used in language. Every language has phomenes, i.e., sounds that it distinguishes. A phomene has one or more physical realizations called allophones. Consider for example the t-sounds in the words stop and top. They are physically different. The first one is accompanied by a puff of air and the other is not. These two sounds are allophones of the same phoneme, because the language does not distinguish them (Covington, 1994). Sound waves are continuous, but phonemes are discrete. If a computer (program) has to understand speech, it must segment the continuous stream of speech into discrete sounds. Each sound has to be classified as a specific phoneme. In fact, now pattern recognition is applied. Here two main problems are met. First, successive sounds overlap. In the word 'man', the 'a' and the 'n' are almost completely simultaneous. The influence of neighbouring sounds on each other is called co-articulation. Second, speech varies from one person to another and even from occasion to occasion with the same speaker. On the other side of speech recognition is speech synthesis. This is the creation of speech by computer. A synthesizer's major task is to simulate co-articulation. This is usually done by providing several allophones for each phoneme, each to be used when a different phoneme is neighbouring.

Phonetics studies the speech sounds that are used in language. One might take as a starting position the physiological mechanisms of speech production, but it is also possible to start from speech sounds in terms of how we hear them. The first approach is known as articulatory phonetics, the second one as acoustic phonetics.

Dialectological research, for example the determination of origin of text dating from the middle ages, has also been mentioned as a level. In my view it is part of the study of language change, which includes several aspects of the levels that have been mentioned.

The first three levels – syntax, semantics and pragmatics – are relevant in both social and behavioral sciences and in humanities. The latter three levels are especially relevant for the humanities. Social and behavioural scientists are most of all interested in the message that is communicated, and in how this is done, this includes discourse. Research in this field may include the development of meaning of words in a specific social or historical context, or differences in naming of issues. As an illustration, Trew (1979) investigates how newspapers reported on riots in Rhodesia in 1975. He shows how the effects of an event are reworded. 'Police shoot dead Africans,' becomes 'police kill Africans,' which is followed by 'Africans die,' and later 'The deaths...' Investigators from humanities are also concerned with structure, stylistics, rhyme, metre, and so on. Pictured in broad lines, social scientists concentrate on the content, while investigators from humanities accentuate the style.

In linguistic research more specialities are distinguished. Some of these specialities point to mathematics and logic. Algebraic linguistics investigates and develops the formal instruments necessary for describing a language. Statistical linguistics is concerned with quantitative properties of phenomena of language, for example frequency of words in a text. Computational linguistics refers to all forms of research on language in which computers are used. Some investigators (Grishman, 1986: 4) consider information retrieval (to be discussed later in this chapter) as an application of computational linguistics. For others (McEnery, 1992) artificial intelligence is a relevant part of it. Here the phenomenon of language is explained within some theory of knowledge representation. One such theory is the frame theory as used by Minsky (1975) and (although other names are used) by Schank (1973). Ethnolinguistics investigates the relation between language, use of language, and culture.

Related to this last mentioned form of linguistics is the discourse analysis. This type of analysis provides insight into the forms and mechanisms of human communication and verbal interaction. The analysis focuses directly and solely on conversations or other language interactions. The goal is two-fold: (1) to discover structure in the language interaction in terms of regularities that can then be described in more general terms as a model, or (2) to find linkages so that the investigator can make assertions.

Linguistics covers a very broad area. Parts of this area are used in text analysis. In the chapter on thematic text analysis all kind of activities have been mentioned to overcome ambiguity without clear reference to linguistics. In my view most investigators used information from linguistics without referring to this field. In this respect one must remember that the developers of the first computer programs of text analysis could not fall back on programs developed by linguists. Therefore they had to develop all algorithms for overcoming ambiguity by themselves.

Considerable parts of the knowledge provided by linguists can be used by investigators doing text analysis. First of all the linguists have tools to overcome lexical ambiguity. Some of the present computer programs for thematic text analysis have their dictionaries in which (part of) this type of ambiguity is met, but there are also several programs that use dictionaries developed by the investigator. Especially such investigators might benefit from the work already performed by linguists in overcoming ambiguity. Natural language processing, i.e., the use of computers to recognize and use information expressed in a human language, might even be used for dictionary construction. I want to point to the special role of the dialectological linguists. Over time words might get another meaning, or words might be replaced by other words.[5]

In semantic and network text analysis the relation between concepts is used. Sometimes the verb that realizes the relation is coded, sometimes it is a type of meaning. It was demonstrated before that the program CETA for network text analysis, uses 15 meaning types. Rahmstorf (1983) distinguished 38 meaning types, named them, gave arguments, paraphrases, and general characteristics. An example is the type of the consequence relation. Arguments are 'x basis', 'y consequence.' A verbal paraphrase is 'y follows from x,' or, taking the converse 'x is the basis for y.' General characteristics are that the relation is transitive, but not symmetric. Note, a consequence is not a cause. It is worth investigating whether the present facilities in programs for semantic and network text analysis can be extended by incorporating these meaning types. They cover most actions that are included in verbs. One class of verbs however, is not covered. These are the modal auxiliaries. The meaning types should be extended into this direction.[6]

Besides the path-algebra should be extended, the join and multiplication operations can handle only a few meaning types.

The problem of recognizing syntactic links can be attached by using methods to find the structure in sentences. Parsing is very relevant here. It is already valuable if it gives a pre-analysis of sentences. So, if it only informs about possible structures without changing the actual structure of sentences. Linguistics also offers special ways for searching in texts. For a greater part these ways are elaborated in information retrieval.

Parsing

The recognition of the structure of sentences by computer is called parsing. Most parsers investigate the syntactic structure of a sentence. Here the computer matches a sentence with the rules that generate it. This can be done either top-down or bottom-up. A top-down parser starts by looking for the structure of a sentence, then looks at the rules to see what a sentence can consist of. A bottom-up parser starts by looking at the string of words, then looks at the rules to see how the words can be grouped together. For examples, see O'Grady et al. (1997: 676 ff). The two approaches can be combined.

Many computer programs for text analysis available today prompt the user for various linguistic relations, but they do not automate the process of identifying them. Only two of the text analysis programs that have been mentioned before provide such capability to divide text into clauses (i.e., phrases containing a single inflected verb and optional subject, object, and modifiers), or to break down clauses into parts-of-speech (most commonly into subject–valence–verb–object, or S–V–V–O combinations). The Gottschalk and Gleser program has a parser that breaks down clauses into parts-of-speech, but requires text to have been manually broken down into clauses beforehand. KEDS has a 'sparse parser' that scans texts for a specific set of verb patterns before assigning an event code to a particular news report. One program for qualitative research that has a parser is RELATUS (Alker et al., 1991), that was developed for representing story grammars. This program requires that the user rewrite the entire text into a form that the program can successfully handle.

More important than pointing out the general poverty of coding tools capability in text analysis software, this listing shows that even those programs with such capability do not afford the user an active role in the coding process. However, user input is desired for a general purpose coding tool, i.e., a tool that can be linked to different text analysis programs. Many decisions depend on the context, and a computer is not able to recognize the context (yet).

A coding tool is nothing more than a set of rules for assigning syntactic features (subject, inflected verb, etc.) to words. The task of rewriting and incorporating such rule-sets into a text analysis program is not the major hurdle to be overcome. The more fundamental need is for a coding tool that both affords the user an active role in the coding process and makes interactive coding results available to a wide range of 'natural language data bases' and text analysis software (cf. Baker, 1997).

It may be clear that parsing might go rather well for finding the syntactic structure of a sentence, and so for recognizing (main and subordinate) clauses. In this way structural ambiguity might be overcome. However, when the semantic characteristics are to be taken into account it becomes very complicated. A computer recognizes structures, but not meanings yet.

A first simple task to be performed by a parser that can handle semantic characteristics is the replacement of personal pronouns by the nouns they refer to (take away referent ambiguity). Another problem in texts that might be overcome by using parsers refers to the problem of knowing when a new noun phrase refers back to a previously encountered referent. Research is going on to solve this kind of problems (Cowie and Lehnert, 1996). The parser might also recognize (and replace) idioms and other forms of ambiguous words or phrases. For this task a coder is absolutely necessary, the parser will guide the coder.

Programs are available for parsing the syntactic structure of sentences, these programs are not related to text analysis programs. They are used to improve texts. At the basis of these programs are a number of key questions in text evaluation, like 'what are the characteristics of an effective text?,' and 'what are the key skills and abilities involved in text evaluation?'. For further details see Schriver (1989). Aspects of the text evaluation that can be automated are incorporated in computer programs.

Research on semantic parsers has also started. They are restricted to a specific issue and text. These parsers start from semantic categories. Now rules are followed like: a sentence consists of a subject, an object, and a value for that object. In sentences having this structure the subject, object and value can be displayed. Sowa (1984: 256) mentions some applications of semantic parsers. I am not aware of applications in text analysis as considered in this book.

Information retrieval

Information retrieval is concerned with the storage and retrieval of information. Traditionally this information has been available as texts. Today these texts are stored on a computer system. They are available and can be approached on such a system in a formalized and consistent way. Information retrieval focuses on the search and retrieval processes rather than on the actual analysis of semantic content. It is universal of application. In information retrieval one seeks a text block that is likely to contain the information one seeks. There are several connections between information retrieval and text analysis research. Before discussing these connections, some background on information retrieval is presented. A general introduction into information retrieval by computer is Salton (1989).

Speaking very generally, information retrieval from large electronic texts follows some basic approaches: data abstraction and text corpora.

Data abstraction. The investigator identifies relevant elements in a text (e.g., words, phrases, numerical data) and stores these in a data base. This data base exists independent of the text itself. Now data are collected systematically in a uniform way. A restriction of the method is that only data that are *interpreted* are kept in the data base and not the original text. In case of doubt about the interpretation of the data the investigator will have to return to the original text. Data abstraction is not used in text analysis as dealt with in this book. Therefore I will only concentrate on the text corpora.

Text corpora. A text corpus is an electronic text enriched with explicit codes that represent information from that text. Two approaches are followed:

• Text is accessed directly by searching for words or phrases in the text, which serve as keys to the specific information being sought. This information might be categorised;
• Text has been assigned to categories denoting the content of specific areas; the user then accesses information in the text via those categories.

The first approach is useful in case the information that is looked for is immediately used, or if one has to start coding. If the text needs to be analysed again, the second approach using categories is preferred. The approaches resemble the process of creating and using an index in a book. Code and retrieve programs follow the approaches to order to find structure in a text. Categories are constructed and revised. Or, to continue the parallel with the book, the index is constructed. Here too, a dictionary might be constructed in which the search entries are linked to the index or categories. Programs for text analysis (as discussed in the book) use the index to find and count occurrences or co-occurrences. Hypertext links also operate in a similar manner.

An information and retrieval system looks like a system presented in Figure 9.1. Information on documents, e.g., books, can be classified, but also information in texts can be classified. Information once stored can be looked for by applying search routines, where users have to define what they are looking for. The great power of the systems is in these search routines. In the first applications of information retrieval the investigator was looking for an exact match, that is, one is checking to see whether an item is present or absent in a text body. Today an investigator might also look for a partial match or a best match.[7] Now relevant items will be found. Therefore the model that has been used has changed from a deterministic one to a probabilistic model. In the query where the investigator defines what he is looking for, logicals and booleans can be used. In a trial and error process the investigator looks for exactly the information he wants. Information retrieval that is concentrated on this activity is an implementation of linguistic theories.

The essention of a user query is presented in Table 9.3. It is assumed an algorithm is available that can detect the stem of verbs (here 'work').[8] The nouns 'child' and 'children' might even be replaced by a noun having as single

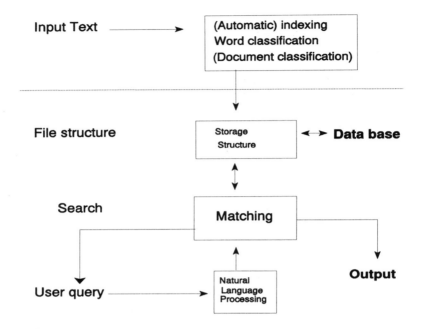

Figure 9.1   *Structure of an information retrieval system*

Table 9.3   *Alghoritm for a user query*

```
find next text block
   find next sentence
      find next clause
         find (((noun = 'child' )
             or  (noun = 'children' ))
            and  (verb = stem ('work' )
         if found
            copy text block to ...
         end find
      until all clauses
   until all sentences
until all text blocks
```

form 'child'. Information retrieval today also allows to use probability statistics. Before it was shown that programs for thematic text analysis sometimes allow for very complex search entries.

In the first chapter the ANES system, developed by Brandow et al. (1995), for automatically summarizing news stories was mentioned. The system is based on information retrieval. In the future it might be used as a method to reduce text blocks. It is necessary then that the summary contains the actual information that is relevant for the investigation at hand.

Sometimes it is stressed that information retrieval might play a role in sampling. I can imagine that in some research situations information retrieval is used to find documents that fullfill some criterium, e.g., deal with the issue under investigation, and that these documents are entered into the sample.

Searching a text might immediately be supported by expert systems. Gauch and Smith (1993) describe an expert-system intermediary that works with the coder as he or she navigates the text with tools allowing smart computer-assisted search procedures and context-sensitive information retrieval. Some degree of textual preprocessing and structuring is necessary for efficient computer access but, as their work shows, it is the tools that assist in textual management that greatly increase the ease with which information can be retrieved from a text.

For computer-assisted analysis the text corpus needs to be in machine-readable form. Therefore, if the corpus at hand is not machine-readable already, transcription procedures including development of transcription schemes, scanning and proofreading techniques are applied.

As more electronic information is going to be produced, the need to preserve this information in an electronic archive demands a lot of attention. The publications stored might be retrieved and consulted for research and, if desired, repackaged into new publications. Standardization to the format in which documents are stored is crucial to the successful operation of an electronic archive. Examples of the standardized generic coding systems are SGML (Standard Generalized Markup Language) and ODA (Open Document Architecture).

SGML (Smith, 1992) is an ISO (8879) standard markup language for representing text corpora. It is in the meantime widely accepted for collecting, transcribing, and preparing textual sources for computer analysis. No efforts are known in which SGML encoded texts are used for text analysis. ODA is another ISO (8613) standard for describing documents.

Apart from these standards, specific projects are going on, which aim at integrating procedures for reading or writing textual data (Duchastel et al., 1995). This means that text formats become available for selected programs, but it is a beginning.

Readability analysis

Text analysis concentrates especially on the content of the messages. If an investigation takes place in the context of communication it might be relevant to know how well a text can be followed and understood by those for whom the text is meant. A text (speech) should be neither too simple or too difficult. The question is how difficult it is to understand a text and when will one have a transfer of information with as little trouble as possible. Readability analysis investigates how well a text can be followed. This is a part of the context of a text. This analysis received a lot of attention at the end of the 1940s and the beginning of the 1950s when lots of propaganda studies were performed. Investigators in this field were concerned with the level of abstraction of a text as an indicator for the apprehension that might occur (Flesch, 1950). The research is especially important for journalists (when are their texts understood best) and for educational researchers (how should the text books and other teaching materials for children be formulated). Many indices for readability have been developed. The basis for several of these indices is the ratio of different words per 1000 words in a text (the number of syllables, the number of words, the number of sentences). An extended overview is given by Lisch and Kriz (1978: 176 ff). The program Intext allows to compute several of these indices.

An example of the use of readability analysis is found in Walters and Walters (1996). They investigate the relationship between public relations practitioners and journalists in the transmission of the language of the science to the public. Output of a public relations office is compared to newspaper stories that appeared as a result of the office's effort. In the comparison the investigators use readability indices, and statistics concerning paragraphs, sentences, and words. They show that newspapers simplify both science and non-science releases. Media sharpen and level science stories. Although syntactically there are hardly differences, science releases are more difficult to read than non-science stories. Within the science releases it was found that stories are edited differently.

Related data collection techniques

Text analysis is a tool for data collection. The data are found in the texts that are analysed. In a lot of research the context in which the text is used is also relevant. This might concern characteristics of the medium in which the text appeared, but it might also be characteristic of those who are sender or receiver of the text. Often such characteristics can be asked for in interviews. The interviewers might be assisted by computer programs that have been developed for this purpose. For an extended discussion on computer-supported interviewing, see Saris (1991).

It is also conceivable that the characteristics of sender and receiver have to be observed. Think of questions like, 'which gestures were made to support the argument (the speech)?', 'how did people look at each other?', 'what is the reaction of the receiver on the message?' These questions all concern sequences of non-verbal behaviour. Non-verbal behaviour that is perceived can be transposed into data. In general, behaviour is directly observable. It is observable in an indirect way when the investigator uses psychophysiologic variables.

The processing of directly observable live behaviour, by video-recording and encoding of behaviour into sequences of distinct events, is rather prone to error and distortion. During encoding, the observer has to recognize the end of an event, to recognize and select a new event from an extensive catalogue, and to store the code and timing repeatedly, often within a fraction of a second. How well the observer performs, depends on the size of the catalogue of events; the lucidity of the definitions; the speed and timing of the events; the simplicity and ergonomics of the technical task; and on vigilance and training. It is essential to give the observer immediate feedback on his or her performance. Paying attention to these factors prevents fatigue, an important cause of erratic encoding.

Video-records make it possible to examine behaviour repeatedly, if necessary at different speeds. Using video, one can encode specific fast events at the appropriate slow speed; encode different simultaneous behavioural traces; or encode different individuals. Such encodings can then be merged into one single encoding, provided that one has retained the same time frame for each encoding. Today several computer programs are available that assist in coding behaviour (Van der Vlugt et al., 1992; Noldus, 1991; Hecht and Roberts, 1996).

In psychophysiology, heart rate variability is used as an index for mental workload. In several studies it is found that this variability decreases as a function of invested effort in the task to be performed. By using specific, well defined test tasks in the beginning and at the end of the working day insight can be obtained in the effects of the work to be performed and in the changes in the physiological state which go along with the performance of heavy mental work during several hours. The different types of fluctuations in heart rate can be distinguished by using spectral analysis on the series of interbeat intervals derived from the R-peak in the ECG. The variability can be determined for several frequency bands. A program for data reduction, correction and spectral analysis of such cardiovascular signals is CARSPAN (Mulder et al., 1992).

Data collected by using these instruments can be added to the data collected in the text analysis.

Other non-textual data can be captured by using multimedia techniques. They allow working with images, audio, and video. Coding and commenting by a human coder of (aspects of) images is now possible in Atlas/ti, Code-A-Text and askSam. Other packages will follow. Here the images are in the program's data base. Automatic extraction of information as in programs for text analysis is not possible. To my knowledge video as part of multimedia does not allow the code sequences of behaviour as do the programs that were mentioned before. But coding characteristics of the video (or of audio) is quite possible.

Notes

1. In the definition by O'Grady et al. (1997) pragmatics is also a grammar. It might also only be considered as a specific subdiscipline in linguistics.
2. In the first two examples 'bank' is assigned to the word class 'noun,' in the third example it is assigned to the word class 'verb.' This kind of ambiguity is also known as homography (Boot, 1978: 120 ff). Linguistics can disambiguate such word meaning based on the word class. The first two examples, belonging to the word class 'noun', can not be disambiguated in this way. Such words are homophones.

   Homonyms can sometimes be disambiguated by means of context sensitive heuristics. On the syntactic level a sentence in German might start with 'Ehe er ...'. *Ehe* might refer to 'before' or to 'marriage'. As the word is followed by 'er' (he) it can not be a stop word (Krause: 1996: 86). On the semantic level one might have the sentence 'The money on the bank'. The 'money' excludes the other meanings of bank.
3. Also 'bright (boys and girls)' is allowed.
4. Speech acts and situations in which language occurs might demand that (characteristics of) people uttering these are observed. The coding of such observations can also be supported by computer. This is discussed later in the chapter.
5. An extreme example of a word that got another meaning is the Dutch word 'heer'. In the past it referred to an army, today to a gentleman. More recent is 'milieu', again a Dutch word. Formerly it referred mainly to social class, today it is mainly to the environment. A consequence of getting another meaning might even be that the word also refers to another concept, as might probably hold in the above example. More complex, but depending on the context also fitting here, is the occupation of 'computer programmer'. Today the status attached to this occupation is not that high as it was two decades ago.

   An example of a word that is replaced by another one is 'farm hand,' which is now often 'agricultural worker.'
6. The problem is partly overcome by using conditional sentences. Now the sentence 'The government should act,' becomes 'If the governments acts, then the government does well.' This way of coding is allowed in CETA. The different nuances in auxiliaries however, are not captured in this way.
7. The best match is found by dividing the word under investigation in parts of for example 3 characters and counting the proportion of parts that match with parts found in the same way from words in the dictionary. The word 'baker' is divided into '__b', '_ba', 'bak', 'ake', 'ker', 'er_', 'r__' (the underscore '_' should be read as a space). These parts are called trigrammes. In general, they are named n_grammes (Kimbrell, 1988). For an application of this method, see Popping (1997a). Other methods are to be found in Salton (1989: 426 ff) under the heading automatic spelling checkers.
8. Chen et al. (1994: 61) use a stemming algorithm, which is the reverse of suffixing. They have a dictionary containing 28,000 root-words, that can recognize about 80,000 words. Besides they have rules to stem suffixes like 'ive,' 'ion,' 'tion,' 'er,' 'ers,' 's.'

10

Conclusion

In the previous chapters, a state of the art in the field of computer-assisted text analysis has been presented, and it was indicated how the method can benefit from developments in the fields of qualitative analysis, linguistics and information retrieval. Three types of analysis have been distinguished, the thematic, the semantic, and the network text analysis approach. In the thematic approach the occurrence of concepts in text blocks is coded, in the semantic approach also the relation between concepts, and in the network approach concepts and relations are even taken together into a network. Computer-assisted thematic text analysis is already available since the 1960s, the other two types started at the end of the 1980s. In thematic and semantic text analysis texts can be coded from an instrumental point of view, i.e., from the point of view of the investigator. In all three approaches text can be coded from a representational point of view, that is, from the point of view from the sender of the text (message). The number of possibilities for the investigator has increased considerably. He or she can choose now, depending on the research question and the design of the research.

At the end of the seventies Janowitz (1969: 157) mentioned three sets of barriers that needed to be overcome:

1. organizational and administrative barriers,
2. substantive barriers, and
3. methodological and theoretical barriers.

Janowitz stated that organizational and administrative barriers are threshold factors that are not satisfactorily solved. Each computer program uses its own format. Sometimes a line has a fixed maximum length. Text blocks are separated by a separation mark or line, some programs demand such a sign at both the beginning and the end of a text block. There is no format to be used in any program. Text editors make it very easy to obtain a text corpus in the correct format.[1]

The substantive barriers concern the time span covered by the data. Data should be gathered covering a long historical period for a particular source or for particular media. I agree with Janowitz, but this barrier can not be solved by any method or computer program.

The third point concerns the methodological and theoretical barriers. The greatest methodological improvement is in my view the attention for the representational view on coding. This includes more than only coding latent meaning, it implies that in the coding the meaning is represented by what the sender of the coded message had in mind.

The semantic and network approach to text analysis allow a better connection to theory than the thematic approach. Co-occurrence of two concepts in the thematic approach is explained as a relation between these concepts. Now the relation is no longer assumed, but specified. It is known between which concepts the relation exists and what this relation looks like. The network approach also informs how a concept in a text block is valenced based on its relation to other concepts.

Janowitz also has mentioned the fusion of text analysis with other methodologies. It is coming. We saw it in the study by Savaiano and Schrodt (1997) on environmental change and conflict in Ethiopia. These investigators found their data in texts, but also in annual reports of organizations. In his oration Kleinnijenhuis (1998) compares the way companies and institutions (big firms, the police, the agricultural sector) are judged on a number of relevant aspects in public opinion polls, and in the media. The judgements show the same direction, but are not running parallel.

This project by Kleinnijenhuis also points to another shift. Topics are studied from a scientific point of view, but are also useful for organizations and institutions. Where possible, the results Kleinnijenhuis found, can be used by the companies and institutions he investigated to turn to the better.[2] Kabanoff (1996) and Kabanoff and Holt (1996) also operate on the point of intersection between science and company. They investigated organizational value structures. They did so by looking for the occurrence of specific concept categories in annual reports, internal magazines and mission statements of companies. Based in the results, four theoretically derived value types could be recognized. Just as in the previous example, these results can be used by the companies that participated in the study, e.g., to change the internal culture. This shows that results of text analysis can well be used for practical purposes without being performed with that intention.

The coding process in the semantic and network approach to text analysis is complicated and time consuming. A computer program guides the coder through all steps. If this coding were to be performed manually, far more time would be needed to write down the results. Organizational confusion would also contribute to this. Take for example the following sentence taken from the article FREE DEMOCRATS OBJECT TO TREATY VENUE in the on-line version of the newspaper Népszabadság of September 10 1996:

'Matyas Eorsi, chairman of Parliament's foreign affairs committee, told Népszabadság Monday that the Alliance of Free Democrats supports the basic treaty with Romania, but does not agree that it should be signed in Timisoara, as it is of purely symbolic significance.'

Using PLCA, this sentence is coded as:

To THE NEWSPAPER HUNGARY's POLITICIAN said, "
HUNGARY's TREATY is of some value,
more negatively however I RECOGNIZE/BELIEVE that
[
HUNGARY's TREATY is obligated not to be ACTED toward,
because ACTING toward HUNGARY's TREATY is consequentially ineffective
]
.

"

This sentence contains four clauses, two of which start as a conjunction (the part with 'more negatively however,' and the one following 'because'), and one as a proxy (starting with 'that').

Although the semantic or the network approaches are promising, investigators using these approaches might still run into problems for which no clear answer is available yet. The meaning types for relations available today need a more theoretical foundation. The meaning types implemented in CETA and the types described by Rahmstorf (1983) have to be combined and elaborated. In this investigation one might also investigate which types can be used in a path-algebra. Here however, it is also necessary to investigate what information is kept, left, and obtained when such path-algebra is applied.

More practical is the issue that knowledge is needed on how to code sentences. Sentences as they appear in a text might be different from the way in which they are coded in a S–V–O statement. Assume the sentence:

'Pete has the impression that John is not performing his task properly.'
The sentence might be coded in at least three ways:

1. 'Pete / is not performing his task properly / John.'
2. 'Pete: John / is not performing his task properly.'
3. 'Pete: Johns performance / is not adequate.'

The first sentence contains a clear S–V–O relation. In the coding the sentences (2) and (3) contain a speaker. These sentences do not contain an object. In CETA an object would be coded however, the Ideal. In PLCA the sentence indicates a judgement, and therefore will not have an object. In (2) it is John who is judged, in (3) it is the performance that is judged. This performance is preceded by a modifier, here John. This way of coding is followed in PLCA.

Agreement is necessary with respect to the way in which sentences like this one are coded. Some restrictions might be caused by the computer program [CETA can not handle (3)], but even then alternative codings are possible. De Ridder (1994: 103) indicates that view (2) [as he refers to CETA, he does not mention view (3)] is only allowed when no other sentences are available in which Pete is paraphrased with sayings about John.[3]

A speaker should only be used in case there is a distinct person, group, or institution that can be pointed to and that is reliable. Often a speaker is used to give authority to the sentence, e.g., 'a reliable person told us ..' or 'a well-informed source said ..'. This source is not a distinct speaker, and therefore should not be included in the coded sentence.

More questions need to be answered. SKI, linking, bundling, they all seem to offer a valuable contribution to research. Nevertheless, research is necessary to find out what exactly they contribute. What would be the difference in results if I would for example apply and not apply SKI? Linking and bundling provoke that networks look simpler, but at which prize was this result reached? In semantic text analysis relations are investigated, between these relations no association is assumed. The presentation of results of a network analysis is for a considerable part also in terms of relations. Statistics have been developed that accept an association between such relations.

Text analysis can benefit from achievements in qualitative research in the phase of development on concept categories. In linguistics many developments have started which help overcoming ambiguity in some way. When these developments have resulted in clear (computerized) tools, they should be adapted by text analysts.

The book contains an overview of approaches to be followed by investigators who want to perform a computer-assisted text analysis that results in a data matrix suited for statistical inference. Several choices are available. Before the choice can be made the investigator has to know what he or she wants to investigate. First the design of the study has to be available. The program to be used follows from the design. In the design phase it might be helpful however, to know which types of analysis can be performed in computer-assisted text analysis. In discussion groups on the Internet people sometimes start with the question which computer program to use, this should not happen.

Availability of sources

Many programs discussed in this text, demand texts on a computer file as input. This should be an ASCII or ANSI-text, a text that contains only standard characters.

Texts are found on paper as documents. Various types of documents exist, like for example public records, newspaper or journal articles, transcripts of broadcastings or films, abstracts, interviews, and scripts. These can be transmitted into electronic form by using scanners and computer programs for optical character recognition or OCR. During scanning an image of the original text is created in the computer memory or on disk. OCR extracts text from the text image. In this way it is quite easy to make texts available for analysis.[4] Many texts, especially newspapers, are also available on micro-film. Such texts can also be transmitted into electronic form.[5]

Although, lots of texts are already available in this electronic form. More and more newspapers, for example, are also published on CD-rom. This occurs afterwards. Several newspapers have also editions that appear on the Internet. One has access to copies of that day, but also to previous issues. The electronic version of the newspaper, however, is different from the real paper version. Pages and columns do not exist any more. Articles must often be selected from an index. The real paper version contains more articles than the electronic version. In the electronic version the background providing articles and editorials is often lacking.

The newspaper articles consist of headline information and text body. Depending on the kind of data that is used, the investigator can use both sources, but also choose only one of the two. In general this will be the headline information. This information also includes facts like the name of the newspaper and the date. For more details, see Hansen (1995). Most papers are available from around 1995. This holds for example for the British *Guardian* (HTTP//:WWW.GUARDIAN.CO.UK). I found articles from the *San Diego Daily* (HTTP//:WWW.SDDT.COM) starting in November 1994, and the *Boston Globe* (HTTP://WWW/GLOBE.COM) even goes back to 1979. Also newspapers that do not appear in the English language sometimes have an electronic version in English. The Hungarian paper *Népszabadság* (HTTP://WWW.NEPSZABADSAG.HU) has each day about three main articles in English from September 1996 on.[6]

One does not only find newspapers on the Internet, but also information from other sources. There are electronic magazines and journals. But there are also (commercial) on-line information providers like Lexis-Nexis (HTTP://WWW.LEXIS-NEXIS.COM) presenting legal, news and business facts from official institutions, or more specific US News & World Report (HTTP://WWW.USNEWS.COM). These providers sometimes are the on-line archival source for newspapers (e.g., Lexis-Nexis is for *The New York Times*). Many official and commercial institutions have put information on the net. Some official institutions are: the Library of Congress (HTTP://MARVELL.LOC.GOV/HOMEPAGE/LCHP.HTML), the Dutch government (HTTP://WWW.NIC.SURFNET.NL/NLMENU/OVERHEID.HTML), National Science Foundation (HTTP://WWW.NSF.GOV).

The references above just serve to illustrate that many sources providing data that can be used in a text analysis study are easily made available.

Soothill and Grover (1997) report on computer searches of newspapers. They mention the advantage of speed. On the other hand they explain that investigators have to recognize that some data will be lost. One might find so called 'false positives', these are text blocks identified by the computer search that are not relevant to the study that is performed. These text blocks are easily eliminated. 'False negatives', however, are pernicious. These are text blocks that are not found during the search, but that are relevant for the study. If no control is performed, the investigator will not be aware of these text blocks. These false negatives usually occur because the investigator did not identify the appropriate key words for searching, perhaps because the meaning of words change over time. Soothill and Grover illustrate this by referring to the changes in use of the term 'rape' between 1951 and 1971. Around 1951 other words were used, like 'carnal knowledge,' 'serious sexual offence,' or 'sexual defilement.'

Other problems that Soothill and Grover mention concern pictures and spatial configurations. A picture, photo or drawing accompanying a text block could not be copied at the time of their study. As technology increases this becomes possible. In my view the problem of the spatial configuration is no longer relevant. Computer output of text alone often fails to highlight the impact of a news story. The output does not indicate where and how the story has appeared in the original newspaper. A final point Soothill and Grover mention is that one will not have the newspaper in their own hands, the investigator will not know how the newspaper looks and smells.

Notes

1. An authority should decide that a text block starts for example with a dollar-sign ($) on a separate line (many programs already have this requirement; the sign might be followed by some text to recognize the text block), and should be closed by a pond-sign (#) again on a separate line. The maximum permitted length of a line can be 255 characters (the length of a [short] string in most computer languages).
2. Of course text analysis has already for a long time been used in market research. An early example in this field is found by McDonald (1982), who allowed respondents to comment on a product. In fact he asked them to answer on open ended questions. The answers were entered into a text file, and were next classified by using the computer. In this way McDonald could get a more detailed judgement of the way the product was advertised in the media than if he would have asked the respondents.
3. A parser might code such a sentence automatically in the way that is agreed upon.
4. The quality of the converted text (appear all characters in the form they were supposed to) depends for a considerable part on the physical quality of the original text. If this quality is not sufficient, additional editing is necessary.
5. A special source is found in the transcripts of interviews. Transcription of oral speech is not yet computerized, but speech recognition becomes possible. Investigators in this field certainly would want this as it is very time consuming and therefore expensive. Lang et al. (1991: 221) report that in their investigation they needed on the average 21.3 hours to transcribe one hour taped interview. Packages for speech recognition are useful here.

   Another problem that is not sufficiently automatized yet is met in international research. Popping and Roberts (1998) have editorials in Russian, Polish, Czechian and Hungarian that have to be translated into English. The subtleties they are looking for cannot be captured by programs that can do translations today.
6. Today texts are found on the Internet. In her feasibility study De Weese (1976) referred to the high costs of computer-assisted text analysis. She stressed that cost reductions could occur with a direct copy approach to obtaining computer-readable text. This refers to optical reading, which is in the mean time rather easy to realize.

Appendix: Computer programs

This appendix mentions the computer programs that are discussed in the text. First, the advantages and disadvantages of computer use are explained.

General remarks

Mergenthaler's (1996) general model for computer-assisted text analysis can help make transparent where exactly the computer comes into play. This model starts by distinguishing a real system within which natural language is used and a formal system in which a more formal language is used. Both systems are divided into object-linguistic and meta-linguistic components. Any text that is analysed is interpreted as an object-linguistic realization within the real system. At this point computer assistance plays no role, leaving the following three-step procedural description of text analysis:

1. Translation of a text from the real system into formal sets of concept categories;
2. If the concept categories are grounded in a theory, interpretation of the formal sets of categories within that theory;
3. Evaluation and verification of the findings with the text being analysed.

By means of computer-assisted text analysis the crucial work of translation as a first step is performed by computational rules implemented as a part of the software used. The second step involves a coding procedure. Within the model this results in a further differentiation of the formal system into object-linguistic and meta-linguistic components. Thus, there will be a correspondence between text and extracted information, and theory and set of concepts system respectively. Figure A.1 depicts this more elaborate procedural description, comprising four steps:

1. Reduction of a text to selected information;
2. Translation of the information to a set of concepts system;
3. Interpretation of a set of concepts within a theory;
4. Evaluation and verification of the findings with the text being analysed.

The first two steps are for the greater part performed automatically using text analysis software, the third and fourth step are based on human skills, making use of the complex contextual environment and universe of meaning.

Table A.1   *Model of computer-assisted text analysis*

```
          Real System                      Formal System
          Natural Language                 Formal Language

                    Text                        Selected
              e.g., Transcript              Information
Object-     ----------------    Information  e.g., Vocabulary
Linguistic    Universe of       Reduction  -> ----------------
Level         Discourse                       Unit of Analysis

                    ^                               |
                    |                               |
            Evaluation                       Algorithmic
--------    Verification                     Computation
                                                    |
                                                    v
                  Results                     Quantification
Meta-       ----------------   <-Representation ----------------
Linguistic                       Reduction                     -
Level             Theory                      Set of Categories
```

Source: Adapted from Mergenthaler (1996: 7)

Advantages of computer-assisted text analysis over the traditional procedure that are listed in the literature (e.g., Heinrich, 1996: 327) include:

* Higher efficiency when large data sets are analysed;
* The possibility of replicating the results;
* Better inter-subjectivity at all steps of analysis through their explication;
* The ability to apply a standardized method to additional texts yet to be analysed.

This assumes that the conventional forms of text analysis have been enhanced. The common forms are based on counting words or phrases in texts. What is new is that other forms of text analysis are now also possible. In these forms relations between concepts are emphasized. This implies attention to the meanings contained within texts.

Given the distinctions discussed computer programs can be classified on two dimensions. One refers to the kind of approach: thematic, semantic, network, or other. The other dimension refers to the way of coding: instrumental or representational. This results in the overview of computer programs in Table A.2.

Table A.2   *Computer programs for text analysis*

	instrumental	representational
thematic	Catpac Genca Intext MCCA Micro OCP Swift Textpack TextSmart VBPro WordStat	CDC-EZ Text FindVerb FlexText Text Base Alpha
semantic	Gottschalk KEDS	PC-ACE Pertex PLCA
network		CETA MECA

Several of the programs mentioned are not designed for the quantitative text analysis resulting in a data matrix to which statistical inferences can be applied. They are programs for qualitative research that allow downloading a data matrix.[1] Although some programs receive more attention than others, I do not want to express a preference.

Information on the programs is given below. The list, however, does not only contain programs for text analysis, but also some programs that are used in analysing the data and that have been mentioned in the text. References are given in the text. The programs are listed alphabetically on name. The following information is presented about each program:

- its name (version numbers are not included as these change very often);
- a characteristic based on key words;
- a short description (not always);
- system requirements (unless noted otherwise it is assumed an MS-DOS program uses 640 kB of RAM-memory, and a Windows program uses 16 mB. Windows-programs often demand a Pentium PC. Packages are often delivered on CD-ROM;
- the vendor.

More detailed overviews of programs for qualitative analysis are Weitzman and Miles (1995), and Prein et al. (1995). All programs use Latin characters. Contact the vendor in case Cyrillic, Hebrew, Chinese, Japanese, etc. characters should be used.

Program descriptions

Agree Intercoder reliability.

This program computes variants of kappa or D2, both intercoder reliability indices for nominal data. Kappa is used when the categories are known before coding starts, therefore all coders use the same categories. D2 is used when the coders also have to develop the categories, each coder might end up with different categories. Analyses can be performed for many different research situations: (weighted) agreement between coders, based on the mean observed and null expected agreement; (weighted) agreement between several coders and a standard; simultaneous agreement between coders (agreement exists when all coders assign an observation to the same category); majority agreement between coders (agreement exists when at least k out of m coders assign an observation to the same category); (weighted) agreement in the situation where per assignment the coder is not known; simultaneous and majority agreement for the same situation; agreement per category for the above situations (except majority agreement); agreement between clusters of coders; multiple assignments per observation. It is also possible to compute the contribution of an extra coder, to select the best coder, to compare lateral distributions, and to use an agreement model.

Operating system: Windows95. Vendor: iec *Pro*GAMMA; P.O. Box 841; NL 9700 AV Groningen; the Netherlands. (Phone: +31 50 3636900. Fax: +31 50 3636687. E-mail: GAMMA.POST@GAMMA.RUG.NL. Website: HTTP://WWW.GAMMA.RUG.NL)

AQUAD Theory builder / hypotheses tester.

The program uses artificial intelligence techniques (Huber and Marcello Garcia, 1991).

Operating system: Windows95, WindowsNT. Vendor: Ingeborg Huber Verlag; P.O. Box 46; D 87643 Schwangau; Germany (Phone and fax: +49 8362 987073. E-mail: GUENTHER L. HUBER@T-ONLINE.DE. Website: HTTP://WWW.AQUAD.COM).

askSam Text base manager.

This is a textbase manager that handles mixtures of free-form and structured text blocks (Weitzman and Miles, 1995).

Operating system: Windows95. Vendor: askSam Systems; P.O. Box 1428; Perry, Fl 32347; USA (Phone: +1 800 8001997. Fax: +1 904 5847481. E-mail: INFO@ASKSAM.COM; Website: HTTP://WWW.ASKSAM.COM).

ATLAS/ti   Network / representational (developed for theory building).

ATLAS/ti (Archive for Technology, the Lifeworld, and Everyday Language) (Muhr, 1991; Weitzman and Miles, 1995: 217 ff) is a text-interpretation program for the purpose of theory construction based on the 'grounded theory' approach by Glaser and Strauss (1967). The program enables the integration of primary texts, text passages, codes, and memos into 'hermeneutic units.' It has hypertext functions on primary texts. The program allows the user to construct a theory based on impressions gained as the texts are explored, this theory is represented in a network. Several types of network relations (i.e., types of links or arcs) are built in, and user-defined relations are also possible. ATLAS also allows the examination of users' various interpretations of the text under analysis. Users' memos can be embedded in the text, and then contrasted according to these users' strategies of text interpretation via clustering in families. Although the program has greatest utility for qualitative text analysis, it can download a data matrix in which cells indicate the occurrence or non-occurrence of user-defined codes for each text block (or quotation).

Operating system: Windows95, WindowsNT. Vendor: SCOLARI, Sage Publications Ltd, 6 Bonhill Street, London, EC2A 4PU, UK (Phone: +44 171 3301222. Fax: +44 171 3748741. E-mail: SCOLARI@SAGEPUB.CO.UK. Website: HTTP://WWW.SAGEPUB.CO.UK/SCOLARI/ATLAS.HTML). Information: E-mail: INFOLINE@ATLASTI.DE. Website: HTTP://WWW.ATLASTI.DE.

CAIR   Thematic / representational.

The program CAIR (Content Analysis in Interactive Regime) is a system for classifying answers to open-ended questions. An answer might consist of a number of sayings. This occurs for questions like: 'Give three arguments for ...'. The program can handle the answers to several different questions.

The programs can generate frequency distributions and some cross-tabulations. It is possible to have a data matrix downloaded containing the names of the concepts used as assigned to each of the questions.

Operating system: MS-DOS. Vendor: Galina Saganenko, Institute of Sociology, Russian Academy of Sciences. 7-th Krasnoarmeiskaya 25/14 198052 St. Petersburg, Russia (Phone: +7 812 3162496. Fax: +7 812 3162929. E-mail: INSO@EGO.SPB.SU).

Catpac   Thematic / instrumental.

Part of the program Catpac are the facilities to perform cluster analyses based on words, and to generate perceptual maps. In these maps word relations are displayed pictorially. Words that are highly associated with each other appear close to each other in the map, while words that are less tightly connected appear further apart. Most importantly, relationships displayed in the map reflect patterns of association identified by the program.

Operating system: Windows95, WindowsNT. Vendor: Terra Research and Computing, Birmingham MI. (Phone: +1 248 258 9657. Fax: +1 248 258 9668. Website: HTTP://WWW.TERRARESEARCH.COM/CATPAC.HTML).

CDC EZ-Text Thematic / representational.

This is a program developed to assist researchers create, manage, and analyse semi-structured qualitative data bases. Investigators have to design a series of data entry templates tailored to their questionnaire. These questionnaires are administered during interviews with a sample of respondents. A response to a question may be entered into the program either as a verbatim transcript or a summary generated from the interviewer's notes. Data from respondents can be typed directly into the templates or copied from word processor documents. The program does not use standard dictionaries, categories have to be entered for all variables by the investigator. The program allows that data are coded by two coders and that the agreement between these coders is computed. A data matrix can be downloaded. This matrix can be imported later into spreadsheet or statistical software for further analysis.

Operating system: Windows95. Vendor: Centers for Disease Control and Prevention; 1600 Clifton Rd., NE; Atlanta, GA 30333; USA (Phone: +1 404 639 3311. Website: HTTP://WWW.CDC.GOV/NCHSTP/HIV_AIDS/SOFTWARE/EZ-TEXT.HTM).

CETA Network / representational.

CETA (Computer-guided Evaluative Text Analysis) (Van Cuilenburg, et al., 1986) has roots in evaluative assertion analysis by Osgood, et al. (1956). The program allows the user to parse text interactively, and to derive from already-encoded nuclear sentences (subject-verb-object triplets), additional nuclear sentences that are not explicitly stated, but are logically implied by the text. Nuclear sentences can also be encoded according to the positive or negative evaluative meanings connoted by their verbs. After nuclear sentences are encoded, data can be generated on interconnections among meaning objects within a network of interrelationships – a network that consists of nodes (meaning objects) and links (connections). The program can download a data matrix (and SPSS setup) with cells containing a variety of measures related to the links between pairs of meaning objects within a network. The ultimate goal is to make comparisons among networks for the purpose of revealing fundamental differences in the underlying structures of various texts. The program is tailored for comparing propositional content among texts sampled from distinct social contexts.

Operating system: MS-DOS. Vendor: iec *Pro*GAMMA; P.O. Box 841; NL 9700 AV Groningen; the Netherlands (Phone: +31 50 3636900. Fax: +31 50 3636687. E-mail: GAMMA.POST@GAMMA.RUG.NL. Website: HTTP://WWW.GAMMA.RUG.NL).

Code-A-Text Theory builder.

This is a package designed to facilitate the analysis of dialogs (Cartwright, 1998). It makes possible the availability of analysis of text, sound or video. The program makes available several quantitative and qualitative methods.

Operating system: Windows95. Vendor: SCOLARI, Sage Publications Ltd, 6 Bonhill Street, London, EC2A 4PU, UK (Phone: +44 171 3301222. Fax: +44 171 3748741. E-mail: SCOLARI@SAGEPUB.CO.UK. Website: HTTP://WWW.SAGEPUB.CO.UK/SCOLARI/ATLAS.HTML). Information: Website: HTTP://WWW.CODEATEXT.U-NET.COM.

Diction Thematic / instrumental.

This program is developed for analysing language. It determines the tone of a verbal message. For this purpose it uses a dictionary that indicates five general features:

- Certainty   Speech indicating resoluteness, inflexibility, and completeness;
- Activity   Speech featuring movement, change, implementation of ideas and avoidance of inertia;
- Optimism   Speech endorsing some person, group, concept or event;
- Realism   Speech describing tangible, immediate, recognizable matters that affect people's everyday lives;
- Commonality   Speech highlighting the agreed-upon values of a group and rejecting idiosyncratic modes of engagement.

More details on the types of analysis the program is designed for are presented in Hart (1984).

Operating system: Windows95. Vendor: SCOLARI, Sage Publications Ltd, 6 Bonhill Street, London, EC2A 4PU, UK (Phone: +44 171 3301222. Fax: +44 171 3748741. E-mail: SCOLARI@SAGEPUB.CO.UK. Website: HTTP://WWW.SAGEPUB.CO.UK/SCOLARI/DICTION.HTML).

The Ethnograph Code and retrieve program.

The program is especially suited for investigators working in the tradition of ethnography and interpretative sociology (Weitzman and Miles, 1995: 191 ff).

Operating system: Windows95. Vendor: SCOLARI, Sage Publications Ltd, 6 Bonhill Street, London, EC2A 4PU, UK (Phone: +44 171 3301222. Fax: +44 171 3748741. E-mail: SCOLARI@SAGEPUB.CO.UK. Website: HTTP://WWW.SAGEPUB.CO.UK/SCOLARI/ETHNOGRAPH.HTML). Information: E-mail: QUALIS@QUALISRESEARCH.COM. Website: HTTP://WWW.QUALISRESEARCH.COM.

FindVerb Thematic / representational.

Findverb uses a dictionary that allows the user to locate the frequency of occurrence of (families of) auxiliary verbs in text blocks. The program downloads the matrix containing these frequencies.

Operating system: Windows95. Vendor: Roel Popping (E-mail: R.POPPING@PPSW.RUG.NL).

FlexText Thematic / representational.

This program was written initially for the content analysis of open-ended responses to interview questions (Baker, 1992). Redundant words can be excluded by using a trivial word list. The investigator defines and labels themes (or concepts) interactively by tagging and classifying multiple word/phrase occurrences from within concordance (or key-word-in-context) windows. Concordances can be constructed (and, thus, data can be encoded) either while perusing individual text-blocks, or while scanning a list of word-frequencies. For any displayed concordance, the user can obtain additional contextual information immediately by accessing the entire text in which it appeared. The program downloads a data matrix, and an SPSS set up for this matrix. The cells in the data matrix contain within-text-block frequencies of concept occurrences.

FlexText can use a trivial word list. This is a list containing words which are not to be included in phrase matching. When the articles 'the' and 'a' are included in the trivial word list the phrases 'playing a game' and 'playing the game' are considered as matches. The list must be specified before a project starts, and it cannot be modified. Words that appear in the trivial word lists cannot be used by themselves to generate concordances.

The program also allows that the first part of a word is fixed, but the remaining part is not, just like with the wild card. The investigator can set the match length, i.e., the part that is fixed. Say the match length is 5, now the words 'computer', 'computing', 'computation' are all considered to match. The length 0 indicates that words only match if they are identical.

Operating system: MS-DOS.[2] Vendor: Albert L. Baker; 2325 Van Buren Avenue; Ames, IA 50010; USA.

GENCA (General Content Analyzer) Thematic / instrumental.

The program GENCA (General Content Analyzer) (Danielson and Lasorsa, 1997) allows researchers to build a dictionary in which thematic constructs are defined in terms of words and phrases that are searched for in text. For example, occurrences of the concept, 'gender', might be identified by searching text for male words (he, his, son, father, boy, man, etc.) or female words (she, her, daughter, mother, girl, woman, etc.). The program outputs a summary of occurrences for each dictionary term employed, and for occurrence totals (expressed as raw frequencies of occurrences, and as percentages of total words in the text). If multiple dictionaries are employed in the analysis of a single text, the program outputs a 'decision' on which dictionary captures the text's dominant domain of discourse.

Operating system: MS-DOS and MACINTOSH. Vendor: Wayne Danielson; 10407 Skyflower Drive; Austin, TX 78759; USA.

General Inquirer III Thematic / instrumental.

The General Inquirer is one of the oldest systems for text analysis (Anonymous, 1989). It consists of a collection of interdependent batch-oriented programs. The program is able to distinguish among the various senses of homographs, or words with more than one meaning. Texts' words are classified into content concepts according to the list of words-within-concepts in its dictionary. This is achieved in two steps. First, a classification program checks each word against the dictionary, and if found determines if the word should be disambiguated. To do so, *disambiguation* rules are applied and the sense of the word determined. These rules are stored in the dictionary. Next, the disambiguated word-senses are assigned to one or more concepts as specified in the text analysis dictionary. The system produces a file of the frequency of occurrences within each of the dictionary's concepts, and a file of the sequence of occurrences of coded items. Stone et al. (1966) contains many details about the General Inquirer.

Operating system: mainframe IBM. Vendor: ZUMA (Zentrum für Umfragen, Methoden und Analysen); P.O. Box 122155; D 68072 Mannheim; Germany (E-mail: ZUELL@ZUMA-MANNHEIM.DE).

Gottschalk-Gleser Content Analysis Computerized Scoring System Semantic / instrumental.

The goal of this program is to quantify the quality and intensity of writers' and speakers' psychological states (anxiety, hostility, cognitive impairment, etc.) as made manifest in their clauses or sentences (Gottschalk and Bechtel, 1993). The program uses a parser for mapping a subset of English. Each clause is assigned a weight on the basis of its verb (or action) and the noun-phrases that function as initiators and recipients of this action. These weights are then combined into text-block-specific scores that measure the psychological states of each text/transcript's source (i.e., its author or speaker). The program generates a data matrix with each of these source's scores on the scales selected. The program can also provide data on word frequencies, on occurrences of the various psychological-state-relatedphrases, on average scores across text-blocks, and on the extent to which sample scores deviate from the norms for each scale.

Operating system: MS-DOS (15 MB disk space); Windows 3.11 (8 MB memory, 20 MB disk space). Vendor: Those who are interested in using the program can contact Louis Gottschalk, Department of Psychiatry and Human Behavior, College of Medicine; University of California, Irvine, CA 92717, USA.

GRADAP Program for network analysis.

Gradap allows one to enter network data and to perform computations on these data.

Operating system: MS-DOS. Vendor: iec *Pro*GAMMA; P.O. Box 841; NL 9700 AV Groningen; the Netherlands. (Phone: +31 50 3636900. Fax: +31 50 3636687. E-mail: GAMMA.POST@GAMMA.RUG.NL. Website: HTTP://WWW.GAMMA.RUG.NL).

HyperRESEARCH Theory builder.

The program allows coding visual images (Hesse-Biber, Dupuis and Kinder, 1991).

Operating system: Windows 3.11, Mac. Vendor: ResearchWare, Inc.; P.O. Box 1258; Randolph, MA 02368-1258; USA (Phone: +1 617 9613909. E-mail: SUPPORT@RESEARCHWARE.COM. Website: HTTP://WWW.RESEARCHWARE.COM).

InfoTrend Thematic / instrumental.

This program tries to predict public opinion from the mass media. For the description of various applications, see Fan (1988, 1997). The program runs using a dictionary defined by the investigator. The codings that are performed appear on screen. This overview gives the investigator the opportunity to alter and improve the dictionary, and perform a new analysis. This process is repeated until the investigator is satisfied with the assignments. The program downloads a data matrix of occurrences.

Operating system: Windows95, WindowsNT. Vendor: Professor David P. Fan; Department of Genetics and Cell Biology, University of Minnesota, 250 Bioscience Center, 1445 Gortner Avenue, St. Paul, MN 55108-1095, USA (Phone: +1 612 6244718, Fax: +1 612 6244718; E-mail: DFAN@EMAIL.LABMED.UMN.EDU).

Intext Thematic / instrumental.

Using a language-independent dictionary of thematic constructs and a set of text-blocks – both specified by the user in advance – the program Intext (Klein, 1992, 1993) counts the frequency of occurrences of these constructs within each block of text. A search entry in the dictionary can be a word (or word-part), a word-sequence, or a word combination. Like the General Inquirer and Textpack, the program downloads a data matrix, but Intext also downloads an SPSS set up for this matrix, and allows the user to execute SPSS from inside the program. The program indexes texts in various ways conducive to qualitative text analysis. The program contains an interactive coding reliability coefficient, and several indices for readability. The program allocates files for ambiguous, negated search entries and uncoded text units.

In my opinion Intext was written to compensate for limitations in Textpack. Although the program has a menu-structure, its routines are as batch-oriented as those in Textpack. Version 3.0 of the program has more interactive facilities, however. This version contains an option in which the program informs the user every time a match with a specific search entry is found in a unit of analysis, and queries the user whether or not it should be coded as an occurrence of the corresponding concept. During the query, a concordance in which the search entry appears is shown on the screen. The user can indicate that the proposed concept is the correct one, or can choose another concept.

Operating system: MS-DOS, Window versions tailored to different processors. Vendor: Social Science Consulting; Königseer Str. 9; D 98708 Gehren; Germany (Phone/Fax: +49 36783 80284. E-mail: INTEXT@GMX.DE. Website: HTTP:\\WWW.INTEXT.DE).

KEDS Semantic / instrumental.

KEDS (Kansas Events Data System) is a system for coding of international event data based on pattern recognition among subject-verb-object triplets (Schrodt, 1993). The program is primarily designed to work with short news articles. The program contains a simple parser, and employs a knowledge base of verb patterns to determine the appropriate event code. The program downloads subject-verb-object relations ordered on a time-scale. A more extended discussion of the program is in Chapter 5.

Operating system: Macintosh, with at least 2 MB memory. Vendor: Philip A. Schrodt; Department of Political Science; University of Kansas; Blake Hall; Lawrence, KS 66045; USA.

Kwalitan Thematic / representational (developed for code and retrieve activities).

Not designed for inferential text analysis, the program (Weitzman and Miles, 1995) was written to perform qualitative interpretive analysis according to Glaser and Strauss's (1967) 'grounded theory approach.' The program allows the user to split texts into 'scenes' that are differentiated in terms of codes or key-words. During execution the program provides data on codes currently attached to the scenes, together with the frequencies of codes within scenes. Scenes can be called up on screen based on a code (or combination of codes) attached to them. Logical operators are available to generate search profiles. During analysis, codes can be combined or subdivided. The program can download a data matrix of within-scene occurrences of the codes.

Operating system: MS-DOS. Vendor: iec *Pro*GAMMA; P.O. Box 841; NL 9700 AV Groningen; the Netherlands (Phone: +31 50 3636900. Fax: +31 50 3636687. E-mail: GAMMA.POST@GAMMA.RUG.NL. Website: HTTP://WWW.GAMMA.RUG.NL).

MCCA (Minnesota Contextual Content Analysis) Thematic / instrumental.

MCCA (Minnesota Contextual Content Analysis) uses verbatim transcriptions of text (McTavish and Pirro, 1990). No special spacing or pre-coding is necessary. Output consists of two sets of normed scores: context scores (C-scores – indicators of relative focus on traditional, practical, emotional, and analytic social contexts), and idea emphasis scores (E-scores – indicators of relative emphasis on idea concepts). C-scores range from -25 to $+25$, reflecting under or over emphasis compared with general English usage. The program uses a dictionary in which a large number of idea concepts are captured.[3] The relative emphasis on each idea concept is captured in the E-score, which varies from a large negative score (when an idea is censored or under-emphasized in a text in comparison to usual English usage), to a larger positive score depending on how strongly the idea is emphasized in a text. Norming E- and C-scores on expected usage of various concepts proves to be quite helpful by providing a framework to coder relative emphasis on different meanings. It also permits an examination of ideas that are relatively under-used, censored or missing from a text.

In MCCA two distance matrices are provided. One is distance between texts in terms of the four context scores (institutional framing), and the other is a distance between texts in terms of differences in the profile of emphasis across all e-score concepts. These can be examined by a multidimensional scaling or cluster analysis procedure for analysis of the relationship between texts.

These are displayed in various ways (e.g., cluster plots). The program generates a data matrix of idea emphasis scores for each text-block. Also provided are data on specific words' contributions to idea emphasis.

Operating system: MAINFRAME CYBER. The MCCA-PC-version is available as an option in the DIMAP (DIctionary MAintenance Programs) dictionary development software. Vendor (PC-version): Ken Litkowski (DIMAP) (Phone: +1 301 9265904; Website: HTTP://WWW.CLRES.COM). For the main frame version contact Don McTavish; P.O. Box 120695; New Brighton, MN 55112; USA.

MECA (Map Extraction, Comparison, and Analysis) Network / representational.

MECA is a set of programs to analyse the 'cognitive maps' of individuals or groups (Carley and Palmquist, 1992). Relations among themes (or concepts) are assumed to represent mental models or cognitive maps that reside in individuals' minds. The program facilitates the parsing of text into statements (i.e., into subject-verb-object triplets with verb-valence modifier), and the assignment of words and phrases to concepts. The user begins by identifying and encoding concepts and the types of relationships that exist between pairs of concepts. Once encoded, data can be displayed graphically as clusters of partially interlinked concept-nodes. These displays can be of unions (knowledge shared among groups) or intersections (knowledge on which consensus exists between groups) of statements among groups of individuals. The program is particularly useful for doing text analysis research on group consensus and dissent. For a detailed discussion, see Chapter 6.

Part of MECA is *Cmatrix2*, a program for instrumental thematic analysis. This program starts with texts and a list of concepts (here words that might occur in the texts and are of interest for the investigator) and downloads a data matrix based on occurrence or frequency.

Operating system: MS-DOS, MACINTOSH, UNIX. Vendor: Kathleen Carley; Department of Social and Decision Sciences; Carnegie Mellon University; Pittsburgh, PA 15568; USA (Phone: +1 412 2683225. Fax: +1 412 2686938. E-mail: CARLEY+@ANDREW.CMU.EDU).

Micro OCP Thematic / instrumental.

This is the version of the Oxford Concordance Program for personal computer (Hockey and Martin, 1987). The program is batch-oriented, and produces word lists, and concordances (i.e., key-word-in-context output) in a variety of languages and alphabets.

Operating system: MS-DOS. Vendor: Oxford Electronic Publishing; Oxford University Press; Walton Street; Oxford OX2 6DP; UK (Phone: +44 1865-267979. Fax: +44 1865-267990. E-mail: ep.help@oup.co.uk. Website: HTTP://INFO.OX.AC.UK/CTITEXT/RESGUIDE/RESOURCES/O125.HTML).

NUD•IST (Non numerical Unstructured Data Indexing Searching and Theorizing) Theory builder.

Comparable to Atlas\ti (Richards and Richards, 1994). Concepts, however, are not related in a network structure, but in a hierarchical structure.

Operating system: Windows, MacOs. Vendor: SCOLARI, Sage Publications Ltd, 6 Bonhill Street, London, EC2A 4PU, UK (Phone: +44 171 3301222. Fax: +44 171 3748741. E-mail: SCOLARI@SAGEPUB.CO.UK. Website: HTTP://WWW.SAGEPUB.CO.UK/SCOLARI/QSR.HTML). Information: Website: HTTP://WWW.QSR.COM.AU/NUDIST-SOFTWARE.HTML.

PC-ACE Semantic / representational.

PC-ACE (Program for Computer Assisted Coding of Events) is a data entry program based on semantic grammar for historical events (Franzosi, 1990). The grammar organizes textual data around an actor-action-object (with numerous modifiers) relational structure. The program combines a front-end program with a relational data base management system. The data base can produce a data matrix on occurrences of relations among actors, actions, etc. within each event under study.

Operating system: MS-DOS. Vendor: Roberto Franzosi; University of Oxford, Department of Applied Social Studies and Social Research; Barnett House;

Wellington Square; Oxford OX1 2ER; UK (Phone +44 1865 270325. Fax: +44 1865 270324).

Pertex Semantic / representational.
This is a program for 'perspective text analysis'. The program detects structural relations in texts via cluster analysis. For details, see Chapter 5.
Operating system: MS-DOS. Vendor: Bernard Bierschenk; Cognitive Science Research; Lund University; PO Box 7080; S-220 07 Lund; Sweden.

PLCA Semantic / representational.
Linguistic content analysis (LCA) (Roberts, 1989) yields data and inferences about the intended (as opposed to the more ambiguous surface-grammatical) relations among words in various socio-temporal contexts. Subject-verb-object (and modifiers) relations are encoded according to an unambiguous semantic grammar appropriate to one of four types of intention. Once encoded, the program reconstructs sentences on screen by 'translating' their encoded form into a sentence that the user can verify for coding accuracy. The program can download a data matrix (and SPSS setup) that provides subject-verb-object relations in each clause, along with an indicator of which of the four types of intention the relation reflects (plus data on valence, tense, modal auxiliary verb, subordination, question type, speaker, audience, and so on). LCA data can be used to make inferences about the conditions under which authors of texts intend to communicate specific meanings to their audiences. The technique is useful for comparing strategies of communication in different socio-historical settings and for measuring shifts in public opinion. The objective is to estimate the probability that specific classes of statements occur.
Operating system: MS-DOS.[4] Vendor: iec *Pro*GAMMA; P.O. Box 841; NL 9700 AV Groningen; the Netherlands (Phone: +31 50 3636900. Fax: +31 50 3636687. E-mail: GAMMA.POST@GAMMA.RUG.NL. Website: HTTP://WWW.GAMMA.RUG.NL).

Protan Thematic / instrumental.
PROTAN is tuned to two tasks (Hogenraad et al., 1995). In the first one, the program addresses the question of how do texts look like: how abstract are they, what is the profile of the main affective connotations of the texts? The second task is to answer the question of what texts are talking about. The way to find the main themes in texts is based on the postulate that there is enough information in the relations between words to allow for themes to emerge by simply analysing these relations.
Operating system: MS-DOS, MacOS, Unix. Vendor: Robert Hogenraad; Psychology Department, Catholic University of Louvain; 10 place du Cardinal

Mercier; B-1348 Louvain-la-Neuve; Belgium (Phone: +32 10 474411. Fax: +32 10 473774; E-mail: HOGENRAAD@UPSO.UCL.AC.BE. Website: HTTP://WWW.PSP.UCL.AC.BE/~UPSO/PROTAN/PROTANAE.HTML).

Swift Thematic / instrumental.

SWIFT (Structured Word Identification and Frequency Table) is a simple interactive, key word-based program for analysing short texts. The program uses a dictionary, and presents a hierarchical outline of the relative frequency of occurrence of specified themes. Frequency data can be displayed on a 'per record' or 'per hit' basis, and multiple occurrences in a single record can be allowed or disallowed. Each sampling unit of text resides in a separate file. Frequencies are not output as a data matrix that can immediately be used available for statistical computing.

Operating system: MS-DOS. Vendor: Ronald B. Heady (E-mail: HEADY@USL.EDU. Website: HTTP://SUZE.UCS.USL.EDU/~RBH8900/SWIFT.HTML).

TACT (Text Analysis Computing Tools) Text base manager, especially for text-retrieval and analysis on literary works (Schutt, 1992; Hawthorne, 1994).

Operating system: MS-DOS. Vendor: Modern Language Association, Customer Services. 10 Astor Place, New York, NY 10003-6981 (phone: +1 212 614-6382, fax: +1 212 477-9863 or +1 212 533-0680). Information: Website: HTTP://WWW.EPAS.UTORONTO.CA:8080/CCH/TACT.HTML.

Text Base Alpha Thematic / representational.

This program was developed for interviews, but can handle any kind of qualitative data (Tesch, 1990). The coding of data is performed directly on the screen. The user is enabled to specify the exact beginning and end of code segments. Codes can be added and deleted during the coding process. The program can perform frequency counts, but it also allows to construct a data matrix which can be used for numeric analysis. This matrix contains frequencies of occurrences of codes.

Operating system: MS-DOS. Vendor: Bo Sommerlund, Arhus University, Arhus, DK (Phone: +45 8942 4983. E-mail: BOS@PSY.AAU.DK. Website: HTTP://WWW.PSY.AAU.DK/BOS).

TextPack Thematic / instrumental.

TextPack (Text package) is a collection of interdependent programs designed to perform frequency counts of words, Key Word In Context lists, Key Word Out of Context lists, comparison of vocabularies, cross-references, procedures for iterative dictionary construction, etc. (Mohler and Züll, 1995). It runs on a personal computer. The program produces a file of the frequency of each code in the dictionary and a file of the sequence of occurrence of coded items in the source text. The programs are batch-oriented, reflecting their earlier development on main-frame computers. Because of this it is criticized heavily (Olsen, 1989: 160). Although Textpack was intended to be a successor to the General Inquirer, it cannot do many things that the Inquirer does. In particular, it does not handle many of the Inquirer's dictionaries, especially those using disambiguation.

Coding is performed by the procedure TagCoder. Words, word roots, and phrases are coded out of context. If texts contain ambiguous words, these words must be manually disambiguated before the analysis starts. Mohler and Züll (1995: 11) suggest using a word processor to append numbers, for example 'spring#1', 'spring#2'. This requires modifying not only the text file, but also the dictionary. The General Inquirer automates such disambiguation.

Operating system: MS-DOS. Vendor: ZUMA (Zentrum für Umfragen, Methoden und Analysen); P.O. Box 122155; D 68072 Mannheim; Germany (E-mail: TEXTPACK@ZUMA-MANNHEIM.DE. Website: HTTP://WWW.ZUMA-MANNHEIM.DE/SOFTWARE/EN/TEXTPACK.HTM).

TextSmart Thematic / representational.

TextSmart is a program for analysing answers to open-ended questions. The program allows the use of a trivial word list, the user has to create a dictionary. The program downloads a data matrix based on frequency of occurrence.

Operating system: Windows95. Vendor: SPSS, Inc. (Website: HTTP://WWW.SPSS.COM/SOFTWARE/TEXTSMART/).

VBPro Thematic / instrumental.

The program VBPro (Miller, 1993) has a menu structure and is batch-oriented. The investigator constructs a general dictionary. It is possible to download a data matrix containing occurrence versus non-occurrence, or frequency of occurrences. Like Intext this program can produce a list containing word counts. Here too different types of search entries are allowed. The program does not use a file containing trivial words.

Operating system: MS-DOS. Vendor: M. Mark Miller; 330 Communications Building; University of Tennessee; Knoxville, TN 37996 USA (Phone: +1 615 9744452; E-mail: MMMILLER@UTKVX.UTK.EDU; Website: HTTP://EXCELLENT.COM.UTK.EDU/~MMMILLER/VBPRO.HTML.

WinMAX Code and retrieve program.

The program allows hierarchical relations between concepts (Kuckartz, 1997).

Operating system: Windows95. Vendor: SCOLARI, Sage Publications Ltd, 6 Bonhill Street, London, EC2A 4PU, UK (Phone: +44 171 3301222. Fax: +44 171 3748741. E-mail: SCOLARI@SAGEPUB.CO.UK. Website: HTTP://WWW.SAGEPUB.CO.UK/SCOLARI/WINMAX.HTML). Information: E-mail: WINMAX@CSI.COM. Website: HTTP://WINMAX.DE/FRAMEE.HTM).

WordStat Thematic / instrumental.

The program uses a dictionary and a trivial word list. Data are stored in a file having dBase format. This file can be entered into a program for statistical computations.

Operating system: Windows95. Vendor: Provalis Research, 2414 Bennett Street, Montreal, QC, H1V 2S4, Canada. (Phone: +1 514 8991672. Fax: +1 514 8991750. E-mail: SIMSTAT@COMPUSERVE.COM. Website: HTTP://OURWORLD.COMPUSERVE.COM/HOMEPAGES/SIMSTAT).

Purchasing a package

If you are to purchase a computer package for text analysis several questions have to be considered. Here follow some of these questions. More detailed is Fielding (1995) in his discussion of packages for qualitative analysis.

In nearly all programs it is assumed that the texts are available in a file on the computer system. This is not a system file of a text editor, but it is a ASCII or an ANSI file, i.e., a text file without any code symbols related to a text editor. The texts have to be organized in such a way that the computer program will know where a new unit starts. Some programs only recognize units of analysis, other programs allow units within units. Ask yourself what kind of units you have. Units are separated by a specific symbol. This might be a blank line, but also a specific character is used (many programs use the pond, #, sign). Be sure that you can organize your text as required by the program you will use.

Ask yourself whether you want to use wild-cards in your thematic analysis to find a word or phrase. You will probably have more hits, but are these the ones you are looking for? You need to check the coding. In some programs the coded text can appear on the screen (or in a file) as KWIC-lists. Other programs allow the examination of which codings are used, e.g., after inspection of the data matrix, but codes and text are separated.

Think about the way the dictionary is organized. In programs that follow the representational view of coding, you need to get access to the dictionary during the coding process. When the instrumental view is followed, it should be easy to have access to the dictionary in case you want to make changes.

You can probably think of more questions with respect to your research project.

Miscellaneous

General information about many programs for text analysis is found on the World Wide Web. Some important URL's follow.

The SiByl data bank, provided by the inter-university expertise center *Pro*GAMMA contains information about all kinds of computer programs for mainly investigators in social and behavioural sciences:

HTTP://GAMMA.RUG.NL/SIBYL.HTML

Text analysis resources might inform about programs for text analysis, but also about texts on text analysis. Very detailed on computer programs is the Web-site by Harald Klein:

HTTP://WWW.INTEXT.DE/ENGLISH.HTM

Information on new texts in the field of text analysis is found on a site made available by Bill Evans (see also Evans, 1996):

HTTP://WWW.GSU.EDU/~WWWCOM/CONTENT.HTML

Information on both computer programs and texts (but not that much as on the ones mentioned above) is found on the side from the Cadqas-project:

HTTP://WWW.SOC.SURREY.AC.UK/CAQDAS/

Notes

1. General statistical packages might also offer some limited possibilities to count the frequency of occurrence of words. When running under Windows or Unix SPSS (SPSS Inc., 1993: 54) allows the user to count the number of times a specific word appears in a text string. The text string can, for example, be an answer to an open question. Consider the following SPSS program:

```
→     DATA LIST / answer 1–40 (A).
→     BEGIN DATA.
→     now and then I think that
→     sometimes I think that
→     still it often is that
→     it is wonderful that
→     it is sometimes and also often that
→     never do this again it has no use that
→     sometimes it goes wrong
→
→     END DATA.
→     *.
→     * The search function index is used to look for a specific string.
→     * The result is 1 when this string is found, otherwise it is 0.
→     * The data are assigned to the variable TYPE.
→     * This variable TYPE gets the value 2 when the string 'sometimes' occurs.
→     *.
→     IF (INDEX(answer,'often')→0) TYPE=1.
→     IF (INDEX(answer,'sometimes')→0) TYPE=2
→     IF (INDEX(answer,'never')→0) TYPE=3.
→     IF (INDEX(answer,'now and then')→0) TYPE=2.
→     LIST.
```

Note that in the SPSS program line 5 contains two indexes to be coded. In the corresponding output, only one is encoded, namely 'sometimes'. If the first two IF-statements in the program were reversed, line 5 would have instead been assigned a value of 1 on the variable TYPE.

```
ANSWER                                     TYPE

now and then I think that                  2.0000
sometimes I think that                     2.0000
still it often is that                     1.0000
it is wonderful that                          .
it is sometimes and also often that        2.0000
never do this again it has no use that     3.0000
sometimes it goes wrong                    2.0000
                                              .

Number of cases read:  8    Number of cases listed:  8
```

A similar facility is available within the package SAS (SAS Institute Inc., 1990: 555).

2. FlexText and PLCA will be integrated into a new program TCA (Textual Content Analysis). This new Windows95 program is scheduled for the autumn of 2000.

3. A new development in MCCA is the correspondence of the MCCA dictionary categories to the WordNet synsets (McTavish et al., 1997; Litkowski, 1997a, 1997b). WordNet (Miller et al., 1990) is a semantic network of about 100.000 words, which are grouped in synsets, i.e., sets of synonyms. These synsets are connected with one another by semantic relations, such as antonomy, synonymy, part of, hyponymy, etc. All WordNet nouns and verbs are hierarchically organized into semantic categories.

4. See note 2 on the integration of PLCA and FlexText.

References

Alker, H.R., Jr, Duffy, G., Hurwitz R. and Mallery, J.C. (1991) 'Text modelling for international politics: A tourist's guide to RELATUS', in V.M. Hudson (ed.), *Artificial Intelligence and International Politics*. Boulder, CO: Westview. pp. 97–126.

Andrén, Gunnar (1981) 'Reliability and content analysis', in K.E. Rosengren (ed.), *Advances in Content Analysis*. Beverly Hills: Sage. pp. 43–67.

Anonymous (1989) 'A Short Guide to the General Inquirer', *Bulletin de Méthodologie Sociologique*, 24: 6–8.

Austin, J.L. ([1962] 1975) *How to do Things with Words: The William James Lectures delivered at Harvard University in 1955*. Cambridge, MA: Harvard University Press.

Baker, Albert L. (1992) *FlexText Reference Manual. FlexText Text Analysis System*. Ames: Software Innovations, Inc.

Baker, Albert L. (1997) 'Text analysis and natural language database systems', in C.W. Roberts (ed.), *Text Analysis for the Social Sciences: Methods for Drawing Statistical Inferences from Texts and Transcripts*. Mahwah, NJ: Lawrence Erlbaum Associates. pp. 251–74.

Bakker, R.R. (1987) 'Knowledge graphs: Representation and structuring of scientific knowledge', PhD dissertation, University of Twente.

Bales, R.F. (1950) *Interaction Process Analysis. A Method for the Study of Small Groups*. Reading, MA: Addison Wesley.

Banks, James A. (1976) 'Comment on "A content analysis of the black American in textbooks"', in P. Golden (ed.), *The Research Experience*. Peacock Press. pp. 383–89.

Banks, David and Carley, Kathleen (1994) 'Metric inference for social networks', *Journal of Classification*, 11 (1): 121–49.

Banks, David and Carley, Kathleen (1996) 'Models of social network evolution', *Journal of Mathematical Sociology*, 21 (1–2): 173–96.

Barton, Allen H. and Lazarsfeld, Paul A. (1982 [1955]) 'Some functions of qualitative analysis in social research', in P.L. Kendall (ed.), *The Varied Sociology of Paul F. Lazarsfeld*. New York: Columbia University Press. pp. 239–85.

Bennett, E.M., Alpert, M.R. and Goldstein, A.C. (1954) 'Communications through limited response questioning', *Public Opinion Quarterly*, 18 (3): 303–08.

Berelson, Bernard (1971 [1952]) *Content Analysis in Communication Research*. New York: Free Press.

Bierschenk, Bernhard (1991) 'The schema axiom as foundation of a theory for measurement and representation of consciousness', Lund: Lund University, Cognitive Science Research, No. 31.

Bierschenk, Bernhard and Bierschenk, Inger (1976) *A System for a Computer–Based Content Analysis of Interview Data*. Lund: CWK Gleerup.

Bierschenk, Inger (1989) 'Language as carrier for consciousness', paper presented at the Annual European Congress of Psychology, Amsterdam, July 2–7, 1989. Lund: Lund University, Cognitive Science Research, No. 30.

Blumer, Herbert (1969) *Symbolic Interactionism; Perspective and Method.* Englewood Cliffs, NJ: Prentice Hall.

Bogdan, Robert C. and Biklen, Sari K. (1992) *Qualitative Research for Education. An Introduction to Theory and Methods.* Boston, MA: Allyn & Bacon.

Bond, Doug, Jenkins, J. Craig, Taylor, Charles L. and Schok, Kurt (1997) 'Mapping mass political conflict and civil society', *Journal of Conflict Resolution*, 41 (4): 553–79.

Boot, M. (1978) 'Ambiguity and automated content analysis', M.D.N., 3(1): 117–37.

Brandow, Ronald, Mitze, Karl and Rau, Lisa F. (1995) 'Automatic condensation of electronic publications by sentence selection', *Information Processing & Management* 31 (5): 675-85.

Brennan, Robert L. and Prediger, Dale J. (1981) 'Coefficient kappa: Some uses, misuses, and alternatives', *Educational and Psychological Measurement*, 41 (3): 687–99.

Budd, Richard W., Thorp, Robert K. and Donohew, Lewis (1967) *Content Analysis of Communications.* New York: Macmillan.

Burton, Dolores M. (1981a) 'Automated concordances and word indexes: The fifties', *Computers and the Humanities*, 15 (1): 1–14.

Burton, Dolores M. (1981b) 'Automated concordances and word indexes: The early sixties and the early centers', *Computers and the Humanities*, 15 (2): 83–100.

Burton, Dolores M. (1981c) 'Automated concordances and word indexes: The process, the programs, and the products', *Computers and the Humanities*, 15 (3): 139–54.

Burton, Dolores M. (1982) 'Automated concordances and word indexes: Machine decisions and editorial revisions', *Computers and the Humanities*, 16 (4): 195–218.

Campbell, Donald T. and Fiske, Donald W. (1959) 'Convergent and discriminant validation by the multitrait–multimethod matrix', *Psychological Bulletin*, 56 (1): 81–105.

Carley, Kathleen (1986) 'An approach for relating social structure to cognitive structure', *Journal of Mathematical Sociology*, 12 (2): 137–89.

Carley, Kathleen (1988) 'Formalizing the expert's knowledge', *Sociological Methods & Research*, 17 (2): 165–232.

Carley, Kathleen (1993) 'Coding choices for textual analysis: A comparison of content analysis and map analysis', in P.V. Marsden (ed.), *Sociological Methodology 1993*. Cambridge, MA: Basil Blackwell. pp. 75–126.

Carley, Kathleen (1994) 'Content analysis', in R.E. Asher (ed.), *The Encyclopedia of Language and Linguistics*, Volume 2. Edinburgh: Pergamon Press. pp. 725-30.

Carley, Kathleen M. (1997) 'Network text analysis: The network position of concepts', in C.W. Roberts (ed.), *Text Analysis for the Social Sciences: Methods for Drawing Statistical Inferences from Texts and Transcripts*. Mahwah, NJ: Lawrence Erlbaum Associates. pp. 79–100.

Carley, Kathleen and Banks, David (1993) 'Nonparametric inference for network data', *Journal of Mathematical Sociology*, 18 (1): 1–26.

Carley, Kathleen and Palmquist, Michael E. (1992) 'Extracting, representing, and analyzing mental models', *Social Forces*, 70 (3): 601–36.

Carré, B. (1979) *Graphs and networks.* Oxford: Clarendon Press.

Cartwright, Alan (1998) 'Personal and professional factors in the development of Code–A–Text', *Qualitative Health Research*, 8 (3): 404–13.

Cartwright, Dorwin P. (1953) 'Analysis of qualitative material', in L. Festinger and D. Katz (eds), *Research Methods in the Behavioral Sciences*. New York: Dryden. pp. 421–70.

Chen, H., Hsu, P., Orwig, R., Hoopes, L. and Nunamaker, J.F. (1994) 'Automatic concept classification of text from electronic meetings', *Communications of the ACM*, 37 (10): 56–73.

Chomsky, Noam (1957). *Syntactic Structures*. The Hague: Mouton.

Cicchetti, Dominic V. (1972) 'A new measure of agreement between rank ordered variables', *American Statistical Association*, Proceedings of the 80th annual convention, 7: 17-18.

Cohen, Jacob (1960) 'A coefficient of agreement for nominal scales', *Educational & Psychological Measurement*, 20 (1): 37-46.

Cone, John D. (1979) 'Why the "I've got a better agreement measure" literature continues to grow. A comment on two articles by Birkimer and Brown', *Journal of Applied Behavior Analysis*, 12 (4): 571.

Conklin, Jeff (1987) 'Hypertext: An introduction and survey', *IEEE Computer*, 20 (9): 17–41.

Contas, Mark A. (1992) 'Qualitative analysis as a public event: The documentation of category development procedures', *American Educational Research Journal*, 29 (2): 253–66.

Covington, Michael A. (1994) *Natural Language Processing for Prolog Programmers*. Englewood Cliffs, N.J.: Prentice Hall.

Cowie, Jim and Lehnert, Wendy (1996) 'Information Extraction', *Communications of the ACM*, 39 (1): 80-91.

Cronin, Blaise, Davenport, Elisabeth and Martinson, Anna (1997) 'Women's studies: Bibliometric and content analysis of the formative years', *Journal of Documentation*, 53 (2): 123–38.

Cropper, Steve, Eden, Colin and Ackerman, Fran (1990) 'Keeping sense of accounts using computer-based cognitive maps', *Social Science Computer Review*, 8 (3): 345–66.

Danielson, Wayne A. and Lasorsa, Dominic L. (1997) 'Perceptions of social change: 100 Years of front page content in The New York Times and The Los Angeles Times', in C.W. Roberts (ed.), *Text Analysis for the Social Sciences: Methods for Drawing Statistical Inferences from Texts and Transcripts*. Mahwah, NJ: Lawrence Erlbaum Associates. pp. 103–15.

Danowski, James A. (1993) 'Network analysis of message content', in W.D. Richards, Jr. and G.A. Barnett (eds), *Progress in Communication Sciences. Volume XII*. Norwood [NJ]: Ablex. pp. 197–221.

Date, C.J. (1995) *An Introduction to Database Systems*, Volume I. Readin, MA: Addison Wesley.

De Ridder, J.A. (1994) *Van tekst naar informatie. Ontwikkeling en toetsing van een inhoudsanalyse–instrument*[From text to information. The development and testing of an instrument for content-analysis]. Unpublished Ph.D.thesis, University of Amsterdam.

De Saussure, Ferdinand (1974 [1916]) *Course in General Linguistics*. London: Owen.

De Sola Pool, Ithiel (1959a) 'Introduction', in I. De Sola Pool (ed.), *Trends in Content Analysis*. Urbana: University of Illinois Press. pp. 1–6.

De Sola Pool, Ithiel (1959b) 'Trends in content analysis today: A summary', in I. De Sola Pool (ed.), *Trends in Content Analysis*. Urbana: University of Illinois Press. pp. 189–233.

De Sola Pool, Ithiel (1980) 'Bridging the gap between content analysis and survey research', in E. Mochmann (Hrsg.), *Computerstrategien für die Kommunikationsanalyse*. Frankfurt: Campus. pp. 245–48.

De Weese III, L.Caroll (1976) 'Computer content analysis of printed media. A feasibility study', *Public Opinion Quarterly*, 40 (1): 92–100.

Duchastel, Jules, Dupuy, Luc, Paquin, Louis Claude, Beauchemin, Jacques and Daoust, François (1995) 'The SACAO project: Using computation toward textual data analysis in the social sciences', in E. Nissan and K. Schmidt (eds), *From Information to Knowledge: Conceptual and Content Analysis by Computer*. Oxford: Intellect. pp. 7–16.

Eltinge, Elizabeth M. (1997) 'Assessing the portrayal of "science as a process of inquiry" in high school biology textbooks: An application of linguistic content analysis', in Carl W. Roberts (ed.), *Text Analysis for the Social Sciences: Methods for Drawing Statistical Inferences from Texts and Transcripts*. Mahwah, NJ: Lawrence Erlbaum Associates. pp. 159–70.

Eltinge, Elizabeth M. and Roberts, Carl W. (1993) 'Linguistic content analysis: A method to measure science as inquiry in textbooks', *Journal of Research in Science Teaching*, 30 (1): 65–83.

Ericsson, K. Anders and Simon, Herbert A. (1994) *Protocol Analysis, Verbal Reports as Data*. Cambridge, MA: MIT Press.

Evans, William (1996) 'Computer-supported content analysis. Trends, tools, and techniques', *Social Science Computer Review*, 14 (3): 269–79.

Evans, William and Hornig Priest, Susanna (1995) 'Science content and social context', *Public Understanding of Science*, 4 (4): 327–40.

Fan, David P. (1988) *Predictions of Public Opinion from the Mass Media: Computer Content Analysis and Mathematical Modelling*. New York: Greenwood Press.

Fan, David P. (1997) 'Computer content analysis of press coverage and prediction of public opinion for the 1995 sovereignty referendum in Quebec', *Social Science Computer Review*, 15 (4): 351–66.

Fielding, Nigel G. (1995) 'Choosing the right qualitative software package', *ESRC Data Archive Bulletin*, 58 (HTTP://WWW.SOC.SURREY.AC.UK/CAQDAS/CHOOSE.HTM).

Fielding, Nigel G. and Lee, Raymond M. (1998) *Computer Analysis and Qualitative Research*. London: Sage.

Flack, V.F., Afifi, A.A., Lachenbruch, P.A. and Schouten, H.J.A. (1988) 'Sample size determinations for the two rater kappa statistic'. *Psychometrika*, 53 (3): 321–25.

Fleiss, Joseph L. (1971) 'Measuring nominal scale agreement among many raters', *Psychological Bulletin*, 76 (5): 378-82.

Flesch, Rudolf (1950) 'Measuring the level of abstraction', *Journal of Applied Psychology*, 34 (6): 221–33.

Frank, Ove (1991) 'Statistical analysis of change in networks', *Statistica Neerlandica*, 45 (3): 283–93.

Franzosi, Roberto (1989) 'From words to numbers: A generalized and linguistics-based coding procedure for collecting textual data', in P.V. Marsden (ed.), *Sociological Methodology 1989*. Oxford: Blackwell. pp. 263–98.

Franzosi, Roberto (1990) 'Computer-assisted coding of textual data', *Sociological Methods & Research*, 19 (2): 225–57.

Franzosi, Roberto (1994) 'From words to numbers: A set theory framework for the collection, organization, and analysis of narrative data', in P.V. Marsden (ed.), *Sociological Methodology 1994*. Oxford: Blackwell. pp. 105–36.

Franzosi, Roberto (1995) 'Computer-assisted content analysis of newspapers', *Quality & Quantity*, 29 (2): 157–72.

Franzosi, Roberto (1997) 'Labor unrest in the Italian service sector: An application of semantic grammars', in C.W. Roberts (ed.), *Text Analysis for the Social Sciences: Methods for Drawing Statistical Inferences from Texts and Transcripts*. Mahwah, NJ: Lawrence Erlbaum Associates. pp. 131–45.

Freeman, Linton C. (1978) 'Centrality in social networks; conceptual clarification', *Social Networks*, 1 (3): 215–39.

Frege, Gottlob (1974 [1884]) *The Foundations of Arithmetic: A Logico–mathematical Inquiry into the Concept of Number*. Oxford: Blackwell.

Gallhofer, Irmtraud N., Saris, Willem E. and Melman, Marianne (1986) 'The empirical decision analysis procedure', in I.N. Gallhofer, W.E. Saris and M. Melman (eds), *Different Text Analysis Procedures for the Study of Decision Making*. Amsterdam: Sociometric Research Foundation. pp. 53–68.

Galtung, Johan (1979) 'Measurement of agreement', in J. Galtung *Papers on methodology. Theory and methods of social research. Volume II*. Copenhagen: Christian Eijlers, 82-135.

Gauch, Susan and Smith, John B. (1993) 'An expert system for automatic query reformation', *Journal of the American Society for Information Science*, 44 (3): 124–36.

Gentner, Dedre and Stevens, Albert L. (eds) (1983) *Mental Models*. Hillsdale, NJ: Lawrence Erlbaum Associates.

George, Alexander L. (1959a) *Propaganda Analysis: A Study of Inferences Made from Nazi Propaganda in World War II*. White Plains, NY: Row, Peterson & Co.

George, Alexander L. (1959b) 'Quantitative and qualitative approaches to content analysis', in I. De Sola Pool (ed.), *Trends in Content Analysis*. Urbana: University of Illinois Press. pp. 7–32.

Gerner, Deborah J., Schrodt, Philip A., Francisco, Ronald A. and Weddle, Judith L. (1994) 'Machine coding of event data using regional and international sources', *International Studies Quarterly*, 38 (1): 91-119.

Glaser, Barney G. and Strauss, Anselm L. (1967) *The Discovery of Grounded Theory, Strategies for Qualitative Research*. Chicago: Aldine.

Goffman, Ervin (1963) *Behavior in Public Places: Notes on the Social Organization of Gathering*. Glencoe, IL: Free Press.

Gottschalk, Louis A. (1995) *Content Analysis of Verbal Behavior: New Findings and Computerized Clinical Applications*. Hillsdale, NJ: Lawrence Erlbaum Associates.

Gottschalk, Louis A. (1997) 'The unobtrusive measurement of psychological states and traits', in C.W. Roberts (ed.), *Text Analysis for the Social Sciences: Methods for Drawing Statistical Inferences from Texts and Transcripts*. Mahwah, NJ: Lawrence Erlbaum Associates. pp. 117–25.

Gottschalk, L.A. and Bechtel, R. (1982) 'The measurement of anxiety through the computer analysis of verbal samples', *Comprehensive Psychiatry*, 23 (4): 364-69.

Gottschalk, L.A. and Bechtel, R. (1989) 'Artificial intelligence and the computerization of the content analysis of natural language', *Artificial Intelligence in Medicine*, 1: 131–7.

Gottschalk, Louis A. and Gleser, Goldine C. (1969) *The Measurement of Psychological States Through the Content Analysis of Verbal Behavior*. Berkeley: University of California Press.

Gottschalk, Louis A., Hausmann, Catherine and Brown, John Seely (1975) 'A computerized scoring system for use with content analysis', *Comprehensive Psychiatry*, 16 (1): 77–90.

Gottschalk, Louis A., Winget, Carolyn N. and Gleser, Goldine C. (1969) *Manual of Instructions for Using the Gottschalk-Gleser Content Analysis Scales: Anxiety, Hostility, and Social Alienation-personal Disorganization*. Berkeley: University of California Press.

Graber, Doris A. (1989) 'Content and meaning: What's it all about?', *American Behavioral Scientist*, 33 (2): 144-52.

Griemas, Algirdas J. (1984 [1966]) *Structural Semantics: An Attempt at a Method*. Lincoln, NE: University of Nebraska Press.

Griffin, Larry J. (1993) 'Narrative, event–structure analysis, and causal interpretation of historical sociology', *American Journal of Sociology*, 98 (5): 1094–133.

Grishman, Ralph (1986) *Computational Linguistics: An Introduction*. Cambridge: Cambridge University Press.

Gutteling, Jan, Boer, Henk, Wiegman, Oene and Caljé, Hans (1991) 'Veranderingen in de berichtgeving over milieurisico's in vier Nederlandse dagbladen', *Massacommunicatie*, 19 (1): 18-36.

Hacking, Suzanne, Foreman, David and Belcher, John (1996) 'The descriptive assessment for psychiatric art: A new way of quantifying paintings by psychiatric patients', *Journal of Nervous and Mental Disease*, 184 (7): 425-30.

Hak, Tony and Bernts, Ton (1996) 'Coder training: Theoretical training or practical socialization?', *Qualitative Sociology*, 19 (2): 235-57.

Hansen, Anders (1995) 'Using information technology to analyze newspaper content', in R.M. Lee (ed.), *Information Technology for the Social Scientist*. London: UCL. pp. 147–68.

Hart, R.P. (1984) *Verbal Style and the Presidency: A Computer–Based Analysis*. New York: Academic Press.

Hawthorne, Mark (1994) 'The computer in literary analysis: Using TACT with students', *Computers and the Humanities*, 28 (1): 19–27.

Hecht, Jeffrey B. and Roberts, Nicole K. (1996) 'VTLOGANL: Coding and analyzing videotaped data', *Behavior Research Methods, Instruments, & Computers*, 28 (1): 76-82.

Heinrich, H.A. (1996) 'Traditional versus computer aided content analysis. A comparison between codings done by raters as well as by Intext', in F. Faulbaum and W. Bandilla (eds), *SoftStat '95. Advances in Statistical Software 5*. Stuttgart: Lucius & Lucius. pp 327–33.

Heise, David R. (1991) 'Event structure analysis: A qualitative model of quantitative research', in N.G. Fielding and R.M. Lee (eds), *Using Computers in Qualitative Research*. London: Sage. pp. 136–63.

Helfgott, M. and Nakell, C. (1992) *Inspiration Idea Book*. Portland, OR: Inspiration Software, Inc.

Helmerson, Helge (1992) 'Representation of the logics in the processing of produced text', text for the workshop on Pertex at the congress on Social Science Information technology. Amsterdam, December 2–4.

Hesse-Biber, Sharlene, Dupuis, Paul and Kinder, T. Scott (1991) 'HyperRESEARCH: A computer program for the analysis of qualitative data with an emphasis on hypothesis testing and multimedia analysis', *Qualitative Sociology*, 14 (3): 289–306.

Hockey, S. and Martin, J. (1987) The Oxford Concordance Program version 2. *Literary and Linguistic Computing*, 2 (2): 125–31.

Hoede, C. (1978) 'A new status score for actors in a social network', Twente University, Department of Applied Statistics.

Hogenraad, Robert, Bestgen, Yves and Nysten, Jean Louis (1995) 'Terrorist rhetoric: texture and architexture', in E. Nissan and K. Schmidt (eds), *From Information to Knowledge: Conceptual and Content Analysis by Computer*. Oxford: Intellect. pp. 48–59.

Hogenraad, R., Daubies, C. and Bestgen, Y. (1995) Une théorie et une méthode générale d'analyse textuelle assistée par ordinateur. Le système PROTAN (PROTocol Analyzer). Louvain-la-Neuve: Psychology Department, Catholic University of Louvain.

Hoivik, Tord and Gleditsch, Nils Petter (1970) 'Structural parameters of graphs; a theoretical investigation', *Quality and Quantity* 4 (1): 193–209.

Holsti, Ole R. (1969) *Content Analysis for the Social Sciences and Humanities*. London: Addison Wesley.

Huber, G.L. and Marcello Garcia, C. (1991) 'Computer assistence for testing hypotheses about qualitative data', *Qualitative Sociology*, 14 (4): 325–47.

Iker, Howard P. (1974) 'An historical note on the use of word–frequency contingencies in content analysis', *Computers and the Humanities*, 8 (1): 93–98.

Iker, Howard P. and Klein, Robert H. (1974) 'WORDS: A computer system for the analysis of content', *Behavior Research Methods & Instrumentation*, 6 (4): 430–38.

James, P. (1992) 'Knowledge graphs', in R.P. van de Riet and R.A. Meersman (eds), *Linguistic Instruments in Knowledge Engineering*. Amsterdam: Elsevier. pp. 97–117.

Janowitz, Morris (1969) 'Content analysis and the study of the "Symbolic environment"', in A.A. Rogow (ed.), *Politics, Personality, and Social Science in the Twentieth Century*. Chicago: The University of Chicago Press. pp. 155–170.

Johnson–Laird, P.N. (1983) *Mental Models: Toward a Cognitive Science of Language, Inference and Consciousness*. Cambridge, MA: Harvard University Press.

Kabanoff, Boris (1996) 'Computers can read as well as count: How computer-aided text analysis can benefit organisational research', in C.L. Cooper and D.M. Rousseau (eds), *Trends in Organizational Behavior*. Volume 3. Chichester: Wiley. pp. 1-21.

Kabanoff, Boris and Holt, John (1996) 'Changes in the epoused values of Australian organizations 1986–1990'. *Journal of Organizational Behavior*, 17(3): 201–19.

Kant, Immanuel (1995 [1781]) *Kritik der reinen Vernunft* [Critique of pure reason]. Frankfurt am Main: Suhrkamp.

Kant, Immanuel (1975) *Die drei Kritiken in ihrem Zusammenhang mit dem Gesamtwerk* [The three critiques together with their connection to the complete edition]. Stuttgart: Alfred Kröner verlag.

Katz, Leo and Powell, James H. (1953) 'A proposed index of the conformity of one sociometric measurement to another', *Psychometrika*, 18 (3): 249–56.

Kaufman, Philip A., Dyjers, Carol Reese and Caldwell, Carole (1993) 'Why going online for content analysis can reduce research reliability', *Journalism Quarterly*, 70 (4): 824–32.

Kelly, Edward F. and Stone, Philip J. (1975) *Computer Recognition of English Words Senses*. Amsterdam: North-Holland.

Kimbrell, R.B. (1988) 'Searching for Text? Send an N–Gram', *Byte*, 13 (5): 297–312.

Klein, Harald (1992) 'Validity problems and their solutions in computer-aided content analysis with INTEXT/PC and other new features', in F. Faulbaum, R. Haux and K.H. Jöckel (eds) *Advances in Statistical Software 3*. Stuttgart: Gustav Fisher. pp. 483-88.

Klein, Harald (1993) 'INTEXT/PC: A program package for the analysis of text', in R. Steyer, K.F. Wender and K.F. Widaman (eds), *PsychometricMethodology*. Stuttgart: Gustav Fischer verlag. pp. 219–21.

Klein, Harald (1996) *ComputerunterstütztelnhaltsanalysemitINTEXT*. Münster, Westf.: LIT.

Kleinnijenhuis, J. (1998) *Strategische Communicatie* [Strategic Communication]. Amsterdam: Free University.

Kleinnijenhuis, Jan and De Ridder, Jan A. (1998) 'Issue news and electoral validity', *European Journal of Political Research*, 33 (3): 413–37.

Kleinnijenhuis, Jan, De Ridder, Jan A. and Rietberg, Ewald M. (1997) 'Reasoning in economic discourse: An application of the network approach to the Dutch press', in C.W. Roberts (ed.), *Text Analysis for the Social Sciences: Methods for Drawing Statistical Inferences from Texts and Transcripts*. Mahwah, NJ: Lawrence Erlbaum Associates. pp. 191–207.

Kleinnijenhuis, Jan , Oegema, Dirk, De Ridder, Jan and Bos, Herman (1995) *Democratie op drift* [Democracy adrift]. Amsterdam: VU Uitgeverij.

Klingemann, Hans–Dieter, Mohler, Peter Ph. and Weber, Robert Philip (1982) 'Cultural indicators based on content analysis', *Quality & Quantity*, 16 (1): 1–18.

Krause, Jürgen (1996) 'Principles of content analysis for information retrieval systems', in C. Züll, J. Harkness and J.H.P. Hoffmeyer–Zlotnik (eds), *Text Analysis and Computers*. Mannheim: ZUMA (ZUMA Nachrichten Spezial). pp. 77–100.

Krippendorff, Klaus (1978 [1969]) 'Models of messages', in G. Gerbner, O.R. Holsti, K. Krippendorff, W. Paisley and Ph.J. Stone (eds), *The Analysis of Communication Content*. New York: Krieger. pp. 69–106.

Krippendorff, Klaus (1980) *Content Analysis: An Introduction to its Methodology*. Beverly Hills, CA: Sage.

Krippendorff, Klaus (1987) 'Association, agreement, and equity', *Quality and Quantity*, 21 (1): 109–23.

Kuckartz, U. (1997) 'Computer aided text analysis and typology construction', in R. Klar and O. Opitz (eds),   *Classification and Knowledge Organization*. Heidelberg: Springer. pp. 363–70.

Lacy, Stephen and Riffe, Daniel (1996) 'Sampling error and selecting intercoder reliability samples for nominal content categories', *Journalism & Mass Communication Quarterly*, 73 (4): 963-73.

Lacy, Stephen, Robinson, Kay and Riffe, Daniel (1995) 'Sample size in content analysis of weekly newspapers', *Journalism & Mass Communication Quarterly*, 72 (2): 336-45.

Landis, J.Richard and Koch, Gary G. (1977) 'The measurement of observer agreement for categorical data', *Biometrics*, 33 (1): 159-174.

Lang, Hartmut, Kokot, Waltraut and Pack, Monika (1991) 'Zum Transkriptionsaufwand in der Analyse oraler Texte' [On the cost of transcription in the analysis of oral texts], *Anthropos*, 86 (1-3): 220-23.

Lasswell, Harold D. (1948) 'The structure and function of communication in society', in L. Bryson (ed.), *The Communication of Ideas*. New York: Harper & Row. pp. 37–51.

Lasswell, Harold D. and Kaplan, Abraham (1950) *Power and Society: A Framework for Political Inquiry*. New Haven, CT: Yale University Press.

Liebrand, Wim B.G, Messick, David M. and Wolters, Fred J.M. (1986) 'Why are we fairer than others: A cross–cultural replication and extension', *Journal of Experimental Social Psychology*, 22 (6): 590–604.

Lindenberg, Siegwart (1976) 'Actor analysis and depersonalization', *Mens en Maatschappij*, 51 (2): 152–78.

Lindkvist, Kent (1981) 'Approaches to text analysis', in K.E. Rosengren (ed.), *Advances in Content Analysis*. Beverly Hills, CA: Sage. pp. 23–41.

Lisch, Ralf and Kriz, Jürgen (1978) *Grundlagen und Modelle der Inhaltsanalyse*. Reinbek: Rowohlt.

Litkowski, Kenneth C. (1997a) 'Category development based on semantic principles', *Social Science Computer Review*, 15 (4): 394–409.

Litkowski, Kenneth C. (1997b) Desiderata for tagging with WordNet synsets and MCCA categories. 4th Meeting of the ACL Special Interest Group on the Lexicon. Washington, DC: Association for Computational Linguistics.

Lofland, John (1971) *Analyzing Social Settings*. Belmont, CA: Wadsworth Publishing Company.

Lonkila, Marrku (1995) 'Grounded theory as an emerging paradigm for computer-assisted qualitative data analysis', in U. Kelle (ed.), *Computer-aided Qualitative Data Analysis: Theory, Methods and Practice*. Thousand Oaks, CA: Sage. pp. 41-51.

Lyons, John (1977) *Semantics*. Cambridge: Cambridge University Press.

Malrieu, Jean Pierre (1994) 'Coloured semantic networks for content analysis', *Quality & Quantity*, 28 (1): 55-81.

Markoff, John, Shapiro, Gilbert and Weitman, Sasha R. (1974) 'Toward the integration of content analysis and general methodology' in D.R. Heise (ed.), *Sociological Methodology 1975*. San Francisco: Jossey Bass. pp. 1–58.

McAleese, Ray (ed.) (1993) *Hypertext: Theory into Practice*. Oxford: Intellect.

McClelland, Ch.A. (1976) *World Event Interaction Survey Codebook* (ICPSR 5211). Ann Arbor: Inter–University Consortium for Political and Social Research.

McDonald, Colin (1982) 'Coding open–ended answers with the help of a computer', *Journal of the Market Research Society*, 24 (1): 9–27.

McEnery, Tony (1992) *Computational Linguistics: A Handbook and Toolbox for natural Language processing*. Wilmslow: Sigma.

McKeown, K. and Radev, D.R. (1995) 'Generating summaries of multiple news articles', in E.A. Fox, P. Ingwersen and R. Fidel (eds), *Proceedings of the 18th Annual International ACM SIGIR Conference on Research and Development in Information Retrieval*. New York: Association for Computing Machinery. pp. 74-82.

McQuail, Dennis (1977) *Analysis of Newspaper Content*. London: Her Majesty's Stationary Office.

McTavish, Donald G., Litkowski, Kenneth C. and Schrader, Susan (1997) 'A Computer Content Analysis Approach to measuring Social Distance in Residential Organizations for Older People', *Social Science Computer Review*, 15 (2): 170–80.

McTavish, Donald G. and Pirro, Ellen B. (1990) 'Contextual Content Analysis.' *Quality & Quantity*, 24 (3): 245–65.

Mergenthaler, Erhard (1996) 'Computer-assisted content analysis', in C. Züll, J. Harkness and J.H.P. Hoffmeyer-Zlotnik (eds) *Text Analysis and Computers*. Mannheim: ZUMA (ZUMA Nachrichten Spezial). pp. 3–32.

Merten, Klaus (1983) *Inhaltsanalyse. Einführung in Theorie, Methode und Praxis* [Content Analysis. Introduction into Theory, Method and Practice]. Opladen: Westdeutscher Verlag.

Miles, Matthew B. and Huberman, A. Michael (1994) *Qualitative Data Analysis: An Expanded Sourcebook*. 2nd edn. Thousand Oaks, CA: Sage.

Miller, B., Faletti, J. and Fisher, K. (1991) *SemNet User's Guide, Version 1.0*. San Diego, CA: SemNet Research Group.

Miller, G.A., Beckwith, R., Fellbaum, C., Gross, D. and Miller, K.J. (1990) 'WordNet: An on-line lexical database', *International Journal of Lexicography*, 3 (4): 235-312.

Miller, M. Mark (1993) 'User's guide for VBPro: A program for qualitative and quantitative analysis of verbatim text'. Knoxville: The University of Tennessee.

Miller, M. Mark (1997) 'Frame mapping and analysis of news coverage of contentious issues', *Social Science Computer Review*, 15 (4): 367–78.

Miller, M. Mark and Riechert, Bonnie P. (1994) 'Identifying themes via concept mapping: A new method of content analysis'. Paper for the Theory and Methodology Division, Association for Education in Journalism and Mass Communication.

Minsky, Marvin L. (1975) 'A framework for representing knowledge', in P. Winston (ed.), *The Psychology of Computer Vision*. New York: McGraw Hill. pp. 211–77.

Mohler, Peter Ph. and Züll, Cornelia (1995) *Textpack PC. Release 5.0*, Mannheim: ZUMA.

Muhr, Thomas (1991) 'ATLAS/ti; A prototype for the support of text interpretation', *Qualitative Sociology*, 14 (4): 349–71.

Mulder, L.J.M., Schweizer, D. and Van Roon, A.M. (1992) 'An environment for data reduction, correction, and analysis of cardiovascular signals', in F.J. Maarse, A.E. Akkerman, A.N. Brand, L.J.M. Mulder and M.J. Van der Stelt (eds), *Computers in Psychology: Tools for Experimental and Applied Psychology*. Lisse: Swets and Zeitlinger. pp. 72–83.

Nacos, Brigitte L., Shapiro, Robert Y., Young, John T., Fan, David P., Kjellstrand, Torsten and McCaa, Craig (1991) 'Content analysis of news reports: Comparing human coding and a computer assisted method', *Communication*, 12 (1): 111–28.

Namenwirth, J.Z. and Weber, R.P. (1987). *Dynamics of Culture*. Boston: Allen & Unwin.

Noldus, L.P.J.J. (1991) 'The Observer: A software system for collection and anlysis of observational data', *Behavior Research Methods, Instruments, & Computers*, 23 (3): 415-29.

O'Grady, William, Dobrovolsky, Michael and Katamba, Francis (eds) (1997) *Contemporary Linguistics: An Introduction*. London: Longman.

Olsen, Mark (1989) TextPack V: Text analysis utilities for the personal computer. *Computers and the Humanities* 23: 155–60.

Osgood, Charles E. (1959) 'The representational model and relevant research methods', in I. De Sola Pool (ed.), *Trends in Content Analysis*. Urbana: University of Illinois Press. pp. 33–88.

Osgood, Charles E., Saporta, Sol and Nunnally, Jum C. (1956). Evaluative assertion analysis. *Litera* 3. pp. 47–102.

Osgood, Charles E., Suci, George J. and Tannenbaum, Percy H. (1957) *The Measurement of Meaning*. Urbana: University of Illinois Press.

Palmquist, Michael E. (1990) The lexicon of the classroom: Language and learning in writing classrooms. Doctoral dissertation, Carnegy Mellon University, Pittsburg.

Palmquist, Michael E., Carley, Kathleen M. and Dale, Thomas A. (1997) 'Applications of computer-aided text analysis: Analyzing literary and nonliterary texts', in C.W. Roberts (ed.), *Text Analysis for the Social Sciences: Methods for Drawing Statistical Inferences from Texts and Transcripts.* Mahwah, NJ: Lawrence Erlbaum Associates. pp. 171–89.

Pfaffenberger, Bryan (1988) *Microcomputer Applications in Qualitative Research.* Newbury Park, CA: Sage.

Popping, Roel (1983) 'Traces of agreement. On the Dot-product as a coefficient of agreement', *Quality and Quantity,* 17 (1): 1-18.

Popping, Roel (1985) 'Nominal scale agreement', in S. Kotz and N.L. Johnson (eds), *Encyclopedia of Statistical Sciences,* Volume 6. New York: Wiley, 261-64.

Popping, Roel (1992a) 'In search for one set of categories', *Quality & Quantity,* 25 (1): 147–55.

Popping, Roel (1992b) *Taxonomy on Nominal Scale Agreement 1945–1990.* Groningen: iec *Pro*GAMMA.

Popping, Roel (1995) *AGREE, Computing Agreement on Nominal Data.* Version 6.0. Groningen: iec *Pro*GAMMA.

Popping, Roel (1997a) 'Reliability of registrations: A feasibility study into registration of occupational and educational titles in hospitals', *Quality & Quantity,* 31 (3): 305–15.

Popping, Roel (1997b) 'The utility of a consultation facility in a program for statistical computing', *Computational Statistics & Data Analysis Statistical Software Newsletter,* 24 (4): 495–503.

Popping, R. and Roberts, C.W. (1997) 'Network approaches in text analysis', in R. Klar and O. Opitz (eds), *Classification and Knowledge Organization.* Heidelberg: Springer. pp. 381–89.

Popping, Roel and Roberts, Carl W. (1998) 'Democracy as reflected in East–Central European newspapers', in H. van der Wusten (ed.), *Proceedings Conference Transformation Processes in Eastern Europe, Part IV: Politics and the Environment.* The Hague: ESR/NWO.

Popping, Roel and Strijker, Inge (1997) 'Representation and integration of sociological knowledge by using knowledge graphs', *Social Science Information,* 35 (4): 731–47.

Prein, Gerald, Kelle, Udo and Bird, Katharine (1995) 'An overview of software', in U. Kelle (ed.), *Computer-aided Qualitative Data Analysis: Theory, Methods and Practice.* Thousand Oaks, CA: Sage. pp. 190-210.

Rahmstorf, Gerhard (1983) 'Die semantische Relationen in nominalen Ausdrücken des Deutschen' [The semantic relations in nominal expressions in German language]. Unpublished Ph.D.thesis, Johannes Gutenberg University Mainz.

Richards, Thomas J. and Richards, Lyn (1994) 'Using Computers in Qualitative Research', in N.K. Denzin and Y.S. Lincoln (eds), *Handbook of Qualitative Research.* Thousand Oaks, CA: Sage. pp. 445-62.

Richards, Tom and Richards, Lyn (1995) 'Using hierarchical categories in qualitative data analysis', in U. Kelle (ed.), *Computer-aided Qualitative Data Analysis: Theory, Methods and Practice.* Thousand Oaks, CA: Sage. pp. 80-95.

Riffe, Daniel, Lacy, Stephen and Drager, Michael W. (1996a) 'Sample size in content analysis of weekly news magazines', *Journalism & Mass Communication Quarterly,* 73 (3): 635-44.

Riffe, Daniel, Lacy, Stephen, Nagovan, Jason and Burkum, Larry (1996b) 'The effectiveness of simple and stratified sampling in broadcast news content analysis', *Journalism & Mass Communication Quarterly* 73 (1): 159-68.

Roberts, Carl W. (1989) 'Other than counting words: A linguistic approach to content analysis', *Social Forces*, 68 (1): 147–77.

Roberts, Carl W. (1997a) 'Semantic text analysis: The problem of linguistic ambiguity', in C.W. Roberts (ed.), *Text Analysis for the Social Sciences: Methods for Drawing Statistical Inferences from Texts and Transcripts*. Mahwah, NJ: Lawrence Erlbaum Associates. pp. 55–77.

Roberts, Carl W. (1997b) 'A theoretical map for selecting among text-analysis techniques', in C.W. Roberts (ed.), *Text Analysis for the Social Sciences: Methods for Drawing Statistical Inferences from Texts and Transcripts*. Mahwah, NJ: Lawrence Erlbaum Associates. pp. 275–83.

Roberts, Carl W. (1997c) 'A generic semantic grammar for quantitative text analysis: Applications to East and West Berlin radio news content from 1979', in A.E. Raftery (ed.), *Sociological Methodology 1997*. Oxford: Basil Blackwell. pp. 89–129.

Roberts, Carl W. and Popping, Roel (1996) 'Themes, syntax, and other necessary steps in the network analysis of texts', *Social Science Information*, 35 (4): 657–65.

Rosenberg, Stanley D., Schnurr, Paula P. and Oxman, Thomas E. (1990) 'Content analysis. A comparison of manual and computerized systems', *Journal of Personality Assessment*, 54 (1 & 2): 298–310.

Rumelhart, David E. (1975) 'Notes on a schema for stories', in D.G. Bobrow and A. Collins (eds), *Representation and understanding. Studies in Cognitive Science*. New York: Academic Press. pp. 211–36.

Salton, Gerard (1989) *Automated Text Processing: The Transformation, Analysis, and Retrieval of Information by Computers*. Reading, MA: Addison Wesley.

Sanil, Ashish, Banks, David and Carley, Kathleen (1995) 'Models for evolving fixed node networks: Model fitting and model testing', *Social Networks*, 17 (1): 65-81.

Saris, Willem E. (1991) *Computer-assisted Interviewing*. Newbury Park: Sage.

Saris–Gallhofer, I.N., Saris, W.E. and Morton, E.L. (1978) 'A validation study of Holsti's content analysis procedure', *Quality & Quantity* 12 (2): 131–45.

SAS Institute Inc. (1990) *SAS® Language Reference Version 6. First Edition*. Cary, NC: SAS Institute Inc.

Savaiano, Scott and Schrodt, Philip A. (1997) 'Environmental change and conflict: Analyzing the Ethiopian famine of 1984-85', in C.W. Roberts (ed.), *Text Analysis for the Social Sciences: Methods for Drawing Statistical Inferences from Texts and Transcripts*. Mahwah, NJ: Lawrence Erlbaum Associates. pp. 147–58.

Schank, Roger C. (1973) 'Identification of conceptualization underlying natural language', in R.C. Schank and K.M. Colby (eds), *Computer Models of Thought and Language*. San Francisco: Freeman. pp. 187–247.

Schank, Roger C. and Abelson, Robert P. (1977) *Scripts, Plans, Goals and Understanding*. New York: Wiley.

Schutt, Russell K. (1992) 'TACT' [Software review], *Social Science Computer Review*, 10 (2): 280-82.

Schmidt, Klaus M. (1995) 'Concepts, content, meaning: An introduction', in E. Nissan and K. Schmidt (eds), *From Information to Knowledge: Conceptual and Content Analysis by Computer*. Oxford: Intellect. pp. 1-6.

Schouten, Hubert J.A. (1986) 'Nominal scale agreement among observers', *Psychometrika*, 51 (3): 453–66.

Schriver, Karen A. (1989) 'Evaluating text quality: The continuum from text-focused to reader-focused methods', *IEEE Transactions on Professional Communication*, 32 (4): 238–55.

Schrodt, Philip A. (1993) 'Machine coding of event data', in R.L. Merritt, R.G. Muncaster and D.A. Zinnes (eds), *Theory and Management of International Event Data: DDIR Phase II*. Ann Arbor: University of Michigan Press. pp. 117–40.

Schrodt, Philip A., Davis, Shannon G. and Weddle, Judith L. (1994) 'Political science: KEDS – A program for the machine coding of event data', *Social Science Computer Review*, 12 (4): 561-87.

Schrodt, Philip A. and Gerner, Deborah J. (1994) 'Validity assessment of a machine-coded event data set for the Middle East, 1982–1992', *American Journal of Political Science*, 38 (3): 825–54.

Schrodt, Philip A. and Gerner, Deborah J. (1997) 'Empirical indicators of crisis phase in the Middle East, 1979–1995', *Journal of Conflict Resolution*, 41 (4): 529–52.

Schrott, Peter R. and Lanoue, David J. (1994) 'Trends and perspectives in content analysis', in I. Borg and P.Ph. Mohler (eds), *Trends and Perspectives in Empirical Social Research*. Berlin: Walter de Gruyter. pp. 327–45.

Scott, William A. (1955) 'Reliability of content analysis: The case of nominal scale coding', *Public Opinion Quarterly*, 19 (3): 321-5.

Seidel, John and Kelle, Udo (1995) 'Different functions of coding in the analysis of textual data', in U. Kelle (ed.), *Computer-aided Qualitative Data Analysis: Theory, Methods and Practice*. Thousand Oaks, CA: Sage. pp. 52-61.

Shapiro, Gilbert (1997) 'The future of coders: Human judgments in a world of sophisticated software', in C.W. Roberts (ed.), *Text Analysis for the Social Sciences: Methods for Drawing Statistical Inferences from Texts and Transcripts*. Mahwah, NJ: Lawrence Erlbaum Associates. pp. 225–38.

Shapiro, Gilbert and Markoff, John (1997) 'A matter of definition', in C.W. Roberts (ed.), *Text Analysis for the Social Sciences: Methods for Drawing Statistical Inferences from Texts and Transcripts*. Mahwah, NJ: Lawrence Erlbaum Associates. pp. 9–31.

Shapiro, Gilbert and Markoff, John (1998) *Revolutionary Demands: A Content Analysis of the Cahiers de Doléances of 1789*. Stanford: Stanford University Press.

Simonton, Dean K. (1994) 'Computer Content Analysis of Melodic structure: Classical composers and their compositions', *Psychology of Music*, 22 (1): 31-43.

Sly, Diane S. (1991) 'Computer-aided content analysis: An application to transcripts of prime-time television', M.S. Creative Component. Department of Statistics, Iowa State University.

Smith, Charles P. (ed.) (1992) *Motivation and Personality. Handbook of Thematic Content Analysis*. Cambridge: Cambridge University Press.

Smith, J.M. (1992) *SGML and Related Standards: Document Description and Processing Languages*. Cambridge, UK: Cambridge University Press.

Snijders, Tom A.B. (1981) 'The degree variance: An index of graph heterogeneity', *Social Networks*, 3 (3): 163–74.

Soothill, Keith and Grover, Chris (1997) 'A note on computer searches of newspapers', *Sociology*, 31 (3): 591-6.

Sorokin, Pitirim (1937) *Social and Cultural Dynamics. Volume 2: Fluctuations of Systems of Thruth, Ethics, and Law*. New York: American Book Company.

Sowa, John F. (1984) *Conceptual Structures*. Reading, MA: Addison Wesley.

Sprenger, C.J.A. and Stokman, F.N. (eds) (1989) *GRADAP Graph Definition and Analysis Package, User's Manual. Version 2.0.* Groningen: iec ProGAMMA.

SPSS Inc. (1993) *SPSS® Base System Syntax Reference Guide, Release 6.0.* Chicago: SPSS Inc.

Stone, Philip J. (1969) 'Improved quality of content analysis categories: Computerized disambiguation rules for high frequency English words', in G. Gerbner, O.R. Holsti, K. Krippendorff, W. Paisley and Ph.J. Stone (eds), *The Analysis of Communication Content.* New York: Krieger. pp. 199–233.

Stone, Philip J. (1997) 'Thematic text analysis: New agendas for analyzing text content', in C.W. Roberts (ed.), *Text Analysis for the Social Sciences: Methods for Drawing Statistical Inferences from Texts and Transcripts.* Mahwah, NJ: Lawrence Erlbaum Associates. pp. 35–54.

Stone, Philip J., Dunphy, Dexter C., Smith, Marshall S. and Ogilvie, Daniel M. (1966) *The General Inquirer: A Computer Approach to Content Analysis.* Cambridge, MA: MIT Press.

Strauss, Anselm L. and Corbin, Juliet M. (1990) *Basics of Qualitative Research.* Newbury Park: Sage.

Temple, Bogusia (1997) 'Watch your tongue: Issues in translation and cross cultural research', *Sociology*, 31 (3): 607–18.

Tesch, Renate (1990) *Qualitative Research: Analysis Types and Software Tools.* New York: Falmer Press.

Trew, Tony (1979) 'Theory and ideology at work', in R. Fowler, B. Hodge, G. Kress and T. Trew (eds) *Language and Control.* London: Routledge & Kegan Paul. pp. 94–116.

Udo, Janny (1998) Is de vluchteling een punt op de agenda? Een oriënterend onderzoek naar een methode om agendavormingsprocessen te traceren [Is the refugee an issue of the agenda? A pilot investigation on a method to trace processes of agenda setting]. Master thesis, Department of Sociology, University of Groningen.

Umesh, U.N., Peterson, Robert A. and Sauber, Matthew H. (1989) 'Interjudge agreement and the maximum value of kappa', *Educational and Psychological Measurement*, 49 (5): 835–50.

Van Cuilenburg, J.J. (1991) 'Inhoudsanalyse en computer' [Content analysis and computer], in R. Popping and Jules L. Peschar (eds), *Goed Geïnformeerd.* Houten: Bohn Stafleu Van Loghum. pp. 71–82.

Van Cuilenburg, Jan J., Kleinnijenhuis, Jan and De Ridder, Jan A. (1986) 'A theory of evaluative discourse: Towards a graph theory of journalistic texts', *European Journal of Communication*, 1 (1): 65–96.

Van Cuilenburg, Jan J., Kleinnijenhuis, Jan and De Ridder, Jan A. (1988) 'Artificial intelligence and content analysis', *Quality & Quantity*, 22 (1): 65–97.

Van Cuilenburg, J.J. and Noomen, G.W. (1984) *Communicatiewetenschap* [Communication science]. Muiderberg: Coutinho.

Van der Vlugt, Maarten J., Kruk, Menno R., Van Erp, Annemoon and Geuze, Reint H. (1992) 'CAMERA: A system for fast and reliable acquisition of multiple ethological records', *Behavior Research Methods, Instruments, & Computers*, 24 (2): 147–49.

Van Dijk, Teun A. (1972) *Some Aspects of Text Grammars.* Paris: Mouton.

Walters, Lynne Masel and Walters, T.N. (1996) 'It loses something in the translation: Syntax and survival of key words in science and nonscience press releases', *Science Communication*, 18 (2): 165-81.

Wasserman, Stanley (1987) 'Conformity of two sociometric relations', *Psychometrika*, 52 (1): 3–18.

Wasserman, Stanley and Faust, Katherine (1994) *Social Network Analysis. Methods and Applications*. Cambridge: Cambridge University Press.

Weber, Robert Philip (1984) 'Computer aided content analysis: a short primer', *Quality & Quantity*, 7 (1–2): 126–47.

Weber, Robert Philip (1990) *Basic Content Analysis*. Beverly Hills, CA: Sage.

Weitzman, Eben A. and Miles, Matthew B. (1995) *Computer Programs for Qualitative Data Analysis*. Thousand Oaks, CA: Sage.

Whissell, Cynthia M. (1994) 'A computer program for the objective analysis of style and emotional connotations of prose: Hemingway, Galsworthy, and Faulkner compared', *Perceptual and Motor Skills*, 79 (2): 815-24.

Whissell, Cynthia (1996) 'Traditional and emotional stylometric analysis of the songs of the Beatles Paul McCartney and John Lennon', *Computers and the Humanities*, 30 (3): 257-65.

Wittgenstein, Ludwig (1953). *Philosophical Investigations*. New York: Macmillan.

Wood, Michael (1980) 'Alternatives and options in computer content analysis', *Social Science Research*, 9 (3): 273–86.

Wood, Michael (1984) 'Using key-word-in-context concordance programs for qualitative and quantitative social research', *Journal of Applied Behavioral Science*, 20 (3): 289–97.

Yuen, Hoi Kau and Richards, Thomas J. (1994) 'Knowledge representation for grounded theory construction in qualitative data analysis', *Journal of Mathematical Sociology*, 19 (4): 279–98.

Author index

Subject index